The code : baseball's unwritten
 rules and its
ignore-at-your-own-risk code of
conduct

WITHDRAWN

THE CODE

THE CODE

Baseball's Unwritten Rules and Its Ignore-at-Your-Own-Risk Code of Conduct

ROSS BERNSTEIN

TRIUMPH
BOOKS

Triumph Books and colophon are registered trademarks of Random House, Inc.

Library of Congress Cataloging-in-Publication Data

Bernstein, Ross.
   The code : baseball's unwritten rules and its ignore-at-your-own-risk code of conduct / Ross Bernstein.
      p. cm.
   Includes bibliographical references.
   ISBN-13: 978-1-60078-010-3
   ISBN-10: 1-60078-010-5
   1. Baseball—Corrupt practices—United States. 2. Baseball players—United States—Conduct of life.   I. Title.
   GV877.5.B47 2008
   796.357—dc22

                                                             2007040527

This book is available in quantity at special discounts for your group or organization. For further information, contact:

   Triumph Books
   542 South Dearborn Street
   Suite 750
   Chicago, Illinois 60605
   (312) 939-3330
   Fax (312) 663-3557

Printed in U.S.A.
ISBN: 978-1-60078-010-3
Design by Sue Knopf; page production by Patricia Frey
Photos courtesy of AP/Wide World Photos.

For Sara & Campbell…

Contents

Foreword by Rob Dibble

The code to me was all about respect, plain and simple. That meant everything to me because in order to earn your teammates' respect, you had to protect and defend them at all costs. No matter what. I always felt that in order for them to do their jobs, I had to do my job. If that meant drilling a guy, so be it. The code has always been about the players policing themselves and making sure that they are accountable for their actions. You know, I grew up playing hockey out East in Connecticut as a kid, so I have a very good understanding of what the code of honor is all about. I learned early on that if you played dirty or disrespected someone out on the ice, then you were going to have to pay a price for that. You might even get the crap beat out of you. The same is true in baseball and, again, it all boils down to respect.

Disrespect someone or try to show them up and you are going to be dealt with accordingly. For instance, if a team went after one of our top guys, like our No. 4 hitter Eric Davis, then we had to go after their No. 4 hitter. If they tried to show us up, then we retaliated, and vice versa. Everybody wants to keep everybody honest in this game, and it has been that way for a long, long time. Or maybe somebody takes out your second baseman with his spikes high up around the hips—you have to make sure that they don't do that again. You have to send a message, loud and clear. As a pitcher, you simply have to stand up for your teammates, no matter what. If that means knocking that guy down and letting him look up at the stars for a while, so be it. If he spends that second or two flat on his back wondering how much it would have hurt if that ball was just a few inches closer and hit him in the head or neck or ribs, then he would think twice about his actions on the field.

As a pitcher, you have to do those things. It is simply part of your job. In fact, I don't even consider it to be an unwritten rule or gray area. You just do it because you have to, and you don't even think twice about it. You do it for your teammates, and you expect them to do the same for you. The bond you have with those guys you sit across from in the locker room—before and after you hit the field—that is what this game is all about in my eyes. So to earn their respect, that meant everything to me.

Intimidation was everything to me as a pitcher. I would even say that in many aspects it defined who I was out there on the mound. The last thing you want as a pitcher is for someone to think that you are not intimidating and that you won't come inside on him. It was all about intimidation and retaliation—they are a huge part of the code. It is not in every guy though, that is for sure. But for me, it was huge. I think the best line I have ever heard in regard to that was by [NASCAR driver] Dale Earnhardt Jr., whose father, the Intimidator, once told him "You can't put it in somebody, and you can't take it out of them." I really believe that.

Nowadays I think about guys like Brad Lidge, Armando Benitez, and Bartolo Colon. Those guys throw way too many "good strikes." And what I mean by that is, in my opinion, in order to be most effective on the mound, you have to be what I would call "effectively wild." I think it is good to let one get away every now and then and keep the hitters wondering. That doesn't mean you have to hit a guy, but to be able to do your job comfortably, you need to be inconsistent once in a while. Again, I don't condone hitting a guy in the head, ever; you can be extremely effective right up under the armpits, knocking guys down and keeping them honest. But you need to be able to control the inside part of the plate, and if that means sitting a guy down every now and then when he crowds the plate, hey, that's just baseball.

I faced 1,979 guys over my career, and I only hit 12. That's it. Yet I had a reputation for being a "headhunter." Needless to say, I never hit anybody in the head in my career, ever. For the most part, having to retaliate was a tough thing to do, but I did it proudly. I stood up for my teammates, and if anybody disrespected them or showed them up, then I sent the other team a strong message. It wasn't always fun, either. You never knew whether or not a guy would charge the mound and come after you. And, being a pitcher with a big ego, I never wanted to give the other team a freebie by putting a guy on base without making him earn it. So it was usually easier just to put one under a guy's chin rather than drilling him in the ribs. The message was sent loud and clear that we weren't about to be messed with. The fact that I could throw the ball 100 mph was also a big plus, because players know how much it hurts to get hit by a pitch coming that fast.

I have to tell you though, hitting a guy is difficult to do. It really is. I mean when you are in a groove and you are just pounding the strike zone, it is hard to throw it in a certain spot two feet away from what you have been programmed to do your whole life. It can get tricky. I have been pitching since I was eight years old, and I have always been conditioned to throw it in the strike zone. Then, when you have to all of a sudden throw it under a guy's chin, or in his ribs, it looks and feels completely different. That is why guys get beaned sometimes, because it is so unnatural to throw at a guy's chest, or up high and tight, that when you do the ball can occasionally get away from you. Most beanballs are unintentional. Nobody wants to injure or kill a guy; they just want to send him a message and either intimidate him or retaliate for something he or one of his teammates did to you or your teammates.

I have been broadcasting games for more than 10 years now, and the code has definitely changed. The players now are so afraid of being injured in a brawl or getting suspended or fined that the game is just different now. I think too many guys adhere to the code of ethics versus the old school code of honor—which is all about protecting your teammates. You look around the league nowadays and see guys like Jose Guillen and many others who complain about their teammates "not having their backs," and that is the last thing a pitcher wants to hear. To me, guys today just don't understand that in order to do their jobs effectively, they need to have a mental edge, which is intimidation.

Intimidation is a state of mind. It is how you carry yourself out on the mound. Look at a guy like [Yankees closer] Mariano Rivera—that guy is so intimidating. He is just even-keeled all the time. He never smiles, he never puts his head down if he gives up a game-winning home run, nothing. He just carries himself so well. Players can never tell if they have gotten to him or not. Pedro Martinez is another guy who is extremely intimidating, maybe more than anyone in the modern era. Pedro was so feared after his first few years in the league that later he never had to throw up and in on anybody because hitters had gotten the message. He commanded such respect from opposing hitters because of that. It was amazing to see. They knew that even if he was up 0–2 in the count, he still might nail them just to send a message. A Pedro fastball under the chin or square in the back was not a fun experience for a hitter, and that was a huge part of his success. Intimidation is a tactic, and if used properly, it can be a tremendous psychological factor.

Take a guy like Roger Clemens. When he went after Mike Piazza a few years back, that was just classic. The more players talked about him nearly hitting Piazza in the head, the more feared and intimidating he became. It just grew and grew. Players knew not to mess with him because, hey, they might be next. That is an incredible advantage if you are a pitcher, to have that little edge of fear over the batter. And at this level, that might be all you need. Fear is a crazy thing.

I also think that baseball is a lot like hockey in the sense that nobody is really afraid of anybody out there. You can knock a hitter down and he is going to get right back up. I mean, do you think Albert Pujols or Manny Ramirez or David Ortiz or Derek Jeter or Alex Rodriguez are intimidated? Absolutely not. Yet if they just have a simple little fear in the back of their minds that a pitcher like myself is not all there, that something is seriously wrong with him, and he might in fact be a little bit nuts and he might nail them at any time…then I have already won the battle. I have the mental edge at that point, and I can do what I need to do to get him out.

It is the same way in hockey—if guys know that an enforcer like Tony Twist is out there, they have to account for him and be aware of him at every moment. They know that he is capable of coming after them, and because of that they may change the way they skate that shift. Maybe they won't go in front of the net, or maybe they won't follow a guy into the boards and check him, because they know that if they do then they will have to answer to Tony. Fear and intimidation are huge in sports, and they are things you can't really quantify. But, boy, do they make a big difference.

The code is also about the little things, like running up the score when you have a big lead late in the game. That is just disrespectful, because you are basically showing up the guys on the other team. I remember once during a lopsided game with the Cubs, Doug Dascenzo laid down a suicide squeeze on me in like the eighth inning. I was like, "OK, if that is how it's going to be, here is my response to that." So while he was running to first base, I drilled him right in the back. It had to hurt. As far as I was concerned, they were trying to embarrass me and my teammates, so I did what I thought was necessary to retaliate and send a message. I took my medicine for it, but it was something I felt I had to do.

Now, to take that a step further, the next day we played Chicago again, and I wound up batting late in the game. Heathcliff Slocumb was pitching for the Cubs that night, and I thought for sure he was going to retaliate and nail me. Hell, I was expecting it, and deservedly so for what I had done. I wasn't so much worried about getting hit as I was concerned about protecting my pitching arm from getting injured. I knew that I was in a vulnerable situation because I was a left-handed hitter and he was a right-handed pitcher. He could have let me have it, but it was a tight game and he wound up walking me. I wasn't even thinking about swinging the bat—I was in survival mode.

As a pitcher you have to pick your spots in close games sometimes, and I just got lucky that night. I am sure he wanted to get me, but it didn't happen. We wound up winning the game, and I was just glad to get out of that situation in one piece, to tell you the truth. Being in the National League, where pitchers didn't have the luxury of having a designated hitter, it often made things pretty interesting. I was always aware of the fact that I could've been drilled by the opposing pitcher. That kept me honest out there. That was just life in the NL, and you had to deal with it. Believe it or not, though, I was never hit over my entire career.

The bottom line for me was that I never tried to embarrass anybody out there. We were all professionals, and we all worked very hard to get to that level. I never did a dance or anything like that when I struck a guy out; that just wasn't my style. I tried to do my job and then jog off the field, plain and simple. People thought that because I was a "Nasty Boy" that I was just a headhunter. The fact of the matter was I considered myself to be a real student of the game.

I roomed with Norm Charlton for a lot of years with the Reds, and he had three degrees from Rice University. He was a really smart guy, and I learned a lot from him. We used to love to discuss the nuances of the game and break down the psychological warfare of hitting versus pitching. We had a ball—it was great. We would talk about how we were going to pitch certain guys and who we were going to dump on his ass. I think Norm was even a little bit crazier than I was, if you can believe that. He would throw behind guys, which really made them nuts. I mean if you ever wanted to see a guy crap himself, throw a 95-mph fastball behind his ass. He doesn't know what to do. It was hilarious. The ball comes at you so fast and guys know that if they move back, which is their initial instinct, that they could be dead. So to see them squirm was pretty fun.

All in all, I just had so much fun out there. To throw a 95-mph pitch under a guy's chin for the pure joy of seeing how he was going to react, that was fun to me. Then, to know that the guy in the on-deck circle was sweating bullets because of that, now you had them where you wanted them. It was the game within the game. If they were just a little bit afraid, then that was all the edge I needed. The head games were priceless. I miss that part of the game. I was truly blessed with a great arm and could do something most people at this level couldn't do, and I really enjoyed that. It was as much fun to intimidate guys as it was helping my team to win ballgames. Hey, baseball was my business, but I had fun doing it. It will always be a game to me, and that is why I enjoyed it so much.

Foreword by Torii Hunter

The code to me is about being accountable for your actions and not trying to show the other guy up out on the field. Really, it's about respect. You just don't want to disrespect someone out there, or you will have to answer for that. I believe in the integrity of the game, and I think I am well respected amongst my peers in the league because of that. So I try to play the game the right way. I play hard, I stick up for my teammates, and I try to have fun. I also try to represent myself and my team like a true professional, which has always been very important to me.

I can't stress enough just how important it is to protect your teammates out there, though, no matter what. You've got to have their backs and, in turn, know that they have yours. That is how you earn respect in this game. You have to be there for them through thick and thin. If there is a bench-clearing brawl, then I am right there, protecting my boys. I can only hope that they will be there for me as well.

As far as retaliation goes, it is all about justice. You grow up playing this game with the mentality that it is an eye for an eye out there. Again, players have to take care of their teammates, no matter what. That is the way it has always been. If the other team goes after your best player, then you have to go after their best player. If a team tries to take me out and hits me, then we might respond to that by going after an important guy in their lineup. That is how the code works. Maybe the opposing pitcher hits me in the elbow, and I get hurt and can't play for two games. Well, according to the code, we would go after one of their guys who is of the same caliber, maybe a Miguel Tejada or someone like that. Certain managers are like, "Okay, you take out our No. 4 hitter, then we're taking out your No. 4 guy," or "You take out our center fielder, then we're coming after yours." It just depends on the situation and the history leading up to it. History is a big part of it, and these guys have long memories—believe me. Bad blood can boil over, and when it does, that is when crazy things can go down. You never know what can happen in a bench-clearing brawl. It can be scary.

Now, in hockey, the players can fight and just get a five-minute penalty. That's it. In baseball, however, if we fight, we get huge fines and suspensions. So it is a different type of code that we live by. Sure, we have to protect each other, but we also have to be careful not to get ejected and hurt our team by being out of the lineup. And, in addition to the suspensions, there are the fines, which are tough. I mean losing $5,000, $10,000, $20,000 is a lot of money, and that is no fun either. We all have family and friends who depend on us, so you think about those things when you are in the heat of battle. Sure, there are times when you would love to whoop some guy's butt and teach him a lesson, but then you think about the consequences that will ensue. Again, it just depends on the situation, because every now and then the fine and suspension are worth it if you feel strongly enough about getting disrespected.

Most of the time, though, it isn't worth it, so you find other ways to retaliate. That is where your pitcher has to step up and be a man. Or, if the situation isn't right, then we can also take matters into our own hands. Maybe we will take out the second baseman on a hard slide, which is another way we can retaliate. Hey, I am going to try my damnedest to knock that guy over in those situations, and that is all a part of the code, too. Now the second baseman will know it is coming, though, and will try to either hit you with the ball or hit you in the face with his arm on his follow-through after throwing it to first base. So you have to watch out for that. It is a battle. There is so much that goes on behind the scenes, it can get crazy.

Retaliation is a huge part of the game. I remember one time back in 2002 playing against Cleveland and getting drilled in the ribs by Danys Baez. I had hit a home run off of him earlier in the game, and he didn't like that at all. Plus, I admired the home run a little too long, which he clearly took offense at. He felt like I was showing him up and felt like he needed to retaliate. Well, the fact of the matter was I wasn't trying to show him up at all. It was just such a good hit that I kind of shocked myself, so I stared at it for a while. As hitters, we call that "pimping it," and we know that we are going to get it for doing it. I guess I couldn't help myself.

Well, Baez had good control the whole game, but I was just hitting the ball great that night for whatever reason. So he came up and in on me to intimidate me. A good pitcher will do whatever he can to get you off your game in that situation. It is a tactic they will use when you are getting hits off them. They want to disrupt your rhythm and get you thinking about something else. They want you to be uncomfortable in the batter's box and to be worried about getting nailed. They want you to know that there is going to be a price to pay for hitting a home run off them. It's all a part of the game, that's all. You just deal with it. I get that. Finally, he drilled me.

Well, on that particular night, I just decided that I wasn't going to be intimidated, so I picked up the ball that he had just hit me with and threw it right back at him and drilled him in the leg. What a feeling—it was amazing. I wanted to send my own message to him, and I did. It was the best feeling in the world, to tell you the truth. I earned his respect that night, and to this day we are friends, so it is cool. Even now, whenever I see him, we laugh about it.

What was funny about the whole thing was that afterward, I wound up getting a ton of phone calls from guys like Ken Griffey Jr. and Reggie Sanders, all these great players who wanted to congratulate me for having the guts to do something like that. They all said that they were so proud of me for throwing the ball back at him because they had all dreamt of doing it. So that was pretty neat, too. The part that sucked was that I wound up getting a big fine and got suspended for a few games to boot. In my eyes, it was worth it. I definitely made a statement that hopefully would make other pitchers think twice about drilling me down the road.

Another huge part of the code is intimidation. Good pitchers can really intimidate their hitters by coming in on them, and once they sense that fear, it is all over. They have them right where they want them. I think that it is usually the mediocre and weaker players who get intimidated by pitchers, though. I look at it more like a chess match. I usually suspect that if they come up and in on me, they are trying to set me up for something. If a guy like Nolan Ryan or Rob Dibble, who threw a lot of strikes, came up and in on me, then I knew that they were trying to set me up for an outside corner pitch. They wanted to back you off the plate and then take advantage of that. A good hitter will know this and be ready for it.

You know, I am not scared or intimidated very easily, and I don't get nervous either. But, there is one guy who scares me a little bit—Daniel Cabrera. The guy is huge, like 6'9" and 275 pounds, and he throws really hard. I don't think he knows where the ball is going half the time, to tell you the truth, and that can be pretty scary. He keeps guys on their toes, that is for sure. It is not so much that he is intimidating, but rather he makes you feel uncomfortable in the batter's box. He is wild, and he walks a lot of guys, but he is effective. You just don't know what he is going to do out there. Plus, he is a right-handed pitcher and I am a right-handed hitter, so the ball is coming out on the same side that I am on, which means you have very little time to react to an inside pitch. I mean, this guy can throw 100 mph, which is insane when you think about it. That is so fast, you just have such a small window to either swing or get the heck out of the way. So facing him can be a real adventure. I definitely don't want to get hit in the head by that dude. No way.

Throwing at a guy's face is almost illegal. It is so dangerous. Even if one of my teammates hit a guy in the face, I would be like, "What the heck are you doing?" Nobody wants to see that. It has no place in the game whatsoever. Sure, guys get hit with pitches and all of that, but to go after somebody and to get him in the head or face is so unnecessary. Guys can get seriously hurt, or even worse. I mean, we are talking about somebody's career here, and a beanball can end it in a heartbeat. We all have respect for each other as teammates and opponents, and nobody wants to see somebody's livelihood be taken away from him. Sure, out on the field we might be enemies and fierce competitors, but for a pitcher to bean a guy in the face is just the ultimate act of disrespect, in my eyes. Retaliation is a part of the code, but going headhunting can't be tolerated.

Certain pitchers are known as headhunters, and they will throw from the shoulders up in order to get you to back off the plate. They are either trying to brush you away or they are trying to hit you. Either way, guys like that aren't very respected by their peers. It is so hard to get out of the way of a rising 95-mph fastball, and if it gets you just right, that could be it. Lights out.

It happened to me in the spring of 2007 during a game against Kansas City. I got hit in the mouth by Zack Greinke on a 2–2 fastball in the second inning. I was pretty upset. But in that particular instance, I don't think he intentionally tried to bean me in the face. It just happened, and I believe it was a mistake. I could see the ball come out of his hand kind of funny, like it slipped. I could see it coming but just couldn't get out of the way. The ball was rising and followed me as I was trying to bail out. It happened so fast, in the blink of an eye. I think he just lost his control that day. Two batters later he drilled Jason Bartlett, so that tells me that he had no command at all.

Well, my first instinct was to go after him and charge the mound. So I took a few strides toward him after I got hit, because my adrenaline was just pumping. But then I started to feel the pain, and I stopped. I also started to think about the fine I would get, as well as the suspension. So I just figured it wasn't worth it to go after him. It all happened so quickly, like when they say your life "flashes before your eyes" when you die. Once I collected myself and realized that it was probably an accident, I just relaxed. I wound up going to the hospital after that and luckily was able to come back with no problems, other than some soreness and a few stitches. The bottom line was that I got lucky. It was important for me to get right back into the lineup that next night, too, so that I could overcome my fear of getting hit again. I was even able to keep my hitting streak alive, which was at 11 or 12 games at that point, which was pretty neat, too.

The vast majority of pitchers don't want to hit a guy in the head because they know that they could be ending his career. Nobody wants that. Plus, they know that tensions will escalate, and then their teammates will start to get nailed in retaliation. A lot of guys don't recover from a beaning, and sometimes they are never the same. It is such a confidence thing to stand up there and face a pitcher, and if that confidence is lost and they have fear—it's all over. They will never be the same again. I will always remember how Kirby Puckett's career ended after he got beaned in the mouth. That was it for him. It was just a surreal moment that I will never forget. You just never know.

Beyond that, the code is about the little things like "what happens in the locker room stays in the locker room," stealing signs, not doing drugs or steroids, and not running up the score late in the game—stuff like that. I mean, if you are up five runs or more in the seventh inning or later, you shouldn't steal or bunt. No way. If you steal a base or drag bunt for a hit at that point, then that is being disrespectful and you will have to pay for it.

It is showing the other team up. Sure, you can bang out hits and do your thing, but if you run up the score or try to pad your stats late in a blowout, then watch out because we will be coming after you—guaranteed.

I would also say that celebrating excessively over your home run is only okay if you get a walk-off homer at the end of a game. Then it is all right. But if you do it in the middle of a game and show up the pitcher, you better watch out because you are probably going to get it the next time you get up to bat. That is just the way it goes. The same is true too for a pitcher to talk smack to you as a hitter if he strikes you out. If he pumps his fist or says something to you, then that, too, is disrespectful and may warrant retaliation of some sort as well. I mean, stuff like that is what the code is all about, in my eyes. You have to be a professional at this level and act accordingly. If you hit a home run, then act like you have done it a thousand times before. The same is true if you strike somebody out. You don't try to embarrass them. What comes around goes around in this league, and if you play like a jerk, then you will get yours. It might not be right then and there, but eventually it will happen. Trust me, it will happen.

Foreword by Jack Morris

Baseball has policed itself for decades upon decades, and really, that is the basis for the code. I firmly believe that baseball is a game of respect. If you love it, then you respect it. There is so much history and tradition behind it, and if you don't love it or respect it, then you shouldn't be allowed to play it. I feel pretty strongly about that.

Hitting guys has always been a part of the game, and it will always be a part of the game. It is what keeps players honest and what makes them accountable for their actions. The bottom line for me was protecting my players. And I had to protect my own job, too. I knew that I wasn't going to be around for very long if I didn't stick up for myself early on in my career.

Look, most hitters hate pitchers, and conversely, most pitchers don't care for hitters. So we had to coexist and do our jobs. We all did what we had to do out there to help our teams win. Sometimes that meant retaliating. As a big-league pitcher, you just knew when you were going to have to sit a guy down or nail him. Things escalate and you have to protect your guys. That is the way it goes. If your key players are being thrown at, then you have to be there for them, no matter what. Sometimes it is tough, but you have to do it or you won't be around for very long in this business.

I remember when I was playing for Detroit, and there was a guy on the opposing team, I won't name names, who really wanted to inflict bodily harm upon my shortstop, Alan Trammell. He came in spikes-high on him at second base and flat-out tried to hurt him. Well, it was up to me to recognize that and let him know that he was going to have to pay for that type of behavior. I had to let his team know that if they wanted to play that way, then we would play that way, too. If that meant putting him down and having him catch a little dust on his backside, then so be it. I went after him because I had to send a clear message to let them know that we were not going to be intimidated.

I didn't believe in throwing at a guy's head. But I felt very strongly in my convictions that I had to have control of the inside part of the plate. So whatever I had to do to make a hitter understand that, then that is what I had to do. I didn't ever want to intentionally hit a guy, but I had to earn his respect. He had to know that I was going to come inside on him and I was going to keep coming inside on him, no matter what. I wasn't looking for fights. I just wanted to keep guys honest out there.

Retaliation is a strange animal. You can't always just do it when you want to. You have to look at two things: the scoreboard and your bullpen. How much confidence you have in both of those things will be the determining factor, in my opinion. Ultimately, if a situation comes up late in the game, then you have to roll the dice and hand the game over to one of your relievers, because you might get tossed for drilling a guy. If it is after the fifth inning and you are winning, then that game is in your name. It is your win on the line. Prior to the fifth inning, you just do whatever you can do in order to stay in the game and give yourself a chance to win.

To me, if you're going to drill a guy and make a point, then it had better be the baddest fastball that you've got. If I see a guy hit a guy with a curveball, as a retaliation pitch…come on. Being hit by a pitch should hurt. It hurt when you were a little kid and it hurts now, and that is the driving force behind every batter being a little bit afraid each time he steps into the batter's box. And believe me, it hurts a lot worse to get drilled by a Goose Gossage fastball than it does a Brad Radke fastball. Guys knew that they could get more comfortable on a guy like Radke because even if he nailed them, they were usually going to be able to shake it off and head toward first base. A guy like Gossage, meanwhile, was a different story. And trust me, even though his fastball was only clocked at 94 mph, I don't buy that for a second. Back then the radar guns were much different than they are today. Nowadays it seems like everybody can throw 100 mph. I saw how fast Gossage could bring it, and it was a lot faster than most of the guys today. That guy was tough.

Pitching is like chess—you are always trying to stay a move or two ahead of the hitter. Smart hitters are always aware of the situations that they are in, though. They know how to read a pitcher; they study his patterns and his tendencies; they understand their own strengths and weaknesses against that particular pitcher; and they are able to process that information in a fraction of a second. They know when that pitcher will go to his bread-and-butter pitch in certain situations, whether that is a curveball or a fastball, and they play the odds. Good hitters are typically good guessers, too, and more times than not, they don't miss when they guess.

One hitter I had a lot of respect for was Al Oliver. He had amazing bat control. He was one of those rare guys who could seemingly hit pitchers at will with line drives as a form of retaliation. He hit me twice in my career: once off my thigh and once off my stomach. I couldn't even get my glove up fast enough to get to it; he just nailed me. He was such a tough hitter. Well, the next time up I gave him one right off his kneecap, just to let him know that I was there. I had to slow him down, and that was my way of getting back at him. He was one of my most feared opponents because he never hit fly balls, only screaming line drives. He was good. He forced me to elevate my game to challenge him, and I really respected that.

You know, hitting guys is a part of the game, but I for one have never been a headhunter. I don't believe that you have to throw above the guy's shoulders to get your point across to him. If I was ever trying to hit a guy, the best place to throw it was right behind his butt—because that was the first thing that was going to move when he bailed out, and it was going to go right into the ball. So, if you really wanted to hit a guy, that was the simplest way to do it, in my opinion.

Beanballs can happen from time to time, though, and as a pitcher, you never feel good about it. I will never forget the time when I was playing with Detroit and I wound up beaning a guy who would later become one of my personal heroes, Gene Larkin. It was back in 1990, the year before he got the game-winning hit in Game 7 of the World Series when I was pitching with the Minnesota Twins. Anyway, it was a tough game, and the Twins had hit us around pretty good. They had pounded out a bunch of hits off me, and I needed to establish the inner half of the plate, so I tried to brush him back. Well, it got away from me a little bit and Geno just froze.

He never saw the ball coming at him, and it got him right in the head. They had to carry him off on a stretcher.

It was really a scary moment for me. I never meant to hit him; it just got away from me. I felt terrible about it. As a pitcher in that situation, you wonder to yourself, "Did I just end his career? Will this have the same effect on him as it did to Tony Conigliaro, who was never the same after getting beaned?" Well, luckily he bounced right back from it, and we became good friends the next year when we were teammates together with the Twins. We could laugh about it, but it still stuck with me for a long time.

Baseball is such a mental game. Once fear and intimidation get into your head, there is no telling what can happen. I remember playing with a guy in Detroit by the name of Kevin Saucier, a left-handed reliever, who started getting very erratic with his control. He began to hit guys and eventually became so worried that he was going to hurt somebody that he had to retire. It just became a mental block for him. He thought deep down that he might kill somebody, so he had to quit. It was rough. Those kinds of things happen, though. Look at Chuck Knoblauch, who in the latter part of his career just somehow forgot how to throw a ball 40 feet to first base. It is a crazy game, and sometimes guys can just lose it.

Anyway, when you go after a guy, you just never know what can happen. He may take offense and come after you by charging the mound. Things can get pretty crazy at that point, but that is all a part of the game. Usually, however, it is just for show. When players charge the mound and a bench-clearing brawl ensues, the reality is that not too much is really going on. There is a lot of yelling, a lot of shoving, a lot of hugging and grabbing, and actually a lot of laughing. Sometimes bench-clearers are downright hilarious, to tell you the truth. Your main objective is to pair up with someone and try to prevent him from punching your teammate. Then you just hope you don't get sucker-punched in the process. The crowd goes nuts, but it is really pretty harmless, for the most part.

Rarely do you ever see a good baseball fight like you do in hockey. Hockey players use fighting as a tactic not only to retaliate, but also to intimidate. Take a guy like Gordie Howe, who was the last great athlete who actually defended himself. Gordie was the greatest hockey player who ever lived, in my opinion, no question. He was so tough, and he really earned the respect of his opponents. That is what made him so unique. Don't get me wrong—Wayne Gretzky was amazing. But Gretzky had his bodyguards, as do most stars today. Not Gordie. He took care of himself. And not only did he not have any goons to protect him, he also played in an era against way tougher guys. So in addition to having to fight the other team's toughest players night in and night out, he still somehow managed to tally two or three points every game on top of all of that. Talk about intimidation.

Certainly in baseball you would have to look at a guy like Bob Gibson, who was probably the most intimidating pitcher of his era. He wasn't afraid to go after guys, and he could really bring it, too. And because he didn't always have the greatest control, being effectively wild on occasion made opposing hitters just nervous enough to fear him. He was a real intimidator. I had a lot of respect for guys like that, who protected their teammates at all costs and did it on their own terms.

Another pitcher who I really respected was a teammate of mine in Detroit by the name of Milt Wilcox, who wasn't a huge household name by any stretch, but was one of the toughest guys I ever knew. He wouldn't hesitate to throw one, two, maybe even three straight balls up and in on a hitter just to make a point. He had to let the opposing team know that he was not going to let them have that part of the plate, and if that meant sitting a few guys down in order to make that point, then that was that. I respected that about him because it wasn't easy to play that way.

As a pitcher, you always wanted to be intimidating. You wanted guys to fear you; that was half the battle. I will never forget when Kevin Seitzer, a third baseman with the Royals, called me the meanest S.O.B. that ever stepped on the mound. It was shocking to me, because I had never intentionally drilled him before. Sure, I had hit him a few times over the years, but it was always unintentional. Well, he thought I just had it in for him for whatever reason, and that really affected the way he approached me when I was pitching. He hated to face me as a result of that and was really intimidated.

Ironically, this was all news to me, but subconsciously, he was taking himself out of the game every time he faced me because of that. What is funny about the whole thing is that I never realized it until late in my career, and it made me realize just how powerful the art of intimidation could be. My only regret is that I didn't figure this out earlier and drill a lot more people!

Overall, the code is about respect: respect for the game, respect for your teammates, and respect for yourself. I just tried to play the game the right way and help my team win. I never tried to be disrespectful to my opponents or to the game. Fortunately, I was able to play for a long time and have a lot of success along the way. Being emotional is part of the game, but taking things too far can warrant retaliation. As for me, I never pumped my fist or did anything to show up another player when I was pitching. But if I ever got a big strikeout or got my team out of a jam, then I might show some emotion. Those things could be big momentum swingers and could even start rallies. Your teammates would sometimes feed on that emotion—it was almost contagious.

As far as hitters trying to show me up? Personally, I didn't care so much if a guy celebrated when he hit a home run off me. I knew that I had already made one mistake, and I didn't want to make another one. So I blew it off and went about my business. You know, the code is much different today than it was when I pitched, and I am sure it was much different when I pitched than it was a generation before me. Back in the 1950s, '60s, and even the '70s, if a hitter took a monster swing and came out of his shoes or gawked at a home run for 10 minutes, then he could expect the next pitch to come right at his head. That is just the way it was back then. Nowadays, that kind of stuff simply does not happen. The umpires have way too much control over the game now, in my opinion. A lot of that stuff started with Reggie Jackson. He was the first guy to watch his home runs clear the fence, but he was also the first guy to charge the mound, too. So he could back it up and defend himself. As a pitcher you had to respect that.

What did bother me, however, was when guys stole signs and things like that. You know, I didn't cheat, and I didn't want anybody else cheating either. As a pitcher, you knew when guys were either peeking back at your catcher or getting signs from somewhere else. The worst was when you had a guy on second base looking down at your catcher and then relaying the signs to the hitter. You could suspect it pretty easily when he started talking, because you knew that he was secretly telling that guy what pitch was coming or where the catcher was setting up. So I would step off the mound and look right at him and let him know I was putting him on notice. I would say something like: "Hey, do you want to get hurt or do you want the hitter to get hurt?" Guys would get mad and think you were nuts, but that was really fun. You were always trying to stay a step ahead of your opposition. It was a constant cat-and-mouse game.

I also didn't like it when a team ran up the score on us late in the game. For instance, if you are up by a pretty good margin late in the game, the code says you don't lay down a bunt, you don't hit and run, and you don't steal a base. Basically, you don't try to run up the score in an effort to embarrass the other team. When that stuff happens, then I hold the managers accountable. Stuff like that will warrant retaliation in a heartbeat. Maybe not that night, but it will happen. Trust me, they will get theirs in due time. The code says so.

Preface

I love this game. I can remember going to see my hometown Minnesota Twins play at old Metropolitan Stadium before it was torn down and replaced with what most would agree is maybe the ugliest ballpark ever built—the Metrodome. I lived in Chicago and New York for a few years and got a taste of what I was missing out on when I would go to Wrigley Field and Yankee Stadium, two of the game's greatest shrines. But miracles can come true, and I can't even tell you how thrilled I am to know that in just two short years I will be able to take my wife and daughter to see my beloved Twinkies playing on real grass once again in a brand-new ballpark in downtown Minneapolis.

I grew up learning the game in the small, southern Minnesota town of Fairmont. My love of the game came from my grandfather, who used to recruit Triple A ballplayers to come to town to play for his adored Fairmont Martins, a 1950s powerhouse town ballclub that played in the old Southern Minnie league. He would get the players jobs at his furniture stores, and many who would come for the summer would wind up falling in love and spending the rest of their lives there.

I played the game all the way up, from T-ball and Little League to American Legion & VFW and on to the high school varsity. There, for the mighty Fairmont Cardinals, I was a pretty lousy No. 3 pitcher. And no, it wasn't as if we had a five-man rotation either. It was just the three of us. Needless to say, I got pretty good at eating sunflower seeds and tracking pitch counts.

My biggest asset was also my biggest liability: I could throw extremely hard but had very little accuracy. It had always been that way, too. In fact, I have vivid memories of pitching way back in Little League and having hitters stand a good two feet outside of the batter's box in utter fear for their lives. My mother even had to field calls from other parents who were concerned about their child's safety. Ah, yes, the good old days.

I eventually went on to attend the University of Minnesota, where I was recruited to play with the Minnetonka Millers, a local team full of college kids. After unintentionally drilling a few guys in my first outing of relief, it didn't take long for my new teammates to tab me with a nickname: "Nuke," as in Nuke LaLoosh, the wild pitcher played by Tim Robbins in the classic baseball flick *Bull Durham*. I stuck to fraternity beer ball after that, which was apparently a little more my speed.

I was so lucky to have been living in a dorm just a stone's throw from the Metrodome back in 1987 when Kirby Puckett brought Minnesota its first-ever World Series title. I felt blessed again to be there in 1991 when one of our own, Jack Morris, threw arguably the greatest complete-game victory in World Series history to give the Twins their second title in just five years. What a way to bookend my college career.

From there, I pursued my passion for writing, and now, more than 30 sports books later, I have taken what I firmly believe to be the most fascinating journey yet—a behind-the-scenes look at baseball's sacred code of honor. As for the genesis of this book, it is the sequel to a similar book I recently wrote about the hockey code. After interviewing more than 100 NHL enforcers, I learned about how their game polices itself and realized that the only other professional sport that has a code is baseball. Hockey players don't wear masks, and as a result everybody has to be accountable for his actions out on the ice. Disrespect someone, whack a guy in the head with your stick, or take liberties with the other team's star player, and you will get punched in the face. That is how the hockey code works.

The same philosophy is true in baseball. If a player celebrates a little too much after a home run, peeks back to steal the catcher's signs, or slides hard spikes-high into second base, he too will have to be accountable. That may mean getting thrown at up and in, or it may mean getting drilled with a 95-mph fastball in the ribs. Either way, the wheels of the code are set into motion, ensuring justice through intimidation and retaliation.

One could only wish that football players would take off their face masks, too, and go back to the old leather helmets, in order to enjoy that same level of respect and accountability as baseball and hockey have found. You certainly wouldn't see a 5'9" cornerback dancing in the end zone and taunting an opposing player after he tackled him if that were the case. Instead, he would lose some teeth while learning a very valuable lesson about not trying to embarrass, humiliate, or show someone up while he is trying to do his job.

My book is intended to celebrate the honor and courage behind the players who have made the great game of baseball what it is. It is about how the code represents good sportsmanship rather than individual gamesmanship and showmanship. And even though fighting and retaliation are at the core of the book, it is really about much, much more than that. Hopefully it will explain why those things exist and what purpose they serve in the game today.

After more than a year of research, I was able to interview more than 75 current and former ballplayers, managers, coaches, and media personalities to get their insights and perspectives on how the code has evolved over the years. They helped me to identify and chronicle dozens of different subcodes, which all collectively make up the baseball code. Some players opened up and poured their guts out, while others chose to stay off the record. That's cool—I know that the first rule of Fight Club is "There is no Fight Club...."

I wanted to examine the roles of intimidation, retribution, and retaliation in the game. I wanted to know why players got drilled. I wanted to know why they stole signs and how they did it. I wanted to know why there are bench-clearing brawls and why players charge the mound. I wanted to know why it is deemed so disrespectful for a team to run up the score or bunt or steal a base with a big lead late in a game. I wanted to know the stories behind the stories and hear what really goes on in those secret meetings at the mound.

My goal in writing the book was to go behind the scenes and let others in on an unexplored facet of the game that had always intrigued me. I hope to inform, entertain, and hopefully educate in the process. Like you, I am a fan with a passion for learning and a passion for the game.

What an adventure it was to meet and interview so many truly fascinating characters along the way. There was Dr. Mike Marshall, a retired big-league pitcher–turned-PhD who is as opinionated as they come; Tim Tschida, one of the most intellectual humans I have ever met, who just happens to be a major league umpire; Al Worthington, an old-timer who actually had the guts to walk away from the game because he didn't feel it was right that his White Sox were stealing signs with a pair of binoculars from the center-field scoreboard; and of course there was Torii Hunter, for years the heart and soul of my beloved Minnesota Twins, and now a member of the Los Angeles Angels of Anaheim—a great guy who I am so proud to now call my friend. So many different opinions, so many different points of view—it was truly an experience of a lifetime.

I wanted to cover a broad spectrum of opinions and capture as many stories as I could. So I interviewed players who played all different positions, came from all walks of life, and were from all different eras. I did try, however, to focus on the relationships between the pitcher and catcher—the battery—who are at the foundation of the code. What the players shared with me was insightful, inspiring, and even hilarious. I hope you enjoy reading about their code half as much as I enjoyed writing about it. Cheers!

1

In the Beginning...

To better understand the history behind the code, let's go back to around the turn of the 20th century and chronicle the evolution of intimidation and retaliation in professional baseball. The game had been steadily growing in popularity over the previous several decades, and by now fans were coming out in droves to see their favorite teams do battle. Terms such as beanballs, drillings, plunkings, high heat, chin music, and just plain ol' throwing inside were all a part of the game's vocabulary. In fact, headhunting pitchers were good for business in those days. They drew fans to ballgames and sold tickets, which made the team owners very happy.

It was a rowdy game, to be sure. Pitchers and hitters dueled at home plate, managers and coaches feuded in the dugouts, and the players clashed in the field. As the pitchers of this era began to throw more sophisticated pitches that could rise and dip, the hitters became increasingly frustrated. Batters became more aggressive, and with that, pitchers began throwing inside more and more often to back them off the plate. When things escalated, players would get drilled. In many instances, beanball wars would break out, with utter chaos ensuing.

When batters did get on base, things often didn't get much easier. You see, there was only one umpire overseeing each game at this point. So the infielders used to have a field day with the base runners as they tried to round the bases: tripping them, holding them, taunting them, and basically doing anything they could to slow them down without getting

Pitcher Bert Blyleven on the Code

"The most important part of the code to me was to protect my players at all costs. If one of my guys was being thrown at or was on the receiving end of a hard slide, then it was my job to protect him. I was brought up that way and I firmly believe in the virtues and values of what the code stands for. I got thrown out of a few ballgames because of it but felt that it was important to stand behind my teammates.

"I came up to the big leagues in 1970, and back then there was no DH rule and the pitchers had to hit. So, you had to be accountable for your actions out there. Unlike in hockey, where you have an enforcer who takes care of the fighting, in baseball you have several guys who have to protect one another. It all comes down to respect, and you have to take care of each other out there. If somebody is disrespecting you, then you hope that your teammates will be there for you and protect you by whatever means necessary."

caught. Players would retaliate and situations would get out of control as the frontier justice mentality of the old Wild West took over.

Because foul balls didn't count as strikes in those days, hitters would foul off as many pitches as they could while waiting patiently for the one that looked just right. Pitchers would get irritated to no end by this, as their pitch counts rose unnecessarily, and eventually they would retaliate. To prevent this, the major leagues ultimately decided to make a foul ball into a strike. With that, batting averages plummeted and pitchers got the upper hand. The balance of power swung even more in their favor as the spitball became an effective weapon. Pitchers used saliva, mud, and just about anything that they could to grease up the balls and get them to perform tricks in midair. It drove the hitters insane.

The game grew and expanded as more and more strategy was introduced into the game by the coaches and players. Teams could no longer just sit back and whale away at the pitches they wanted, running up the score. They would have to manufacture runs by getting men on base, bunting, stealing, squeezing, and executing hit-and-runs. Signs from the coaches to the players, as well as between the pitchers, catchers, and middle infielders, were used to orchestrate all of these maneuvers.

While the game was evolving in some aspects, it was regressing in others, especially when it came to the issue of respect. Over the following decades, more and more pitchers would strike fear into their opponents by hurling beanballs. To retaliate, the batters would charge the mound to exact revenge right on the spot, or the opposing pitchers would just simply return the favor. It was a tit-for-tat approach to getting even, and the basis for what the code would evolve into. Fights were commonplace in those days, especially with hothead players like Ty Cobb stirring it up out on the base paths. Cobb was one of the most feared men of his era, and his dirty tactics were often the impetus for inciting fights.

Things would become brutal, literally. According to famed historian Bill James, at least four minor league players died from beanings between 1909 and 1920. Then, sadly, tragedy struck the major leagues on August 16, 1920, when Cleveland shortstop Ray Chapman was fatally struck by Yankees pitcher Carl Mays during the fifth inning of a game being played at the Polo Grounds. Mays, who had a unique "submarine-style" delivery, threw the ball up and in, and it wound up sailing inside and striking Chapman in the temple. Chapman, who tended to crowd the plate, seemed to freeze as the pitch came at him. He fell to the ground instantly with blood streaming from his left ear. He managed to get up and start walking toward the dugout, only to collapse on the field a few moments later. Chapman, who was one of the most popular figures in the game at the time, was then carried away by his teammates and taken to the hospital, where he would be pronounced dead just 12 hours later.

First Baseman Kent Hrbek on the Code

"The code in my eyes has kind of gone away from what it used to be in recent years. Retaliation used to be almost automatic back when I was a kid watching the game. If a guy hit a home run, then the next guy would get bopped. Now you see all the showboat stuff going on too. Guys today stand there and do the "Thank you, lord" as they look up at the sky and celebrate before they take their sweet time getting around the bases. Some of these guys take like 20 seconds to get around the bags. It is ridiculous. I think [Minnesota Vikings coach] Bud Grant said it best when commenting on guys scoring touchdowns. He would tell his guys to respectfully hand the ball to the referee and act like they've been there before. That is a classic line from a classic guy and really speaks volumes about what is wrong with all sports today. It should be about playing the game the right way and not about showing guys up or hotdogging it out there."

Outfielder Dave Winfield on the Code

"First of all, you have to know the rules—written and unwritten—in this game. That is essential. I played very hard because I wanted to win. If you knock a guy over, that is okay—you don't have to be friendly out on the field. But you should never try to intentionally hurt anyone out there. That is when you have gone too far in my eyes. You can't show people up out there because baseball is a dangerous sport."

The sports world was shocked and horrified after hearing the news of the terrible tragedy. While there had been other high-profile beanball incidents in past years, this one was especially unique in that it happened in New York City. The media had been out in droves that day to cover, among other things, Babe Ruth, who would go on to set a new home-run record that season with 54—shattering the old one by 25 round-trippers. Ruth would witness the entire incident from his position in right field.

Mays felt terrible and insisted that he didn't bean Chapman on purpose and that the pitch had simply slipped. Many felt that the reason Chapman froze on the play and didn't duck out of the way was because he had trouble picking up the dirty-gray baseball as it came rifling toward his head. Dirty, weathered, and beat-up balls were a much bigger problem than anybody had realized. As a result, a silver lining would emerge. Major League Baseball, fearful of future tragedies, announced shortly thereafter that it would abandon the practice of keeping weathered and dirtied balls in play. New balls would be required to be used during games, replacing the filthy ones that were usually stained dark brown with tobacco juice and phlegm from the spitballers of this era.

Pitcher Tommy John on the Code

"The code to me was just playing the game hard and playing the game the right way. If you wanted to do something cheap or disrespectful, then you had to expect that you were going to get something in retaliation, either by getting thrown at or by having your guy get taken out extra hard at second base. That is just the way it is in baseball, and it has been that way for a very, very long time."

Manager Tom Kelly on the Code

"The code is about not embarrassing anybody. I don't want to be embarrassed, and I don't want anybody to embarrass me. The code is also about just playing the game hard and with respect; the fans deserve that. They deserve to see players running balls out, doing the fundamental things, and just trying their best. I liked to have guys who could lead by example, guys like Kirby Puckett and Paul Molitor, who would show the younger guys how to play the game the right way."

In fact, the league would take it a step further and soon announced it would take measures to eventually outlaw spitballs, as well as trick pitches that required scuffing or dirtying balls. While veteran spitballers would be allowed to continue their craft, all newcomers would be banned from the practice. The league was trying to clean up its act and make the game more family-friendly. The infamous "Black Sox" World Series cheating scandal had hurt the game's image, and the owners decided to take action. Kenesaw Mountain Landis was named as the first commissioner and set out to give the game a makeover.

The new rules requiring clean baseballs did more to clean up the game, both literally and figuratively, than perhaps anything in baseball history. As the decades of the 1920s and '30s were ushered in, a new offensive era would soon follow. Lighter bats and clean white balls could only mean one thing—more home runs. The fans ate it up and came out in droves.

With more offense, however, also came more defense, as in pitchers doing whatever they could to defend their livelihoods and protect their teammates. For the players, it was all about respect. As such, each and every violation of the game's sacred honor code had to be dealt with accordingly. A whole new breed of fireballers entered the fray, and with them came more beanball incidents and more hitters charging the mound to get revenge.

In 1941, after several teammates got beaned, members of the Brooklyn Dodgers took matters into their own hands and inserted thin protective liners into their caps as a safety precaution. Once word got out, the players immediately started to take heat from their opponents for being cowards. The Dodgers weren't the only ones who felt like something needed to be done. In fact, Negro League star shortstop Willie Wells reportedly modified a construction helmet after being knocked out cold from a pitch by Baltimore spitballer Bill Byrd. Once, Wells apparently even used a miner's helmet.

Second Baseman Al Newman on the State of the Code Today

"The code to me is about playing the game the right way and respecting the history of the game. I think back to what my old manager Tom Kelly used to tell us: 'Respect the game and it will respect you; the game will still go on even without you.' That is what it is all about to me.

"The code has changed a lot, though, nowadays. It used to be that if a guy hit a home run and then danced around the bases, he was going to get drilled the next time he came up to bat. But now, with the fat contracts and insurance policies that the players have gotten through their agents, all bets are off. Between free agency and the fact that so many players have the same agents now, they are much more reluctant to retaliate against each other. Hell, when I started out half of the players didn't even have an agent. And if you did have one it was so he could handle your contract—not like today, where they are the player's mouthpiece.

"Now the managers have to deal with the agents more than they do the players. Whenever anything comes up, the players now run off and call their agents. Back in our day you just stood up like a man and spoke for yourself. So that is a problem, in my eyes, when you talk about the respect for the game. That part of the game has been hurt so much.

"The agents now have to 'sell' their client's abilities in the free market and hype them up. In fact, that is where the saying 'don't believe the hype' comes from—the agents hyping up their players through the media. Players used to let their talent speak for them, and if recognition in the media followed, that was just a bonus. Now it seems like so much of it is just fabricated. Guys want to be on ESPN every night. They know that the fans love that, and in the end it may help them get a bigger contract. Hey, that is just the way it is.

"These new general managers in the game today are so different than when I was playing. They are all about 30 years old, and what that tells me is that they never played the game. I am not saying they don't know the game, but they see the game and the players as numbers, in a business sense. As a result, a player like myself wouldn't survive in today's game. The things that I brought to the table weren't stats-related. I could steal bases, draw walks, move runners over, pinch hit, pinch run, come off the bench, be the utility guy, and do the dirty work. I was a good locker-room guy, too, but none of that stuff, those intangibles, shows up on paper.

"You know, Tom Kelly walked away from millions of dollars and a guaranteed job a few years back because he just didn't feel like he could relate to and effectively teach this new breed of player. All of the distractions, the lack of respect for the game, and the money that was being thrown around to mediocre players finally got to him. That to me says a lot.

"Look, great teams need all sorts of players, from superstars to role players. I worked hard, played the game the right way, and walked away with a pair of World Series rings. That is what it was all about to me. All of that other stuff didn't matter. I just hope more players in today's game realize those things and stay true to the code."

The issue of race and baseball would finally come to the forefront in 1947, when Jackie Robinson was eventually allowed to play in the major leagues with the Brooklyn Dodgers. The civil rights movement was in full swing, and it was an historic time in American history. Our boys were returning home from overseas military service in World War II and were full of aggression. Many of the more-prejudiced ballplayers couldn't deal with an integrated baseball diamond and did whatever they could to make life absolutely miserable for No. 42.

Players taunted Robinson with verbal attacks and spiked him on the base paths. As for the pitchers? They knocked him down, drilled him, and beaned him early and often. Robinson's forearm was nearly broken on several occasions from having to use it as a shield from would-be beanballs. As more and more black players entered the league, more and more incidences of racism would occur.

Robinson wasn't able to exact revenge very often, but when he did, he made it count. On one occasion, after being thrown at by New York Giants headhunter Sal "the Barber" Maglie, Robinson got even by plowing over Giants second baseman Dave Williams. The collision was so violent that it ultimately ended Williams's career.

In 1953 the Brooklyn Dodgers' top minor league shortstop prospect, Don Zimmer, playing for the St. Paul Saints of the American Association, was nearly killed when a beanball fractured his skull and left him unconscious for a week. Zimmer, who spent a total of seven weeks in the hospital following the incident, underwent brain surgery and even had to learn how to talk again.

Zim later garnered a reputation as a player who would freeze when the ball was thrown up and in. "Plate paralysis," as it was known, would prove to be costly for Zimmer yet again a few years later when Reds pitcher Hal Jeffcoat tossed a slider that got away and knocked Zimmer unconscious, breaking his cheekbone in the process. Doctors warned Zim that further

Pitcher Jim Perry on the Code

"You had to always protect your players. That was the bottom line. If they were being thrown at or hit, you had to go out and let the other side know that you weren't going to tolerate it. Retaliation is necessary in those instances, otherwise your guys would be thrown at all game. And if somebody did something to show me up, then I had a long memory for that kind of stuff. They would get what was coming eventually. You just had to be patient and pick your spots."

beanings could result in blindness or worse. Zim was a tough dude, though, and came back strong.

"'Popeye' scared me half to death," wrote Hall of Fame pitcher Don Drysdale of Zimmer in his autobiography. "He stood in there, right over the plate, daring you to come inside on him. He had a motto about that, too: 'If you're going to hit me, don't wound me. Get me good. I don't want to lie there quivering. Just end it.'"

That next season another horrific beanball incident occurred, this one taking place on August 27 in a game between the Philadelphia A's and the Chicago White Sox. A's pitcher Marion Fricano hit Chicago third baseman Cass Michaels so hard that he wound up in critical condition at the hospital and was even given his last rites. Michaels would recover from his injuries, but never played the game again.

Eventually the leagues decided to take action in order to prevent any further tragedies. With that, in 1956 Major League Baseball mandated that all batters must wear protective batting helmets made from hard plastic whenever they came up to bat. (Helmets with an earflap wouldn't be required for nearly another three decades.) While most applauded the decision, others felt like it gave certain headhunting pitchers a free pass to throw up and in on hitters. In fact, a handful of minor league and amateur ballplayers were killed over the next decade as a result of being beaned, even though they were wearing helmets.

This seems like a good place to transition into each one of the codes and what they are all about. With a brief overview of the first 100 years or so under our belts, let's now take a much closer look at how the next half century has shaped and affected the game's revered code of honor.

2

On Retaliation

The code is, was, and always will be about one thing: respect. If a player or team feels disrespected or "shown up," then retaliation in some form will undoubtedly occur. Players have to be held accountable for their actions at this level of play, and that is why the game polices itself.

The most common way for a team to retaliate for a code violation is to have its pitcher either throw a brushback pitch, which is a pitch up and in and intended to serve as a warning, or simply drill the batter. To drill a guy, or plunk him, means that you are hitting him anywhere but in the head or face—which is better known as a beanball. Beaning a guy can maim or kill, so it is a pretty rare occurrence. Most beanings are accidents, but there are still a handful of headhunting pitchers out there who aren't afraid to go upstairs.

For the most part, however, a pitcher will drill a guy as a form of retaliation in the arm, thigh, butt, back, or ribs. What happens after that split-second moment of fear and pain is what makes the game so damn exciting. Everybody has got an opinion on the subject, too.

Players and managers alike know that you have to keep players honest out there, no matter what. "I know if somebody throws at one of our players, then something's going to happen," said longtime manager Larry Bowa. "You've got to stick up for your teammates. I'll take a loss to get the point across."

Certain pitchers were better at retaliating than others. "I had an automatic thing," said Don Drysdale, one of the game's all-time great

First Baseman Harmon Killebrew on Retaliation

"As a hitter, you had to hold your ground; otherwise, pitchers would just throw at you all day. If you did get hit, the best thing to do was to just dust yourself off and run to first base like nothing had happened. If you ever let the pitcher know that it bothered you to be thrown at, then they would use that against you and keep doing it. You really had to hide your emotions over stuff like that and keep those things close to your vest. In fact, if we got drilled back in our day, we didn't even want to rub it. You just did not want to let the pitcher have the satisfaction of thinking he hurt you or was able to intimidate you. Later, after you were in the dugout, the trainer would then come over and freeze it with ethyl chloride to numb it up and take down the swelling and bruising.

"I got hit a lot over the years, but the worst shot I ever took was a Ryne Duren fastball back in the late '50s. He got me right above the elbow, and that thing puffed up like nothing I had ever seen before. The doctor stuck a needle in it, and it was just like a spigot with all of the fluid that had gotten in there. Even to this day, whenever I see Ryne he always smiles at me and asks 'Hey Harmon, do you know what the weather is going to be like tomorrow?' He thought that was the funniest thing in the world, but let me tell you, it hurt like crazy."

intimidators. "It was two for one. One of our guys, two of theirs." The late Hall of Famer even used to keep a list written under the bill of his cap of the pitchers who had drilled his teammates, and then check them off one by one as he got the opportunity to retaliate against them.

The players call it "protection," as in if a guy gets drilled, the opposing pitcher will have to protect his players by retaliating in kind. For example, on July 27, 1976, then-Baltimore slugger Reggie Jackson got beaned by Yankees pitcher Dock Ellis and had to be carted off the field on a stretcher. Jackson would later refer to the incident as "the most frightening thing that's ever happened to me in baseball." Honoring the code, Orioles pitcher Jim Palmer responded by drilling New York's leadoff hitter, Mickey Rivers, square in the back. "Our best hitter gets hit in the face, and who knows how long he's going to be out? You've got to do something to protect your hitters," said Palmer.

Retaliation was pretty cut and dried to pitcher Kevin Millwood, who had his own rules on when and where to hit a batter in retaliation. "It comes down to whether you think your guys are getting thrown at on purpose, and when they are, you have to protect them," said Millwood. "If you don't, you won't be able to show your face in the clubhouse again." As far as where to hit them, Millwood added, "My rule is to keep it below the shoulders; that is written in stone for me. You don't throw at somebody's head."

While nearly every big-league manager would agree that throwing inside is an important part of the game, they also know that drilling players intentionally is a very slippery slope. Take, for instance, the melee that erupted between the Angels and the Padres in March of 2002 that featured not one, but two bench-clearing brawls. The festivities commenced when Angels starting pitcher Aaron Sele tried to back Ryan Klesko off the plate and wound up drilling him in the back. Klesko charged the mound and the benches cleared. Padres pitcher Bobby Jones then retaliated by throwing some chin music to Angels third baseman Troy Glaus, at which point Glaus also charged the mound for round two. After the game the fireworks continued, with Angels manager Mike Scioscia offering up some suggestions for the league to consider.

"If they [Major League Baseball] think a guy is throwing at someone's head, they should step in and suspend a guy to make it a deterrent," said Scioscia. "Not a one-day or two-day suspension. Something so that pitchers know, if they're not pitching responsibly, there are consequences. Then players wouldn't have to take it into their own hands."

"This game is meant to be played aggressively and pitched aggressively," added Scioscia. "There's plenty of room for pitchers to execute the inside pitch. We're human. Pitches are going to get away. It's the deliberate attempt I question a lot. There are other ways to send a message than throwing at a guy's body. You're running the risk of putting your team in more risk. Where does it end? You're throwing 93 mph, and if you're off by a foot, you kill a guy."

Other high-profile managers have expressed strong opinions on the topic as well.

"I think they've taken it to the point where they've made it too safe for everybody," said longtime manager Sparky Anderson. "I think you have to live dangerously. Without that, you take away some of the competitive edge. I'm not saying I believe in throwing at somebody just to put them in the hospital, but I do believe you ought to be allowed to knock a man off that plate, and then it's his responsibility to get out of the way."

"I think the brushback pitch is becoming a dinosaur," added current Cubs manager Lou Piniella. "The umpires have made it so, along with the league presidents, the owners, and the players. Nobody wants to see anything that could cause a scuffle on the field. Too much money is being made and a very important, high-priced commodity could get hurt."

Where you drill a guy says a lot, too. Just ask pitcher Mike Marshall:

> My favorite spot to drill a guy was right in the middle of the back. I probably enjoyed that the most. My ball would go in on them and they would turn and expose their back just as it was about to hit them. You knew that was going to sting, which made me happy. If I had to hit a guy, it was for a reason, so I took pride in doing it. I never went above the shoulders, though. That wasn't necessary. I was also pretty good at coming in on guys with my fastball if I had to. I had a lot of movement on it and could bring it in tight on guys' hands. I remember one time facing Felix Millan, and for some reason he started yelling at me, taunting me. So I took him to 3–2 in the count and then drilled him in the forearm. That shut him up.

Retaliation in baseball isn't just about pitchers getting back at hitters, either. The code says that teammates must stick up for each other, no matter what. That is one of the reasons why enforcers exist in pro hockey,

Coach Steve Liddle on Retaliation

"I remember catching a game in Triple A ball one time, and my pitcher had given up a couple of back-to-back home runs. He had hung a couple of breaking curveballs, and the hitters just jacked them out of the park. Well, I could see it in his eyes that he was frustrated and was going to drill the next guy up. So I went out to the mound and told him that if he drilled the next guy up because he was mad about the fact that the two previous hitters had homered off of him, I wasn't going to even try to stop the hitter from charging the mound.

"I told him that those homers were his fault and nobody else's, so the next guy up didn't deserve to get it. If a guy digs in and cheats to get an advantage over you, then that is one thing. But if the pitcher makes a bad pitch and is punished for it, well that is just a part of the game. I just didn't agree with drilling that next guy in that situation. That was my pitcher being lazy and not respecting the game as far as I was concerned, and that is what I told him."

Pitcher Kevin Tapani on Retaliation

"For me, when I had to drill a guy or even just flip him over, I would almost always give him a chance to get out of the way. I never wanted to intentionally hit guys, so I would always give them the option of getting out of the way. I could throw it up and in, but they could duck out if they had to. It was more about sending a message in those situations. I tried to be a professional when I had to do those types of things and hopefully opposing hitters respected that about me. If I really had to hit him, then I would get him on the back side where there was a lot of padding. I never wanted to take a guy out of the lineup.

"I remember a situation one time where I had to retaliate against Cal Ripken Jr. in Baltimore. I had to be real careful not to hit him. I just remember thinking to myself 'Oh man, what if I accidentally drill him and end the streak [his consecutive-games-played streak]?' But luckily that never happened. As soon as you came in on a guy like that, though, a respected veteran, you were going to wake up his teammates. They weren't going to be too happy about it, and you would definitely hear from them."

to protect the smaller guys from being intimidated and abused by bigger opposing players.

As for the breakdown of how a team decides on the how, when, why, and where to drill a guy, former Oakland catcher Terry Steinbach explains the process:

As far as how a drilling will go down out there, each team is different. Some teams will have the pitcher make the call and let him figure out when and where he wants to handle it. Other teams will have the catchers or even a veteran position player make the call. It varies from team to team and from situation to situation.

When I was playing in Oakland, we had a sort of system where we would take input from several key people. I mean if a guy gets nailed, he is pissed and of course wants to get immediate retaliation right then and there, to get revenge. If it were up to him, he would nail the next four guys and let them suffer like he was. Well, you have to take that guy out of the equation sometimes, to get an unbiased opinion. You have to decide what is the best course of action for the team. We asked our most respected guys on the team, the guys who really knew the code, to help make those decisions. Then we would go out and do it. In our system, there was no signal from the catcher. The call to drill a guy would come from the bench. It was all predetermined before we hit the field that inning. There were no random acts of retaliation or anything like that.

I would also add that we never tried to hit a guy in the head. That was forbidden. Pitchers know that they need to stay between the shoulders and knees; that is part of the code, too. I don't think it mattered so much where you hit them in that area, whether it was in the back or in the ribs or thigh—each one was supposed to send a specific message.

From there, I had to make sure that I was able to protect my pitcher if that guy decided he wanted to charge the mound. That was my job out there, and I didn't take that lightly. If you are going to have the balls to drill a guy, then you have to have the balls to back it up. As a team, we expected our pitchers to protect us, whether that meant throwing purpose pitches up and in or drilling a guy. So it was up to us to protect him at all costs in return. If we had an opposing pitcher who was trying to intimidate us, then that would factor into the decision, too. You had to weigh each situation and retaliate accordingly. Otherwise things could escalate and that is when guys get hurt. You have to play with emotion, but you also have to play smart.

You also had to look at the history of each situation. Some teams just didn't like each other and that was a part of it, too. Look, I believe 100 percent that you have to be able to pitch inside. It is a must for your team to have any success out there. But when you do that, the other team will take offense at that and question whether or not you are intentionally trying to hit one of their guys. It was a big game trying to keep up with it all.

Patient Revenge

Baseball players have long memories, too, and will wait to retaliate—even if it means waiting years—to get the justice they feel is necessary. There is a term for that in baseball: "patient revenge." It means "what comes around goes around," even if it takes a season or two. A good example to illustrate this happened in 1980, when Tigers outfielder Al Cowens charged White Sox pitcher Ed Farmer on his way to first base. Farmer had drilled Cowens the previous season when he was with the Royals, and Cowens finally saw his opportunity to get back at him. Cowens was running out a routine ground ball and decided to just skip first base altogether and instead go after Farmer.

Like Cowens, Twins manager Tom Kelly was also willing to wait for justice to be served. "I remember an incident several years back during spring training where our shortstop rounded third and slid in hard at home plate," recalled Kelly. "Well, I didn't think anything of it. It wasn't a dirty play or anything like that. Two innings later our shortstop got up to bat and the pitcher threw the first pitch behind his head and then drilled him with the next pitch. Turned out he was upset that he had run over his catcher and felt like he needed to retaliate. Now, because I didn't think that the play at the plate was dirty or disrespectful, I had an issue with my guy getting drilled. So two months later we faced those fellas again, and I told my pitcher before the game to drill their shortstop in the ribs as retaliation, sort of an eye-for-an-eye thing. I just felt like that was the right thing to do. He did it and nothing much came of it, but I am sure he wondered why the hell he got drilled for no apparent reason. I would assume that the veteran guys probably filled him in afterwards."

Another example of patient revenge occurred in 1971, when outfielder Billy North got beaned by pitcher Doug Bird in a minor league game. Three years later, North finally got his opportunity to get back at Bird when he was pitching for the Royals. North, playing for Oakland, was up to bat against Bird and "accidentally" let his bat fly out of his hands. So he walked out toward the shortstop to retrieve it. However, as he was walking out there very nonchalantly, he picked up a head of steam and charged the mound, getting in a few good licks on Bird before the skirmish could be broken up.

Current Twins manager Ron Gardenhire recalled a similar incident. "My first manager in professional baseball was a guy by the name of Jack Aker, and he told me a funny story one time," Gardenhire said. "I think

Pitcher Dave Goltz on Retaliation

"The biggest thing for me was when a guy would disrupt my rhythm. There was one guy in particular, Mike Hargrove, who really irritated me every time he would come to the plate. He would step into the box and then go through all of these idiosyncrasies, like a routine, before he would come set. It drove me nuts. And he would do it after every pitch. I would just as soon drill him and put him on first base rather than waste my pitches on the guy. It was ridiculous. He would then get mad for throwing at him, but that was just the way it was. I had to let hitters know what I was and wasn't going to put up with out there."

First Baseman Kent Hrbek on Retaliation

"I never appreciated it when a pitcher came up above my chest. To me that was just stupid. It is really dangerous to throw at a guy's head, and that is not what retaliation is all about anyway. I mean, a good shot to the coconut could kill you. So if a guy needs to be drilled, I say get him in the thigh or butt or back, but not up and in. I would rather see the two guys fight like men out in the parking lot, to tell you the truth, rather than see a guy get nailed in the head. That goes beyond the code in my eyes. It is almost grounds for manslaughter if you think about it. A guy throwing a 100-mph sphere right at another guy's head—that can go really wrong in a hurry."

he was pitching with the Mets at the time, and somebody drilled one of his guys. Well, they never had the opportunity to get even that night. So they had to wait until the middle of the next season before they saw that team again. Finally, when they faced them, Jack drilled the guy on the first pitch. He then looked right at him, pointed, and said, 'That was for last year, you son of a bitch!'"

For pitcher Dave Boswell, it took over a year to get his payback. "Retaliation is a necessary aspect of baseball, and my motto was 'as long as it takes,'" said Boswell. "Things were never forgotten out there, and it was my job to make sure retribution was carried out. Players need to be accountable for themselves, and they usually knew why they were getting drilled. I remember when I was with the Twins one year and Harmon Killebrew got tripped on a play and wound up missing three months of the season. That was a really big deal; he was our main run-producer, our meal ticket. Well, I won't name any names, but it took me over a year to get that guy, but I got him. I had to protect my guys. That was something I strongly believed in. You know, in all my years of pitching, not once did I ever hit a guy on purpose…they just didn't get out of the way."

For pitcher Mike Marshall, the retaliation was for personal reasons:

I remember one time having to wait to get Joe Rudi. He wound up hitting a home run off of me in the World Series, and I had to wait two years before I could get him back. I eventually got to face him, and he was moving out of the batter's box for the first couple of pitches, to avoid me. Finally, on a 3–2 count, where he had to stay in there, I drilled him in the forearm. I didn't do it because of the home run, though. Rather, it was because he talked about the home run in the newspapers after the game. He talked about how he outsmarted me and about how he thought he was so clever. That was unnecessary, as far as I was concerned, and it warranted retaliation on the basis of how he disrespected me. So I got him.

He said that he knew I was going to throw a fastball on the first pitch because I had just come into the game as a reliever and didn't get much time to warm up. That was nonsense. I didn't warm up because I very seldom ever warmed up when I came out in relief. And I threw the fastball inside because that was the game plan I had before the game had even started. I studied players and their tendencies and planned for everything. I tried not to leave much to chance, but that time he got the better of me. Yes, he guessed right and hit a home run off of me, and that is just baseball. But to rub it in, that was where he crossed the line. Well, in the end I put that 5¼-ounce baseball right where I wanted it to go, and I got the last laugh.

Frank Viola had his own unique take on patient revenge:

As a veteran pitcher, you just knew when you had to drill somebody, but you also had to pick your spots. If it was late in a tight game, you couldn't just drill a guy and put him on first base. That might cost you the ballgame. Maybe the payback wouldn't be until the next time you saw that team, even if the next series was weeks or months away. You would just have to wait and then drill the culprit at the appropriate time. Baseball players are like hockey players in the sense that we never forget. I had a great memory, and trust me, I was going to get that guy back one way or another. Sometimes it was fun to make guys sweat it out a little bit. If they knew it was coming, then they would be nervous every time you faced them. The suspense and buildup was half the fun. Then, when they least expected it, wham!

Third Baseman Ron Coomer on Getting Drilled

"Sometimes you just know that you are going to get drilled, either for something you did or for something one of your teammates did. When that happened, and you knew it was coming, you just tried to grin and bear it. There was no sense in charging the mound or anything like that if you got drilled in a spot that wasn't dangerous. If the pitcher got you in the middle of the back or in the ass, then you had to suck it up. If you knew he wasn't trying to hurt you or your career, and he was just doing what he was probably told to do, then that is just baseball. Sure, it would hurt and sure, it would suck to have seam marks on your ass, but sometimes you had to take your medicine."

THE CODE

The King of the "HBP" (Hit By Pitch)

The all-time career record for being hit by a pitch is held by Houston Astros second baseman Craig Biggio, who set the record back in 2005 when he was plunked for the 286th time. Prior to Biggio, the record had been held by Don Baylor, who was preceded by Ron Hunt, who still holds the modern single-season record with 50. Hunt was so used to getting drilled that he even occasionally wore a wetsuit underneath his uniform to deaden the pain when he knew he was going to face a pitcher that liked to throw inside.

I only drilled about a half-dozen players over my career on purpose. Believe it or not, I found it to be way tougher to hit a guy than it was to throw a perfect pitch down and away for a strike. It was so unnatural. The target you were looking at was so foreign to you. Your whole life you have been programmed to throw it at your catcher's mitt, and then all of a sudden you are aiming at a guy's ribs. And on top of that, you had to make sure it didn't get away from you so that you hit him in the head. Trust me, it was not an easy thing to do. Plus, you didn't know if he was going to get pissed and charge out there after you, either.

When it came to retaliation, perhaps no one was more old-school than pitcher Bert Blyleven:

> It was my job as a pitcher to take care of my guys, no matter what the situation was. The pitcher needs to recognize those instances and react accordingly. Pitchers only play once every four or five days, whereas your teammates are out there giving it their all night after night. So if a pitcher has an opportunity to protect one of his players, he has to do it, no matter what. He has got to be ready to react, regardless of the consequences. I firmly believe in that.
>
> If a player got a bunch of hits off of me, I was going to go after him and drill him when I got the opportunity. I was going to let him know that "Damn it, I am out here too...." I wanted him to know that his success against me was taking bread off of my table. I wasn't going to stand for it.
>
> I looked at myself as the enforcer of our team when I was out on the mound. Just like the hockey enforcer, I too had to protect my players at all costs. That was my job and I relished the role. It was my responsibility to take care of my players and to make sure that they didn't get thrown at or hurt. If the opportunity was there, you *had* to protect your everyday players. If that meant drilling somebody,

then you drilled them. If an opposing team threw up and in on a guy like Kirby Puckett, then that was it. I was coming after them and somebody was going down, guaranteed.

I usually tried to aim at the guy's hips if I had to hit him. That way, if you came up you would get him in the ribs, or if you came down you would get him on the thigh. But if I ever had to hit a guy who was pretty quick, like a Willie Wilson or Rickey Henderson, then I would go for his legs. I would go for the knee area or maybe the ankle, to try and slow him down because I knew he was going to get first base, and the last thing I wanted was for him to steal second on me and get into scoring position. So, I figured if I was going to have to nail him, then it might as well be in a place that was going to prevent him from doing any further damage out on the base paths.

Another thing you thought about as a starting pitcher was getting in your five innings, so you could get the official "W" in the books. For instance, if you had a 6–1 lead in the fifth inning and they hit one of your teammates, I would make sure to finish the inning and have the chance to get my win. Otherwise I might get ejected for drilling a guy and it wouldn't count in my record. But if it was early in the game, say the second or third inning, and you had a lead in a similar situation, then it wouldn't matter. You take the guy out and roll the dice. If you get tossed, so be it. You have to do what you have to do.

3

On Fear and Intimidation

Fear and intimidation have been a part of baseball since the very beginning. The specter of getting drilled or beaned is the fear that keeps every hitter honest. It's a primal fear everyone can relate to, athlete or not. It's like looking down the barrel of a loaded gun: you just never know if and when it could go off. A good pitcher will throw inside and be able to keep the hitter at bay. Every hitter wants to crowd the plate so that he will be able to reach out and drive an outside pitch while still being able to pull the inside offering. Pitchers, however, don't want that to happen, so they will do whatever they have to in order to keep them honest. The fear of what a 95-mph fastball hitting your flesh feels like is an emotion we can all imagine. It hurts…a lot.

Yes, intimidation is a powerful elixir. All of the great ones had it. Take a guy like legendary Dodgers flamethrower Don Drysdale. He would throw at anybody and everybody to back them off the plate, including the likes of Henry Aaron, Willie Mays, or Frank Robinson. He would come hard up and in and had no problem throwing at guys' heads, either. He wanted to instill a sense of fear in his opponents and wanted to keep them on edge, always wondering if he might be just crazy enough to seriously injure them.

One of the game's first intimidators was a kid by the name of Amos Rusie, who pitched for the New York Giants back in the 1890s. As legend would have it, "the Hoosier Thunderbolt," as he was affectionately known, used to make money at the Tennessee State Fair by throwing baseballs through wood panels. What made Rusie so scary to hitters wasn't just the fact that he could throw harder than probably anybody playing baseball at the time, but that he was just a little bit wild. Hitters could deal with fast. What they couldn't deal with was the knowledge that Rusie had very little idea as to where the hell the ball was going.

Once Rusie knocked a few batters out cold, word spread quickly. *Watch out for this guy, he might be a little bit nuts.* Before long, opposing hitters were standing as far back in the batter's box as possible, fearful for their lives. So unpredictable was Rusie that in four different seasons he led the league in both strikeouts and walks. It was that inconsistency that kept his foes on their toes. As a result, the National League increased the distance between the pitcher and the batter from 50 feet to the present 60'6".

Athletes inflicting pain and bodily harm on one another on the sports field is certainly nothing new. It happens in football and hockey games

Pitcher Jim Kaat on Intimidation

"Fear is the biggest thing you have to overcome in this game. It is a natural instinct to be scared of getting hit in the head with a ball, but you have to overcome that fear if you want to make it at this level. Look at the Tony Conigliaro incident. That fear of getting hit and never being able to recover is real. I faced guys like Nolan Ryan and Sandy Koufax plenty of times in my day, though, and was really never intimidated by them. If you allow yourself to be intimidated, then it is all over, you don't stand a chance. I was a competitor and wanted to be challenged.

"If a hitter is scared of the ball, you can pick up on that, too. I remember talking to Wally Moses one time, the great hitting coach for the Yankees during the '60s, and we were watching a young player in the instructional leagues. We watched this one particular kid take some cuts, and Wally leaned over and told me that he thought that the kid was going to have a lot of trouble making it to the big leagues. I asked why, and he said he thought the kid was afraid of the ball. I asked him how he knew that, and he told me to watch his front shoulders and how they dipped when the pitch was coming. He was scared of getting hit. I learned a lot from Wally and was able to pick up on things like that throughout my career. When you saw guys with tendencies like that, you had an immediate advantage as a pitcher.

"Intimidation went both ways, as far as I was concerned, though. I mean, Frank Robinson and Al Kaline were extremely intimidating hitters. They got up in there and crowded the plate and challenged you. They were tough, too. They made you earn it."

hundreds of times per game, and for boxers it is just a way of life. Fans don't cringe when a left wing gets checked or when a quarterback gets sacked or even when a middleweight gets KO'd, quite unlike when a pitcher knocks down a hitter with a blazing beanball. The horror it induces is like no other. It is simple physics really; force equals mass times acceleration. So when a 100-mph fastball comes screaming in toward a player's head…well, you do the math. It's just downright scary.

One of the most notorious beanings happened on May 25, 1937, when the Tigers' Hall of Fame catcher Mickey Cochrane's skull was fractured by an errant fastball thrown by New York Yankees pitcher Bump Hadley. Cochrane had hit a homer off Hadley in the third inning, and the payback was devastating—straight heat that found the area above his right eye, breaking Cochrane's skull in three places. Cochrane spent three weeks in the hospital and never played in another major league game. Later, in a remarkable display of compassion, Cochrane exonerated Hadley by acknowledging that he had simply lost the ball in the horizon and that Hadley wasn't to blame.

There has been one singular incident in professional baseball that has defined this very topic like no other over the years, and it is synonymous with the man behind it: Tony Conigliaro. In 1964, the 19-year-old Conigliaro hit 24 home runs as a rookie with the Boston Red Sox, and the next season he led the American League with 32 home runs. Two years later, on August 18, this kid with Hall of Fame potential made history for all the wrong reasons. In a game against the California Angels, Conigliaro came up to bat against pitcher Jack Hamilton. Hamilton reared back and fired a fastball that struck Conigliaro square on the side of the head. He went down like a sack of dirt and wound up with a broken cheekbone, a dislocated jaw, and worst of all, a damaged retina.

Conigliaro would recover physically, but the emotional scars would remain forever. He made several comebacks into professional baseball, but he never regained his old form. Many felt that even though he was able to overcome the fear of getting back into the batter's box, he would always be labeled as "plate-shy." Pitchers worried that he might freeze up and get "hitter's paralysis" if a ball got away and sailed toward his head. It was surely a difficult situation. For all intents and purposes, his career was finished.

Beanballs are, in a word, devastating. However, not all beanball incidents are destined for the same sad outcome. Take, for instance,

Steve Dalkowski: The Fastest Pitcher Nobody Has Ever Heard Of...

Back in 1998, when *The Sporting News* wrote a book about baseball's 100 greatest players, they asked a handful of former players and managers to rank their top 10 in various categories, including "Hardest-Throwing Pitchers." While Nolan Ryan, Roger Clemens, and Bob Feller topped the list, coming in at number five was a guy by the name of Steve Dalkowski. Steve who?

Steve Dalkowski was a career minor leaguer from the late 1950s and early '60s who apparently had a fastball that clocked in at a heart-stopping 110 mph. To put that into perspective, Nolan Ryan is in the Guinness Book of Records for the fastest pitch ever recorded, at 100.9 mph. But due to the advancement of radar-gun accuracy, it was believed that Ryan could actually throw as high as 103 mph. (Although not official, two other pitchers also had fastballs clocked in at 103 mph: former Atlanta Braves reliever Mark Wohlers, during a spring-training game in 1995; and Detroit pitcher Joel Zumaya, in a 2006 contest against the Yankees. And let's not forget Sidd Finch, *Sports Illustrated*'s 1985 fictional April Fool's Day pitcher from Tibet, who could throw a whopping 168 mph.)

Regarded as the most frightening pitcher of all time, Dalkowski would have made it to the big leagues had it not been for one small problem: he was wild as hell. In 1960 he recorded an incredible 262 strikeouts while playing in the California League. That same season he also set a league record with 262 walks. Nobody is sure how many guys he beaned, either, but it was more than a few. Get the picture? There was very little rhyme or reason to his success, or lack thereof.

Many believed that he was the hardest thrower of all time, without a doubt. "He was unbelievable," said former Orioles manager Earl Weaver. "He threw a lot faster than [Nolan] Ryan. It's hard to believe, but he did."

Dalkowski scared the crap out of his opponents, including arguably the greatest hitter of all time, Ted Williams. "Fastest ever," said Williams, who once faced the fireballer in a spring-training game. "I never want to face him again."

Dalkowski was raised in New Britain, Connecticut, and by his junior year in high school his fastball was starting to attract some attention. The Orioles gave him a $4,000 advance and assigned him to minor league Kingsport, Pennsylvania, where he threw a fastball that literally took off part of a hitter's ear and sent him to the hospital with a concussion. His legend just grew from there. Teammates dared him to throw balls through wooden outfield fences, and he did.

Many speculated that his long-standing fear of killing someone with a pitch shattered his confidence and contributed to his departure from the game. He eventually tore a ligament in his throwing arm, which led to his retirement. He would go on to become a migrant farm worker after retiring, but his chronic alcoholism eventually caused his health to deteriorate. In the late 1980s, Dalkowski was evidently living in a small apartment in Southern California, out of work and almost broke.

Dalkowski's legend has only continued to grow over time. In fact, the character named Nuke LaLoosh in the 1988 film *Bull Durham,* played by Tim Robbins, is based loosely on Dalkowski. Turns out that screenwriter and director Ron Shelton played in the minor leagues alongside Dalkowski in the old California League.

According to Jared Hoffman's 1999 article about Dalkowski in *The Sporting News,* here are some amazing facts about the man they used to call "White Lightning":

- In one minor league game, Dalkowski threw three pitches that penetrated the backstop and sent fans scattering.

- In a high school game, Dalkowski threw a no-hit shutout with 18 strikeouts and 18 walks.

- In an Eastern League game, Dalkowski struck out 27 and walked 16 while throwing 283 pitches. In another game, he was pulled in the second inning after throwing 120 pitches.

- At Aberdeen in the Northern League, Dalkowski threw a one-hitter and lost 9–8.

- In 1960 at Class A Stockton, Dalkowski threw a pitch that broke an umpire's mask in three places, knocking him 18 feet back and sending him to a hospital for three days with a concussion.

- In 1959 Dalkowski set a Northern League record with 21 strikeouts in a game.

- In 1960 at Stockton in the California League, Dalkowski struck out 19 and limited Reno to four hits but walked nine and lost 8–3.

the plight of Cubs slugger Andre Dawson, who was hit in the face by a beanball from Padres pitcher Eric Show back in 1987. "The Hawk" went down hard, bleeding from the mouth, and didn't get up for several frightening moments. A bench-clearing brawl ensued as Show had to be escorted out of Wrigley Field by the umpires for his own protection. Incredibly, though, Dawson came right back and even went on to win the NL MVP Award that season.

Many contend that the hardest part of coming back from a situation like this isn't the short-term physical recovery but the long-term mental rehabilitation.

"To be a good hitter, you can't have fear," said longtime player and manager Lou Piniella on the subject of coming back after getting beaned. "You've got to feel comfortable that the helmet offers you ample protection, number one, and number two, that these things happen very rarely and the chances of it happening to the same player twice are very remote. The first few at-bats after you get plunked pretty good, it's a little difficult. When I played I got hit one time, and the first couple of at-bats were not the most comfortable. But then I did what I had always done, which was go into the ball."

Another similar comeback situation happened to former Minnesota Twins star center fielder Torii Hunter on April 26, 2007, at the Metrodome in Minneapolis. Hunter was hit in the mouth in the second inning by Kansas City Royals pitcher Zack Greinke and went down in a bloody mess. He quickly popped up, however, and took a few quick steps toward Greinke, with the intention of charging the mound. He realized that it wasn't intentional, though, and backed off. Greinke was having control problems, as evidenced by the fact that he nailed Twin Jason Bartlett just three batters later.

It is interesting to note that in the seventh inning, the wheels of the code were set in motion when Kansas City's Reggie Sanders was hit in the ribs by Twins reliever Matt Guerrier. Sanders took a couple of steps toward the mound and then took his sweet time going to first base, showing his disgust for what was clearly a retaliatory shot. That is how the code works: you hit our star, we hit yours.

After getting some stitches in his mouth at a nearby hospital, Hunter returned to the dugout dressed like a mummy, with a gauze pad wrapped around his head. His making light of the situation put his teammates at ease and probably served as a rallying point in the team's dramatic victory.

"I was very surprised he took a couple of steps," said Guerrier after the game of Sanders's move toward the mound. "No matter whether it is intentional or not, you've got to expect us to do something about it, either today or whenever. He's been around. Maybe he didn't think it was right. But stuff like that happens. That's the way the game has been played. They hit Torii in the face, then they hit Bartlett in the same inning. If we don't hit anybody, then people question that. I'm not saying I did it on purpose. The pitch got away and hit him. That's it. There's no big deal."

One of the game's greatest intimidators is pitcher Randy Johnson, who at 6'9" is as imposing a figure on the mound as there has ever been. "The Big Unit," as he is known, beaned San Francisco Giants first baseman J.T. Snow with a fastball during a spring-training game in 1997. The crowd fell to a hush, horrified by the awful sound the ball made when it nailed Snow square in the face. Snow would miss the rest of the preseason, as well as the first six weeks of that regular season, but was able to overcome his fear and make a comeback.

Not all victims of beanballs are so lucky, though. In addition to the aforementioned tragic incidents that included the likes of Ray Chapman and Don Zimmer, there have been plenty of close calls that could have gone either way. Among them was the 1979 beaning of Mike Jorgensen of the Texas Rangers by Red Sox pitcher Andy Hassler. Jorgensen was taken to the hospital, where he suffered a nearly fatal seizure that cut off the oxygen to his brain.

In 1995 Minnesota Twins All-Star outfielder Kirby Puckett was beaned by Dennis Martinez, suffering a broken jaw and a burst artery in his mouth. Sadly, it would be the future Hall of Famer's last at-bat ever, as it was discovered shortly thereafter that he was suffering from a career-ending case of glaucoma in his eye.

It is interesting to note that drilling batters can also be used as a tactic to swing the momentum, or as an effort to start a rally. One classic instance of this rare form of intimidation came in the spring of 1974. The Pittsburgh Pirates had won three straight divisional titles from 1970 to 1972, and pitcher Dock Ellis could sense that his teammates were becoming scared of their hated rivals, the Cincinnati Reds, whom they had lost to twice in the playoffs during that span. So in an attempt to bust his club out of their slump and help restore their aggressive nature, Ellis took matters into his own hands.

The Pirates faced off against the Reds on May 1 that season, and Ellis was hell-bent on instilling his own brand of fear into "the Big Red Machine." Ellis drilled the very first batter, Pete Rose, right in the ribs. Next up was Joe Morgan, whom he drilled in the small of the back. Dan Driessen came up next, and like the batters before him, he too got drilled in the back.

With the bases now loaded, Ellis faced Reds cleanup hitter Tony Perez. The elusive Perez knew what was coming, though, and managed to duck and dodge his way to first base via a walk. Johnny Bench was next, and the burly right-hander went right at the big catcher's head, narrowly missing him with a pair of would-be beanballs. That was the final straw, as Pirates manager Danny Murtaugh finally came out and removed his pitcher from the ballgame. As for Ellis's unconventional motivational tactics, they worked. That's right—the Bucs went on to win the division crown.

4

Should Beanballs Be Illegal?

In hockey, fighting is not only allowed, it is welcomed. Players have to be accountable for their actions—that is why they don't wear face masks at the professional level. The game is permitted to police itself, with the players meting out discipline when their code is broken. Occasionally, however, a player will lose his cool and whack a guy over the head with his stick. This is in no way acceptable behavior and is definitely not a part of the code. Or a player will hit a player from behind, as was the case in the infamous Todd Bertuzzi incident of 2004, when the rugged Vancouver agitator sucker-punched Colorado's Steve Moore from behind and broke his neck. Legal proceedings have gone on for several years.

In addition to ejections, suspensions, and fines, in some instances the legal system has stepped in to assess its own judgments and penalties. All of a sudden a player who thought he only had to worry about going to the penalty box now has to consider going to prison on charges of aggravated assault and battery. A new line has been crossed in professional sports history. And that is not necessarily a bad thing, either.

Now let's take the Bertuzzi incident and apply it to baseball. What if a pitcher intentionally beans a batter and tragically kills him? Is that not murder? Nobody knows for sure. In 1920 Cleveland's Ray Chapman became the first and only major leaguer to die from injuries resulting from a beanball. Yankees pitcher Carl Mays insisted that he didn't do it intentionally, and everybody took his word for it. But what if it happened today after a manager ordered his pitcher to drill a guy? Maybe that pitcher

> "A brushback is a brushback, but throwing at somebody's head…that is another matter."
>
> —Joe DiMaggio
>
> "He is the only guy who puts fear in me…and not because he can get you out, but because he can kill you."
>
> —Reggie Jackson on pitcher Nolan Ryan
>
> "The beanball is one of the meanest things on Earth, and no decent fellow would use it. The beanball is a potential murderer. If I were a batter and thought the pitcher really tried to bean me, I'd be inclined to wait for him outside the park with a baseball bat."
>
> —Walter Johnson, Hall of Fame pitcher

lets it get away from him, and instead of hitting the batter in the ribs, it sails up and catches him in the temple?

This is the doomsday scenario in baseball, just like the fight scenario in hockey. Sadly, it is probably not a question of "if," but rather "when" it will occur. It will happen one day, because the players today are just that much bigger, faster, and stronger. Something can and, tragically, probably will go wrong, even if it is a one-in-a-million shot. We're due.

Believe it or not, there is actually one bit of legal precedent on the issue, regarding a beanball incident back in 2001 during a community-college game in California. Jose Avila of the Rio Hondo Roadrunners was beaned during a game against the Citrus Community College Owls. The pitch, which cracked his helmet, was allegedly thrown in retaliation after the Roadrunners pitcher had hit an Owls batter earlier in the game. Avila, who now suffers from sporadic seizures, later sued the Citrus Community College District for negligence in failing to control its pitcher. However, after an appeals court ruled Avila could sue for damages, the California Supreme Court reversed the decision.

"Being hit by a pitch is an inherent risk of baseball," wrote Justice Kathryn Mickle Werdegar in her dissent. "Pitchers intentionally throw at batters to disrupt a batter's timing, or back him away from home plate, to retaliate after a teammate has been hit or to punish a batter for having hit a home run. It is so accepted by custom that a pitch intentionally thrown at a batter has its own terminology: brushback, beanball, and chin music."

"Even if the Citrus College pitcher intentionally threw at Avila, his conduct did not fall outside the range of ordinary activity involved in the sport," concluded Justice Werdegar, citing the fact that anyone who plays a sport consents to physical contact and understands the rules of the game. "Thus, the boxer who steps into the ring consents to his opponent's jabs; the football player who steps onto the gridiron consents to his opponent's hard tackle; the hockey goalie who takes the ice consents to face his opponent's slap shots; and, here, the baseball player who steps to the plate consents to the possibility the opposing pitcher may throw near or at him."

Seemingly nothing will rile up a team more than seeing one of their own get beaned, especially if that guy just happens to be a superstar. What makes one recent incident in the majors so unique, though, is that the guy throwing the ball was also a superstar. The result was a major-market media blitz that led to some pretty tasty drama. It is now known simply as the "Clemens versus Piazza" incident and has become one of the most storied beanball skirmishes of the modern era.

It took place on July 8, 2000, in the nightcap of a rare day/night doubleheader between the Yankees and the Mets at Yankee Stadium. Yankees fireballer Roger Clemens, one of the few remaining headhunters in the game and a real intimidator, had grown weary of Piazza's success against him at the plate. A lifetime .365 hitter against Clemens, Piazza stepped up to the dish and got decked in the front of the helmet with one of the Rocket's trademark blistering fastballs. The All-Star catcher went down in a heap and lay motionless in the dirt for several moments while players from both teams slowly began to creep out from their dugouts in anticipation of a bench-clearer.

The sell-out crowd went nuts, but cooler heads would prevail. Piazza, who sustained a concussion from the incident, would later say that he thought the beanball was intentional. Clemens's explanation on what had transpired, meanwhile, was firm: "I was only trying to pitch him inside."

It seemed as if everybody had an opinion on the high-profile incident, including Giants outfielder Barry Bonds, who came to the pitcher's defense.

"I have known Roger Clemens for a long time," said Bonds. "I have played against him in college, talked with him in airports and All-Star Games, and I don't think he's that type of guy. If he has become that way, then it's a shame. You know when a pitcher is intentionally trying to hit you, and I can understand Mike's feelings, but I really don't think Roger would try to do that."

"Roger is a good guy, and I really can't see him throwing at anyone's head," added then–Seattle Mariners shortstop and future Clemens teammate Alex Rodriguez. "I just think Mike's a little emotional. That happens when you get hit. You're mad about it."

Ironically, the two teams would meet up again in the World Series a few months later in what was dubbed "the Subway Series." The media was out in force as the much anticipated rematch between Clemens and Piazza was about to go down in front of the entire world.

What happened this time was even more bizarre than anybody could have imagined. Facing Piazza for the first time since the notorious beaning, Clemens was pumped full of adrenaline up on the mound at Yankee Stadium. The two dueled, with Piazza finally hitting a grounder foul up the first base line. As he hit it, though, part of his bat broke off and flew toward Clemens. The Yankees hurler then inexplicably picked up the jagged piece of lumber and flung it back at Piazza, who was running toward first base. In what must have been one of the craziest scenes in baseball history, the two alpha males just looked at each other in utter disbelief.

Moments later the benches cleared for a good old-fashioned finger-pointing party, complete with plenty of pushing, shoving, and verbal taunting. The fans went berserk and a near-riot broke out in the stands between the rival Yankees and Mets fans. Clemens later claimed that he was simply clearing the bat from the playing field, but Piazza and the Mets weren't buying it for a second. When the dust finally settled, the Yankees went on to win yet another World Series title.

Clemens and Piazza would have to wait two more seasons to once again face off in interleague play. It finally happened in June of 2002, with a media frenzy resembling that of a professional wrestling pay-per-view match rather than a baseball game. And because it was a National League game played at the Mets' Shea Stadium, there would be no designated hitter—Clemens would have to bat for himself. The fans in attendance were beside themselves with anticipation, waiting eagerly for Mets pitcher Shawn Estes to drill Clemens for some much-deserved retaliatory payback.

But when Estes's first pitch to Clemens came nowhere close to nailing him, the fans cried foul. They felt as if they had been mugged; it was a huge letdown. After the game ESPN analyst Rob Dibble berated Estes for failing

---

Sometimes Beanballs Occur Because Players Put Themselves into Bad Situations

Longtime Cubs third baseman Ron Santo was beaned in the cheek by Mets pitcher Jack Fisher in 1966 and had to be carted off the field on a stretcher and taken to the hospital. Santo later acknowledged that he knew why he had been hit. He explained that because the Mets had put on a defensive shift, he altered his batting stance in order to be able to drive the ball into right field. "I moved my body and locked myself up," he said. "The ball was up and in where a normal knockdown pitch was that I would get away from. But I locked in and got it. And I knew it was my fault. I had no ill feelings because I knew why I had been hit."

---

to honor his duty in protecting his teammate. Estes, who was with the Giants at the time of the previous Clemens-Piazza incident, shied away from the topic and instead chose to talk about the inherent risks of retaliation.

"Primarily guys have stayed away and come in when they had to, for effect," said Estes. "I've always been a guy who did it for effect [rather than to intimidate]. It's a question of how bad would you feel [if you ended a player's career]."

The fans love a good storyline, and this one was full of drama and intrigue, complete with a genesis and a flashpoint. Both players would move on to other teams after that, however, and the bad blood finally came to a halt.

As for the future of beanballs? It's business as usual, but players today certainly understand the inherent risks of throwing inside. Headhunting is risky business for the hitter as well as the pitcher. For the hitter, it means potentially being injured, or worse. For the pitcher, it could mean instant retaliation in the form of that hitter charging the mound; it could mean being retaliated against personally, if he plays in the National League or was playing in an interleague game; or it could mean legal penalties if he indeed threw the ball intentionally. At the end of the day, most would agree that it is simply not worth it. Pitchers can clearly get their point across by drilling hitters elsewhere in retaliation, and that should be the way it stays.

"As a pitcher, you never wanted to hit a guy in the head, ever," said pitcher Bert Blyleven. "If you wanted to make a statement, you would hit him in the hip or the leg or right in the ribs. Headhunting is a whole part of the code that is really looked down upon. People can really get hurt when that stuff happens, and to be honest, nobody wants to see that. Nobody wants to be labeled as a headhunter in this business—that is a real dishonorable thing. It is almost an unwritten law that you live by, not to throw at a guy's head. Up and in is acceptable in certain situations, but never right at the guy's head.

"I did hit a few guys in the head over my career, though, and that was tough. I never meant to do it, but once in a while the ball would just get away from you. I shattered a few helmets in my day, but believe me, those were all unintentional. I remember drilling Rick Burleson one time in Fenway Park right on the earflap of his helmet. He went down hard and had to be taken away on a stretcher. I damn near thought I killed him. You feel about two inches tall at that point, with everybody staring at you and the fans screaming at you. It is a tough spot to be in. Burleson knew that there was nothing behind it, though, and that it was not on purpose. He even said later that he just froze. As a pitcher, situations like that certainly make you think long and hard about what type of damage you can do to a person and his career if you are not careful out there."

A Beanball Bounty of the Sickest Kind...

In one of the more disturbing stories you will ever read, on June 27, 2005, a T-ball coach from Dunbar, Pennsylvania, was busted for offering a player a $25 bounty in exchange for beaning an autistic teammate. The coach, Mark Downs, apparently did not want the victim, Harry Bowers, to be able to play in the game. The player who hit the autistic child, Keith Reese, testified that his coach offered him the money in the parking lot before the game in exchange for him beaning Bowers during warm-ups. Reese complied and hit Bowers with two balls, one in the groin and one in the ear.

Once the news got out, the authorities were contacted and criminal charges were filed against Downs. From there, he was convicted of conspiracy to commit simple assault and corruption of a minor, following a jury trial. A judge later ruled that there was no basis for an appeal in the criminal conviction and sentence, thus debunking claims that Downs's one- to six-year prison sentence was excessive. As of 2007 the case was pending in the state Superior Court, where Downs, who was free on bond, was appealing his conviction and sentence.

Pitcher Frank Viola feels similarly. "Whenever you see a beanball incident, where a guy gets it in the head, that is so scary," he said. "Forget baseball, you are talking about a guy's life. It is so dangerous to throw at players' heads, it should never be done. Beanball incidents can stick with you, too. They haunt you. I remember drilling Brady Anderson square in the head one time. I had absolutely no intention whatsoever to do it, but it just totally got away from me. I wasn't even trying to throw inside. It was crazy. He went down like a rock. It scared the living daylights out of me. Luckily he got up, but I was shaken by that for a while. I just kept thinking that I could have taken his livelihood from him and his family, and that is such a sobering feeling. I called him up that night to apologize, and thankfully he forgave me. He knew it just got away and that I had no intention of hitting him. Brady was a true professional and he handled the situation with class."

Former third baseman Ron Coomer has his own unique take on the subject:

> Beanballs can end careers, and that is no joke. I was in the dugout for Kirby Puckett's last at-bat ever, and I saw him get beaned in the mouth by Dennis Martinez. They were friends, so it wasn't intentional or anything, but it ultimately ended Kirby's career. He had his eye problems after that, and sadly it was the start of a lot of health problems for him. So, you just never know in those situations. We retaliated right away after that. We had to. So we drilled their first batter up after that on the very first pitch, and it just happened to be one of their best players, Albert Belle. Albert knew why. He didn't say a thing, he just quietly ran to first base. He knew the code.
>
> I only got beaned once in my career, by pitcher Esteban Loaiza, and my first reaction was to charge out there and kill the guy. I mean you are instantly raging mad and ready to go. The problem was that my brain was like scrambled eggs, and I wasn't able to do a thing. You just want to get revenge. I think that is your natural instinct. But at the time you can't think real clearly. Luckily I was okay, but that was pretty scary.
>
> Psychologically, getting beaned can have a profound effect on how you play the game. It takes a brave man to stand in front of a 95-mph fastball, and an even braver one to stand in there right after he got one in the face. So the courage of players like Torii Hunter, who came right back from getting one in the face early in 2007, I just have to tip my hat to guys like that. What guts. Unless you have played this game, you have no idea how much courage that really takes. No idea.

It is pretty easy to get psyched out after that and lose your edge. It is a tough thing to do, but you have to overcome that fear if you ever want to be successful in this game.

5

On Charging the Mound

One of the most exciting yet horrifying events in baseball is the act of charging the mound. It is a rare occurrence, but it is one that happens from time to time immediately after a batter is drilled with a pitch—the hitter runs out to the mound as fast as he can, with the intent of getting a couple of punches in before anybody else gets there to break it up. The catcher will usually try to tackle him from behind, but each situation is unique.

If the hitter does make it out there unscathed, he will try to do whatever he can to retaliate. He may deke and throw a punch; he may just tackle the pitcher; or he may try a combination of both. The pitcher, meanwhile, has to stand his ground. If he runs and hides, he will be considered a coward. If he stays and fights, like he is supposed to, he risks breaking a knuckle on his throwing hand. It is a wild few moments.

From there, a melee will usually ensue as both benches will undoubtedly clear. The players will rush out from the dugouts, and the relievers will come streaming in from the bullpens in a beautiful symphony of utter chaos. Sometimes things can get ugly. Bats, spikes, and even catcher's masks can become a part of the fray.

Everybody pairs up and tries to make sure there are no unfair two-on-one scenarios. The umpires try to keep order, but things can get ugly in a hurry. The code says that if a guy charges the mound, then the rest of the team had better follow…or else. There is no room for cowards on a baseball team, so players know that they better "show up," or else they may find themselves sent down to the minors, traded, or even released.

Pitcher Frank Viola on Charging the Mound

"I was fortunate in that I only had one guy ever charge me out on the mound. It was during a Triple A game in Toledo when I was just a kid coming up. Luckily, I was fortunate enough to have a first baseman by the name of Boomer Wells who was like 6'6" and 280 pounds. Anyway, I was told to hit the batter by my manager just before the inning started, and Boomer told me that he had my back. So I drilled the guy on the first pitch, and when he took a couple of steps towards me, I wanted to look tough, so I took a couple of steps towards him. Then out of the blue, this guy, who was actually a big-leaguer with the Mets who was sent down on rehab at the time, came sprinting out of the bullpen straight towards me. He was not about to let his teammate get nailed by me, and he was coming out there as fast as he could to kill me. Well, my back was turned to him, but all of a sudden I felt Boomer push me aside and I heard this horrible sound of flesh on flesh. Boomer threw one punch and absolutely laid the guy out cold. Boomer then comes up and hugs me and says, 'I told you I had your back....' It was one of the most amazing things I have ever seen."

Each player's fuse is a different length, and it is hard to predict why and when he will charge the mound.

"I think that while we all have a disdain for violence and we don't want to see guys hurt, we also believe fiercely in competition played with great compassion and emotion on the field," said longtime manager Phil Garner. "You cannot, and I stress that, you cannot as an athlete play this game and not have emotion, and sometimes not push those emotions to the brink. And if you're going to compete, if you're going to be a winner, you're going to get to the point sometimes when you're willing to fight. And I say that to a lot of players when I get some that are sort of pacifists. I say, 'Listen, there is a point in your life when you will fight. If I start smacking you around on the face, pretty soon you're going to get up to me and you're going to stand up to me.' The same thing happens on the field when you're trying to win, and you want players to play like that."

For some players, it is all about their gut reaction.

"When something like that happens, you know, I don't think most guys think about the consequences," said Detroit Tigers left fielder Bobby Higginson. "They just go out and react. And maybe they'll have to deal with the consequences after they do what they do. But in the heat of the battle, they don't really think about that when they're going out to the mound."

Sometimes a trip toward the mound is the result of a pitcher being too aggressive. This was the scenario for Milwaukee Braves first baseman Joe Adcock, who became a marked man after hitting four home runs in a game back on July 31, 1954, against the Brooklyn Dodgers at Ebbets Field. The Dodgers pitchers felt shown up by Adcock and let him know how they felt about it the next day by beaning him. But it wasn't over there by a long shot. Six weeks later the teams met again, and this time Adcock got drilled in the hand, putting him on the shelf for the rest of the season.

Word got out about Adcock's perceived showboating, and the next season the New York Giants continued the retaliation when pitcher Jim Hearn broke Adcock's right forearm on a nasty fastball. Then on July 18, 1956, at Milwaukee's County Stadium, Giants pitcher Ruben Gomez nailed Adcock again on the right hand. This time Adcock was visibly upset. So as he started jogging to first base, he decided to give Gomez an earful. Thinking Adcock was going to charge the mound, Gomez fired the ball into Adcock's leg and then hightailed it into the dugout with several Braves players chasing after him. Gomez would spend the rest of the game hiding in the clubhouse.

Sometimes hitters will charge the mound if they feel like an opposing pitcher is trying to intimidate them excessively. Such was the case for White

Pitcher Rick Aguilera on Charging the Mound

"One time when I was playing in college, I spent a summer playing ball up in Alaska. I got called into a 9–1 game in, like, the ninth inning. We were just getting killed. The first guy up drag-bunts for a hit. Well, I was already pissed about being put into the game at that point, and that just added to my frustration. So I drilled the next batter right between the numbers on the very first pitch. Little did I know, however, that the batter was future NFL star Jack Del Rio, who was a two-sport star at USC at the time. Sure enough, he charged the mound on me, and it was ugly.

"As soon as he threw his bat and started sprinting out towards me, I knew that I was in trouble. He just kept getting larger and larger as he got closer. I had nowhere to run to, so I figured I had just better stay in there and take my lumps. We both started swinging and eventually he got me down and started pummeling me. It seemed like an eternity before my reinforcements showed up, but they finally got him off of me. The moral of the story there, I suppose, is if you are going to intentionally drill a guy, make sure he isn't a linebacker."

Sox third baseman Robin Ventura on August 4, 1993, in a game against the Texas Rangers. Ventura had been having success against legendary Rangers pitcher Nolan Ryan at the plate, and when Ryan decided to drill him with one of his patented 100-mph fastballs, Ventura decided to charge out after him. What made the situation so unique, however, was the fact that the then-46-year-old Ryan cleaned Ventura's clock. Nolan stood his ground, tossed his glove, and then put Ventura into a perfectly executed headlock, at which time he proceeded to pummel Ventura in the head with a barrage of right uppercuts. Incredibly, when the dust had cleared, it was Ventura, not Ryan, who got a two-game suspension and fine.

Another pitcher who held his own on the mound was Boston's Al Nipper, who after drilling Seattle's Phil Bradley in the back went to extraordinary measures to make sure he didn't hurt himself in the ensuing melee. You see, when Bradley charged the mound, the right-handed Nipper tossed his glove and made a deke move that put him in a perfect position to pound away on the charging Mariner with his left hand. Smart. Just like Nuke LaLoosh from the movie *Bull Durham*, he made sure not to mess up his throwing hand.

While Ryan and Nipper certainly set the bar with regard to technique for pitchers, there have been a myriad of offensive tactics employed by hitters over the years. While pitchers will toss their gloves, hitters can either toss their batting helmet or even their bat, if they choose to bring it. The code forbids such behavior, but crazier things have happened in the heat of battle.

In all, there have been some good, some bad, and, yes, some really ugly mound-charging incidents over the years. There was then-Toronto outfielder George Bell's flying karate kick at Red Sox pitcher Bruce Kison

Catcher George Mitterwald on Charging the Mound

"When I was with the Cubs back in the late '70s, we were playing the Dodgers one afternoon. Rick Reuschel was pitching and Bill Russell hit a long drive down the foul line that just barely hooked foul. He ended up striking out, but the next batter was Reggie Smith, who had been jumping up and down like a maniac in the on-deck circle over Russell's near home-run ball just a few moments earlier. So Reuschel threw the first pitch in on him to send him a message, and it hit him in the knee. Well, he started to walk towards first base and then took off towards the mound. I immediately ran out and tackled him but then got piled on from behind when the dugouts emptied. Sure enough, my shoulder got separated, and it ultimately cost me my career."

Pitcher Bert Blyleven on Charging the Mound

"I pitched for 23 years in the big leagues, and never once did I ever have a guy charge the mound on me. I think that I had a hard-ass attitude, but for whatever the reason, I wasn't perceived as a real hard-ass. I guess I was around long enough to earn the respect of my peers, and I took pride in that. I just tried to be as competitive as I could, and I never backed down from anybody. I have been in a good share of melees over the years, however, as a bystander. When the benches clear, you just get up and get out there as fast as you can.

"I actually charged the mound once myself, believe it or not. I remember playing against Philadelphia one time, and I threw a pitch up and in on Mike Schmidt. He liked to lean in over the plate, and I had to back him up. Well, the next inning he said something to me as he was walking down the third-base line. I responded, and we had some words. So the next inning I was up to bat and got drilled on the first pitch. It was retaliation; I understood that. He was a future Hall of Famer and [his teammates] were protecting him. But I wasn't about to let them intimidate me, so I charged the mound and went after their pitcher. I got fined and suspended for it, but it was worth it to me. I was a competitor and wasn't about to be pushed around or intimidated, no way. So I did what I had to do."

back in 1985. And San Francisco outfielder Kevin Mitchell's linebacker-impersonation tackle of San Diego Padres pitcher Bruce Hurst in 1991. Those were the good.

As for the bad? That would go to Baltimore Orioles reliever Tippy Martinez, who hightailed it out of Dodge back in the late 1970s when George Scott chased him into center field at old Memorial Stadium.

Another bad one happened on March 12, 2003, during a spring training game between the Mets and the Dodgers. Dodgers pitcher Guillermo Mota drilled Mets catcher Mike Piazza in the back, and it was go-time. Piazza charged the mound with his fist cocked, ready to pound. Mota, meanwhile, threw his glove at Piazza's head and started to backpedal into the outfield as fast as he could. As Piazza gave chase, he was eventually tackled by a trio of Dodgers, who dragged him to the ground like a rodeo calf. Piazza, who had been drilled before by Mota, really wanted to get back at him. In fact, he even reportedly went looking for him after the game in the opposing team's locker room, but to no avail. Lucky for Mota!

Now for the ugly. That would go to Pawtucket (minor league) Red Sox outfielder Izzy Alcantara, who was suspended for six games back in July

Outfielder Dave Winfield on Charging the Mound

"I went out to the mound many times during my career. When pitchers want to establish themselves and come inside on me, I will go out there and have words with them. I have even introduced them to the 'five of clubs' as they say, and mixed it up out there. You have to stand up for yourself sometimes and take a stand.

"I got into it one time with Nolan Ryan. He felt he had to do what he had to do, and I felt like I had to do what I had to do. So, we had some words. He was a great pitcher and I was a serious hitter, so we respected each other. We were both true competitors. He never let up and neither did I. I don't think we had spoken a word to each other out on the field our entire careers, but we had some words that day."

of 2001 after a game against the Scranton/Wilkes-Barre Red Barons. Alcantara, who was leading the league in batting and home runs at the time, became enraged after Red Barons pitcher Blas Cedeno brushed him back with some chin music. The pitch was in response to an earlier home run in which Alcantara celebrated a bit too much by taking a slow trot around the bases. What transpired next was pretty crazy. In what might have been a first, instead of charging the pitcher, Alcantara first turned back toward Red Barons catcher Jeremy Salazar and kicked him in the face, eliminating any chance Cedeno's battery mate would prevent Alcantara from reaching his target. With the catcher down, Alcantara took off toward the mound, managing to throw one wild haymaker before being tackled and subdued by the third baseman.

As for the future of mound-charging in baseball, maybe former pitcher Tommy John has the answer:

> As far as I am concerned, if a guy wants to charge the mound, then let him charge the mound. But just let it be those two, the pitcher and the hitter, nobody else. Take the third-man-in rule in hockey, for instance, where that third guy is automatically suspended or ejected. That is how it should be in baseball. Hey, if two willing combatants want to go at it out there, fine. Let them go, let them fight like men. They can whale away at each other until they are tired, and then the umpires can break it up and toss them out so that the ballgame could resume. That would be fair. That is how it should be, in my opinion.

6

On Bench-Clearing Brawls

Whenever a mound-charging incident occurs, a bench-clearing brawl almost always follows. It is just inevitable. Bench-clearing brawl, donnybrook, fracas, imbroglio, basebrawl, skirmish, melee, or just plain old fight—call it what you want. It is the part of the code that says, "We are not going to be pushed around or disrespected anymore. We are going to stand up for ourselves and take a stand. Bring it on!"

"Brawling has been a part of baseball for decades," says ESPN's Jeremy Schaap. "Like bullfighting, charging the mound is a strange and sacred tradition, a ritualized dance. The bullpens and dugouts empty as players, sometimes out of genuine anger, sometimes merely out of a sense of obligation, storm the field."

No matter how a brawl starts, Rule Number One for bench-clearers is that you have to jump in and help protect your boys. Get up out of the dugout or bullpen as fast as you can. Nothing will put you in your teammates' doghouse quicker than playing possum and not showing up. In baseball you are a family, and you have to stick up for your family at all costs.

A few years back Indians manager Charlie Manuel got ejected from a game and, as such, was prohibited from going back on to the field. But when a brawl broke out, he hustled out there to help out his boys. For his actions he was given a two-game suspension, but he didn't care, saying that there was no way he was going to sit by in the clubhouse while his team was in a fight.

Bench-clearers have been a part of the game since its inception more than 150 years ago. The pundits talk about how bad they are for the game and what a terrible example they set for kids. That may be true, but very few fans have ever gotten up and left a ballgame during the middle of a bench-clearing brawl. It's the voyeur in all of us that wants to see grown men go at it like gladiators.

And just like in hockey fights, the old adage holds true: "If we don't stop all of this fighting, we are going to have to build bigger arenas." The bottom line is that most fans love brawls, and for all intents and purposes, most players enjoy them from time to time, too. In fact, a good bench-clearer can unite the team. It can swing the momentum for a team and let their opponents know that they won't be intimidated. Sometimes it can be the perfect wake-up call for a team that is slumping. While most brawls are pretty harmless, a few over the years have gotten out of hand. One that certainly fit that bill occurred back in 1953 when a brawl in the old Pacific Coast League needed no fewer than 50 Los Angeles cops to break it up. An *L.A. Daily News* scribe described the scene as "an orgy of gouging, spiking, and slugging."

While scenes like that have pretty much gone the way of the dinosaur, there have been some vicious bench-clearing brawls in recent years. One in particular happened in Game 3 of the 2003 American League Championship Series between the Boston Red Sox and their archrival, the

Player/Manager Frank Quilici on Bench-Clearing Brawls

"My most memorable bench-clearing brawl came when I was managing with Minnesota, and we got into it one night in Milwaukee. Ray Corbin was pitching, and he had a rising fastball that could take off inside once in a while on a right-handed hitter. Well, sure enough a kid was leaning over the plate on him and just froze when the pitch came up and in. It got him right in the jaw and he went down hard. So the benches cleared, and we got into it pretty good. George Scott came after me, but Craig Kusick bear-hugged him. Once he got loose, Bobby Darwin hit him with three quick rights. It was great. Scott was screaming at me and accusing me of throwing at their guys. I just looked at him and said 'Sorry George, but we don't throw at .230 hitters,' and that really pissed him off. From there, I went after a guy who was trying to get one of my ballplayers, and the next thing I knew, their manager Del Crandall had me on my back. It was all over for me at that point."

Pitcher Charlie Walters on Bench-Clearing Brawls

"I was in what many consider to be the greatest bean-brawl in baseball history. It was in July of 1970, and I was playing with the Washington Senators' [Triple A] team, the Denver Bears. We were playing the Wichita Aeros in Mile High Stadium, and the fight lasted over 40 minutes. It was crazy. There were a couple of beanballs thrown, and then the place just exploded. Our pitcher, Art Fowler, was right in the middle of the whole thing. Everybody was just going at it, and I wound up getting clipped from behind on a real cheap shot. I even ended up with torn knee ligaments and had to spend the next six months with a big cast on my leg, which ended my season. It was brutal. You never know what can happen in those situations. It can get scary. I mean, I wasn't even pitching that day, and I wound up suffering what could have been a career-ending injury."

New York Yankees. It all started when the Yankees' Karim Garcia slid hard into Boston second baseman Todd Walker. Sox pitcher Pedro Martinez retaliated by throwing at Garcia's head. The umpire came out waving his arms, warning both sides that he wouldn't tolerate any more retaliation. Boy, was he in for a surprise.

Tensions mounted and then finally boiled over, however, in the fourth inning, when Yankees pitcher Roger Clemens threw high heat to Sox All-Star slugger Manny Ramirez. "Man-Ram" took offense and started out toward the mound with his bat in hand. The benches emptied, and the players met at the mound in what would turn out to be one of the zaniest postseason melees in history. At the center of it all was 72-year-old Yankees bench coach Don Zimmer, who leaped out from the dugout and lunged at Pedro Martinez. Martinez, shocked at what he saw, sidestepped Zim and sent the old man hurtling to the ground. It was surreal.

And it wasn't over there. There was a ninth-inning altercation in the bullpen between Yankees reliever Jeff Nelson, Karim Garcia, and a Red Sox groundskeeper. In the aftermath, New York's Mayor Michael Bloomberg suggested that maybe Pedro Martinez should have been arrested for assaulting Don Zimmer. Boston police then responded in kind by threatening to arrest Jeff Nelson for his role in the bullpen fight. The perfect ending to the story came when the crusty old warhorse, Zimmer, showed up at a press conference to apologize, sporting a bandage on

Manager Tom Kelly on Bench-Clearing Brawls

"The first rule I had whenever there was a bench-clearer or if a guy charged the mound was to get out there and protect the pitcher. You really had to hammer that home with your catcher, that he had to be quick and tackle that guy from behind before he could get out there. You didn't want to see your pitcher get hurt and break a hand or something, because then you were stuck. Certain teams really emphasize that, like Boston. When Pedro Martinez drilled a guy, there would be eight guys standing in front of him within seconds practically. Hey, he was their bread and butter, so they had to take care of him. He was untouchable, and rightly so."

his schnoz. As ESPN's Jim Caple wrote, the game became "the ultimate reality show."

While some bench-clearing incidents are downright wild and crazy, others are simply ironic. Take, for instance, the game between the Durham Bulls and the Winston-Salem Warthogs on May 22, 1995, where the boys did their best to celebrate "Strike Out Domestic Violence Night" at the Durham Athletic Park. Warthogs pitcher Jason Kummerfeldt had drilled three Bulls batters when left fielder John Knott led the charge out to the mound to kick off the festivities. The benches emptied and when it was over, Winston-Salem pitcher Glen Cullop ended up hospitalized with a broken jaw and five lost teeth after being kicked in the face. All in all, 10 players had been ejected and 124 days of suspensions were doled out to boot. It was surely a great show for all the anti–domestic-violence fans in attendance.

For the most part, the vast majority of bench-clearers arise out of retaliation for a player getting drilled. Such was the case during a wild one that took place on April 22, 2000, at Comiskey Park between the White Sox and the Tigers. Not one but two brawls erupted in this one. Tigers pitcher Jeff Weaver drilled Carlos Lee in the sixth, and in retaliation, Chicago's Jim Parque plunked Dean Palmer in the top of the seventh. Palmer charged the mound, throwing his helmet at Parque on the way out there. Things finally cooled down, but then heated right back up in the ninth inning when another fracas erupted after a couple more batsmen were hit. When it was all said and done, 16 players, coaches, and managers were suspended, with another nine getting fined, in what Major League Baseball referred to as "the biggest mass-suspension ever."

Shortly thereafter, MLB's Vice President of Operations, Frank Robinson, commented on bench-clearing brawls:

> I'm not trying to stop a pitcher from pitching inside, and maybe even hitting hitters accidentally or even on purpose. I'm not saying that. But if they do that, and it escalates into something…they have to be willing to pay the penalty. I think if we can stop players from coming out of the bullpen or coming out of the dugouts and spilling onto the field, I think we can start to control these types of things and start to eliminate them.

Another reason for bench-clearing incidents is when a pitcher gives up a home run and then drills the next guy up to send a message and keep him off guard. An example of this happened on May 19, 1998, in a game between the Orioles and the Yankees. It all started in the eighth inning, when Orioles closer Armando Benitez gave up what turned out to be the game-winning three-run homer to Bernie Williams. Frustrated, Benitez drilled the next batter, Tino Martinez, square in the back. All hell broke loose at that point, and the benches cleared. Yankees reliever Graeme Lloyd was so upset that he sprinted in from the bullpen with the hopes of getting a shot at Benitez. He would have gotten it, too, had it not been for Yankees slugger Darryl Strawberry, who beat him to the punch, literally. Straw threw what the *Baltimore Sun* called a "sucker punch" at Benitez, swinging so hard that he actually fell into the Baltimore dugout. Seeing what happened, O's pitcher Alan Mills then smacked Strawberry right in the face, leaving him a bloody mess.

"I've never seen anything like that in 25 years," said Yankees owner George Steinbrenner. "That guy should be suspended for the rest of the year. That was a classless act. He's got no class."

"It was so blatant," added Yankees manager Joe Torre. "Benitez caused a riot. That's the downside to the designated hitter. The pitcher gets braver when he doesn't have to face the music."

Second Baseman Al Newman on Bench-Clearing Brawls

"One thing a lot of fans might not realize is that after every bench-clearing brawl, the players will go back and watch the tape. They want to know who did what and if anybody got sucker-punched. If they see something that doesn't look right, justice will be served the next time those two teams get together, guaranteed."

First Baseman Kent Hrbek on Bench-Clearing Brawls

"For the most part things are pretty harmless when the benches clear, but you never know what can happen out there. You just run out and try to find somebody to pair up with, a dance partner. Things can get ugly, though. I once got the crap knocked out of me in Milwaukee back in the early '80s when I was with the Twins. I was having a good day against them at the plate, and they finally just had enough of it. Well, we were in the middle of the game, and Robin Yount tried to take out our second baseman on a hard slide. Both benches emptied, and the next thing I knew I was being pummeled at first base. I think most of their guys were looking for an excuse to get me, so they just ran past second base and ganged up on me at first. Our pile spilled into right field, and it got crazy. I suppose it was their way of saying 'Welcome to the league, kid.' There was a great picture of me in the paper the next day as I was walking off the field, with my hat in one hand and my shoe in the other. They wanted to send me a message, but it only made me dig in even harder. I loved that kind of stuff."

One thing is for certain: when it comes to retaliation, there is a genesis to each incident. Some of the most notorious brawls in history have a plot that reads like a novel, complete with multiple players retaliating against one another in multiple games that might span days, weeks, months, or even years. Players have long memories in this business, and they never forget when they have been disrespected. Justice will be served—the code says so.

Many brawls will escalate during a long series as well, when teams face each other for four straight days. Such was the case between Anaheim and Texas back in August of 2006, when tempers flared during a home-and-home series that transpired over the course of eight days. It started in Anaheim when Rangers pitcher Adam Eaton was ejected for throwing at Juan Rivera of the Angels. The Rangers' Vicente Padilla then retaliated for the ejection by drilling Anaheim slugger Vlad Guerrero. Guerrero responded by hitting a three-run dinger in his next at-bat. Two batters later, Padilla plunked Rivera and got tossed.

Peace was restored, but the next night Anaheim pitcher Kevin Gregg threw behind the Rangers' Ian Kinsler in the eighth and then nailed Michael Young before getting ejected. His replacement, Brendan Donnelly, drilled the next batter, Freddy Guzman, and promptly got the heave-ho, too. Finally, with two outs in the ninth, Rangers reliever Scott Feldman drilled the Angels' Adam Kennedy to empty the benches. What transpired was later referred to in the *Dallas Morning News* as "the wildest fight scene at Ameriquest Field in Arlington in, well, maybe ever." By the time the games were complete, there had been five hit batters, five players ejected, and both managers tossed, with Rangers skipper Buck Showalter getting the hook twice.

7

On Throwing Inside

Many baseball insiders contend that the practice of throwing inside has become a lost art. "Purpose pitches" have been and always will be an effective tool for pitchers to keep batters from crowding the plate. Being able to throw the ball inside is just as important for a pitcher as being able to keep the ball low in the strike zone—if they don't do it, balls will be deposited into the outfield bleachers in a hurry.

Pitchers need to keep their opponents on edge and keep them honest. Batters need to know that they could get drilled at any moment, and therefore must stand back just a little bit in order to be able to duck out of the way. If a hitter has no fear of retaliation or is not intimidated, it is going to be a long day for the pitcher.

Some have suggested that the reason so many hitters are getting beaned nowadays is because they have had no practice at bailing on beanballs. Back in the day, if a hitter went up against a fireballer such as Nolan Ryan, Don Drysdale, or Bob Gibson, he was on his toes and ready for the inside pitch to come in and knock him down. That is simply not the case today.

Today, some pitchers are more reluctant to come inside. One reason is the fact that the strike zone has gotten smaller in recent years—with the umpires calling much tighter games nowadays, pitchers feel they can't afford to waste a pitch inside and get behind on a batter.

Others contend that the culture of the game has changed, in that the players on different teams are friends now and wouldn't want to hurt each

Manager Frank Quilici on the Difference between a Brushback and a Purpose Pitch

"The purpose pitch was not intended to hurt anybody; it was to send a message. It was to let the other team know that they had done something disrespectful or thrown at one of your team's top guys and you were protecting them. Now a brushback pitch is something totally different. There is a line on the batter's box that runs six inches off of home plate. If a hitter has his elbow over that line, then a pitcher needs to brush him back, or throw inside to back him up. It is not intended to hit him, but rather to get him to move his feet and back away a little bit. If he is cheating towards that line, then he has a better chance to drive an outside pitch. So as a pitcher, you want to take that advantage away from him by intimidating him a little bit. You want him to know that if he doesn't move back and respect your warning, then you might have to drill him. A good pitcher will never let the hitter get the upper hand."

Infielder/DH Paul Molitor on Throwing Inside

"It is almost ridiculous how much players today complain about how pitchers throw inside on them. Now if it is a brushback at your head, then that is a little bit different. But that usually isn't the case. Heck, I remember facing Roger Clemens so many times over my career, and it was almost a given that in my first at-bat I was going to see at least one pitch that made me move my feet. It was going to happen, no doubt about it. I took it as respect, really, because he challenged me the way he did. It was like 'game on,' let's go. He never really put me in danger by throwing at my head, he just threw inside on me and forced me to move back. He didn't want me digging in on him and getting too comfortable, and I certainly understood that. We had some great battles over the years, and I had a lot of respect for him as a competitor."

Pitcher Dave Goltz on Throwing Inside

"You had to be able to throw inside. You only had 18 inches to work with. So if a guy leans in on you, you had to brush him back. That is just the way it is in this business. If you don't throw inside, then you will get smashed all over the place. Things have changed now with the warning system. The game is more about hitting now. People come to the ballpark to see runs scored. They don't want to see a 1–0 game. The only people who enjoy that are the pitchers."

Manager Tom Kelly on Throwing Inside

"I really feel like young pitchers today need to learn how to pitch inside while they are in the minor leagues. That is not something you want a guy to learn while he is in the major leagues. Yet that is what we are seeing more and more of today. There is a lot of pressure on young pitchers, and they need to develop slowly, with good teaching. The bottom line is that if a team tries to teach a guy who has no experience how to throw inside against big-league ballplayers, there are going to be problems. As soon as they do that, then their top hitters are going to get hit, and before long the benches will empty."

Catcher Tim Laudner on Calling for an Inside Pitch

"Catching, to me, was like playing chess. My pitcher had strengths and weaknesses, and the hitter had strengths and weaknesses. So it was more of a battle of wits than a battle of courage up there. My goal was to do whatever I could to help get the [hitter] out. If we had to take care of some other business, then that was all a part of it, too. I mean as a catcher, I had no problem calling for pitches on the inside part of the plate. You had to be able to pitch inside in order to set up your other pitches.

"If we had to drill a guy for some reason, then we handled that as well. But we tried to do it with respect so that things didn't get out of hand out there. One thing I know for sure about drilling guys is this: of all the pitchers that I caught over my 10 years of playing, the guys who talked about drilling guys never drilled anybody. The guys who never talked about drilling guys, they were the ones you had to watch out for. Before I could even get a chance to throw a number down to call a signal in those situations, they were already in their windup, ready to take care of business."

other. Back in the day, there was more animosity between opposing teams. Managers would fine their players for saying hello to an opponent, and they wouldn't dare make chitchat on the base paths. In today's game, the players get to know each other in college, the minor leagues, and at celebrity charitable events. They share the same agents and are all concerned about making big bucks. Nobody wants to hurt anybody to the point that he might not get that next contract. As a result, today's players hug and high-five before games, talking away about their personal lives. It is a much different atmosphere than it was 20, 30, or 50 years ago, when those types of things were practically forbidden.

Catcher Terry Steinbach on Throwing Inside

"Throwing inside is not taught today like it was back in the day. Guys don't do it as often and, as a result, have less confidence in their abilities to do it effectively. Plus, a lot of the college players that come into the league today don't learn how to throw inside that well because at that level guys can still hit inside pitches over the fences with aluminum bats. So they get used to throwing outside a lot. In fact, I would say that 90 percent of the young pitchers in the game today throw predominantly to the outside part of the plate. Well, at the major league level, players can drive the outside pitches over the fence, too, so they have to be able to use both sides of the plate if they want to have any sort of success at this level. The objective of coming inside is to keep the hitter off balance. [The pitcher] can do that two ways: by changing speeds with fastballs and change-ups or with location, either in or out. Whatever way he so chooses, it must be done."

Pitcher Jim Kaat on Throwing Inside

"When I was coaching with the Reds, I would take our pitchers down to the bullpen mounds after throwing batting practice and work with them on how to throw inside. I would actually stand in the batter's box wearing a double-flapped helmet and have them throw right under my armpits. The object was to get them to feel comfortable throwing inside and, ultimately, to get the batter to move his feet. I didn't want to teach them to drill the guy. I wanted to teach them how to throw a purpose pitch inside, effectively. It is almost a lost art because it is not something that is taught anymore. But it is still a very important part of the game. So I wanted my guys to know how to do it properly so that they could send a clear message of protecting their players and also do it in a safe way that wasn't going to get anybody hurt."

It used to be that a young pitcher would learn how to throw inside while making his way up through the minor leagues. Players today aren't being developed like they used to be and don't spend as much time learning the fundamentals of the game. Teams are coming back to it, though, and are making an effort to teach their young pitchers how to come inside with confidence.

Some minor league teams even keep charts on how many times a pitcher will make the hitter move his feet. That is the objective—to get the batter moving up there and thinking about how he can't get too comfortable and

Manager Ron Gardenhire on Throwing Inside

"Throwing inside effectively is so important. You have to be able to knock a guy off the plate. That is just baseball. A hitter can't have both sides of the plate, so it is critical for our pitchers to be able to throw inside to back them up and get their feet moving. They also have to be able to throw purpose pitches that send messages, too. Throwing inside has become a bit of a lost art, though. Some of the younger guys, for whatever the reason, just can't do it. I don't know if they are scared to hit the guy or if they just don't know how to do it, but they struggle either way. Our organization teaches it, and we work on it, but certain guys are just able to execute it better than others. It takes a certain mentality to be able to do it."

dig in, or he might just get drilled. Young pitchers are being taught to take away the inside corner and force the hitter to move off the plate. It is said that even the best hitters can only cover about three-quarters of the plate, so if a pitcher lets the hitter have the inside corner, there is a very good chance that he will also own the outside corner, too. The bottom line is that pitchers must be able to come inside for their very survival.

Outfielder Dave Winfield on Throwing Inside

"I can't begin to tell you how comfortable I would be at the plate in this day and age. I wouldn't have to worry about getting drilled all the time like I used to—the umpires don't allow pitchers to throw inside anymore. The rules have changed now, and it is what it is. It used to be a rite of passage to get thrown at: if you didn't get up from a knockdown or a brushback, and you let the other team intimidate you, then they had you. Also, the strike zone is smaller today because the umpires use an electronic monitoring system that grades their performance. The umpires don't want to make mistakes, so they tend not to call pitches outside of that strike zone."

8

On Verbal Taunting and Bench Jockeying

Verbal taunting, or "bench jockeying," has been a part of baseball since the game's beginning. It falls under the category of "getting inside a player's head" and is used as a tactic to try to get your opponent to become distracted or angered so that he won't be focused on completing the task at hand—either hitting the ball or pitching the ball. If you can break his concentration, then you have effectively succeeded.

While some forms of taunting are harmless, others can be downright brutal. Personal attacks and insults about race, religion, and family life have all been fair game over the years. In fact, years ago managers and players alike even directed racial epithets at the African American, Hispanic, and Jewish ballplayers. For whatever the reason, it was seen as a sort of gamesmanship rather than the sick prejudice that it really was.

One of the worst offenders of racial bench jockeying was none other than Leo Durocher, the legendary manager of the Dodgers, Giants, Cubs, and Astros, who was both offensive as well as effective at his unique craft. Josh Prager, author of the book *The Echoing Green*, provided some interesting insight into what it was like in the dugout with "Leo the Lip."

"I have a quote in my book from Earl Rapp, a part-time outfielder who played in the early '50s, about Leo Durocher," said Prager. "Apparently, Durocher gathered up all of the black players on his Giants team one time and said, 'Look, I am going to be screaming "nigger," "watermelon," and all of these horrible things to the black players on the opposing teams, but I just want you to know that it isn't personal. I am doing it to get under their skin and to take them out of their games. I want all of you to know that you are still a part of my team and don't want you to take offense to it.' Hard to believe that stuff really happened, but it did."

Durocher encouraged his pitchers to throw high heat at opposing ballplayers and would even reward them with $100 bounties if they beaned certain players. Leo really hated a handful of players, including St. Louis Cardinals outfielder Stan Musial. Leo would scream out to his pitcher, "Hit him on the six!" referring to the location of the number on Musial's back. Durocher would yell just about anything to get a rise out of a player and didn't care about hurting anybody's feelings. Baseball was like war to Leo, and he took no prisoners.

Another great bench jockey was manager Billy Martin, who loved to try to get under his opponents' skin. And, like Durocher, Billy also believed in offering bounties to his pitchers to throw at enemy heads. In fact, on September 18, 1979, Martin paid rookie pitcher Bob Kammeyer $100 to drill former Yankees player Cliff Johnson, whom Martin detested.

The people who undoubtedly suffered the worst from the verbal taunting were the African American players who came into the league in the late 1940s and early '50s. Cruel and vile taunts were hurled from dugouts coast to coast at ballplayers such as Jackie Robinson, who just had to suffer and take it. Not only was he taunted, but he was also thrown at quite frequently as well, all in an attempt to intimidate him both mentally and physically. The civil rights movement was starting to unfold, and many ballplayers weren't ready to accept the integration of the game.

One player who had a unique insight into Robinson's situation was teammate Howie Schultz. "My claim to fame was that Jackie Robinson replaced me at first base in 1947 when I was with the Dodgers," he recalled. "Jackie was a good person, and it was tough to see him go through what he had to go through. [Phillies manager] Ben Chapman was notoriously hard on Jackie. He could just not accept the integration of African American ballplayers gracefully, and that was very difficult to see. He expected the opposing pitchers to really give it to Jackie whenever he came up to the plate. And they did. But Jackie was such a good ballplayer, and he handled that whole situation so well. Pitchers would throw at him, but he just went about his business. Eventually it all backfired on them, and it got old in a hurry. It was amazing to see it all transpire, though."

Black pitchers were another story. Sure, they had to deal with just as much racism as the black hitters, but the pitchers were in the unique situation of being able to retaliate whenever they saw fit. And they did. One of the first African American power pitchers in the big leagues was Joe Black, who once threw at the heads of seven consecutive Cincinnati batters who had been taunting him from their dugout. Needless to say, he didn't hear a peep from them for the rest of the game.

Sometimes players will just say things in an effort to get under another player's skin. Such was the case back on August 20, 1990, when Philadelphia's Lenny Dykstra had a few choice words to say to Dodgers catcher Rick Dempsey as he stepped into the batter's box during the seventh inning. The 40-year-old Dempsey stood up and took off his mask, at which point Dykstra dropped his bat and stepped toward him. Dempsey quickly smacked him in the face with his glove and then followed it up with an immediate right. The two then went at it and wrestled each other to the ground before the benches could empty to break it up.

9

On Using a Bat as a Weapon

The code says that no matter how mad you get, or how badly you want to bash your opponent's brains in, you cannot under any circumstances use your bat as a weapon. Sure, the regular rule book says the same things, but the code reinforces it and makes it an even bigger crime in the eyes of the players. As in hockey, if a player uses his stick (or bat) to hurt another man, he is crossing a line that will ensure immediate and swift retaliation. Not only will he get a suspension and fine from the league, he will also get a serious ass-whooping from the teammates of the victim.

There are many stories about hitters getting revenge on pitchers who beaned them by charging the mound with their 44-ounce hunks of lumber. Fortunately, those days are long gone. But there have been a few high-profile bat-as-weapon incidents over the years, with the most infamous one taking place on August 22, 1965, in a game between San Francisco and Los Angeles at Candlestick Park.

The Giants and the Dodgers were bitter rivals and had been running neck and neck in the National League pennant race until that point in the season, which only added to the drama of the highly emotional series. It was billed as a pitching duel between Giants ace Juan Marichal and Dodgers fireballer Sandy Koufax. Things heated up in the second inning when Marichal knocked down the speedy Maury Wills, spinning him into the dirt. Marichal was a headhunter who went after Wills on account of his reputation as a confrontational base runner who had been known to spike players. Marichal also knocked down Ron Fairly in the third inning.

The drama boiled over when Marichal then came up to bat in the bottom of that inning, with everyone expecting Koufax to retaliate. But he didn't. Instead, his catcher, Johnny Roseboro, threw a ball back to Koufax that whizzed past Marichal's face. Intentional or not, Marichal was furious, and the two had words with each other. As Roseboro came up out of his crouch, Marichal went berserk and clobbered him over the head with three swings of his bat. The umpire grabbed him, but Marichal continued to taunt the bloody catcher, screaming, "Come on! You want some more?"

It was a surreal moment as Roseboro, now bleeding profusely, grabbed Marichal, and the fight was on—both benches emptied, and a 15-minute brawl followed. When it was all said and done, both Marichal and Roseboro were ejected. Roseboro, meanwhile, went to the hospital, where he got sewn up with 14 stitches. In the aftermath, Marichal was suspended for eight games and fined $1,750 by the league. Roseboro later sued Marichal for $110,000 in damages, as well.

Years later, Roseboro would admit to instigating the attack. "When Marichal came up to bat, I tried a knockdown from behind the plate, throwing the ball close to his nose when I returned it to the pitcher," recalled Roseboro. "I expected Marichal to attack me in some way. If he had said anything to me, I had studied karate, and I was ready to annihilate him."

Many speculated that the violence was in response to the longstanding bad blood that had brewed between the two rival franchises. Others pointed to the race riots that had just transpired in the Watts section of Los Angeles, and even the escalating tensions surrounding the looming war in Vietnam. The nation was shocked that a game could get so out of control with a man being bludgeoned before their very eyes. For whatever the reason, it was a bizarre spectacle that will forever live on in baseball infamy.

It is interesting to note that Marichal and Roseboro would actually become friends years later. Some speculated that because they had reconciled, Marichal would finally get voted into the Hall of Fame. Sure enough, it came to fruition.

"There were no hard feelings on my part, and I thought if that was made public, people would believe that this was really over with," said Roseboro. "So I saw him at a Dodgers old-timers' game, and we posed for pictures together, and I actually visited him in the Dominican Republic.

The next year, he was in the Hall of Fame. Hey, over the years, you learn to forget things."

Ironically, less than a year later, another bat attack occurred in a minor league game between the Vancouver Mounties and the Seattle Angels. Seattle pitcher Jim Coates drilled a Vancouver batter, and a brawl ensued. Seattle catcher Merritt Ranew was trying to restore order when Vancouver's Santiago Rosario bolted from the on-deck circle and bashed Ranew over the head with his bat. Ranew was rushed to the hospital, where he underwent brain surgery and would spend the next six weeks recovering. He would also suffer from facial paralysis but luckily was able to recover and later returned to the diamond.

Years later, in 1976, a bat attack of a different kind occurred during a nasty bench-clearing brawl between the Cubs and the Giants. After a series of brushback pitches were exchanged by both clubs, Cubs third baseman Bill Madlock got beaned on the helmet. To retaliate, he then "accidentally" let his bat slip out of his hands and sent it flying toward the mound. Nobody was hurt, but it certainly sent a clear message to the Giants pitching staff.

A similar situation took place on May 22, 1988, during a game between the Dodgers and the Mets, when Pedro Guerrero threw his bat at David Cone. The incident took place the day after a brouhaha between the two teams that featured Mets pitcher Dwight Gooden drilling Alfredo Griffin on the wrist, followed by Dodgers pitcher Brian Holton plunking New York's Howard Johnson. In the sixth inning of the game, Mets pitcher David Cone came inside on Pedro Guerrero and got him on the batting helmet with a curveball.

Guerrero issued an evil glare at Cone and then threw his bat with both hands toward the pitcher. As Guerrero began to walk out to the mound, Mets catcher Barry Lyons grabbed him. Both dugouts cleared, but no punches were thrown. Guerrero later told reporters that his intent was to "brush back" Cone with his bat, the same way that Cone had done to him. The league didn't buy it, though, and he was suspended for four days and fined $1,000.

Perhaps the most infamous bat-throwing incident took place back on August 4, 1960, when Billy Martin, then a second baseman with Cincinnati, took offense when Cubs pitcher Jim Brewer threw at his head. So on the next pitch, Martin tried to retaliate by heaving his bat back at Brewer.

He missed and then pretended it was an accident and that the bat had slipped. While walking out to retrieve the bat, he had some words with the pitcher. Then, as he bent down to pick up the bat, he quickly sucker-punched Brewer right smack in the eye with a devastating overhand right. The benches then cleared, and things got ugly as the fans at Wrigley Field booed in disgust. When the dust had cleared, Brewer wound up suffering a broken orbital bone that required surgery and ultimately caused him to miss a month of playing time. Martin was fined $500 for the cheap shot and was later sued by both Brewer and the Cubs for a whopping $1 million. Years later the courts awarded Brewer $100,000, but there was no report of whether or not Billy actually paid up.

Another dangerous bat-throwing incident occurred in the 1972 American League playoffs when Bert Campaneris of Oakland threw his bat at Detroit pitcher Lerrin LaGrow and was suspended for the first few games of the 1973 season.

More recently, former major league infielder Jose Offerman was attempting to make a comeback with the Long Island Ducks of the independent Atlantic League when he regrettably joined the bat-brandishing club on August 14, 2007. After belting a home run in the first inning off Bridgeport Bluefish pitcher Matt Beech, Offerman got plunked when he returned to face Beech in the second. Enraged, Offerman charged the mound with his bat and delivered the rare two-for-one blow—as he swung the bat at Beech, the backswing hit Bluefish catcher John Nathans in the head. Beech suffered a broken finger, Nathans sustained a concussion, and Offerman was arrested by Connecticut police on two counts of second-degree assault. The fact that a 15-year major league veteran like Offerman could lose his temper illustrates one thing—no matter the consequences, there will always be players willing to break the code.

10

On Plays at the Plate

Although they are a rare occurrence, plays at the plate are one of the most exciting yet dangerous aspects of the game. According to the code, there is a right way and a wrong way for both the catcher and the base runner to properly execute a play at the plate.

If the base runner chooses to be aggressive, he will put his shoulder down and try to run over the catcher in an attempt to knock him off the plate so that he can score. His objective is to get the catcher to drop or fumble the ball as he collides with him. He also wants to intimidate him and keep him guessing as to whether or not he is going to smash into him, versus just sliding behind him harmlessly.

The catcher, meanwhile, can't take his eyes off of the ball because it is coming in fast and will often be in the dirt. So he has to block the plate, both to be able to smother the ball and to try to prevent the runner from sliding successfully past him. He needs to put up a roadblock of sorts and hold his ground. The catcher will see the runner coming out of the corner of his eye but can't risk taking his eyes off of the ball or it will fly past him. It puts the catcher in an extremely compromising position.

For the catcher, leaving a safe path or lane for the runner to slide in is the proper thing to do. If he doesn't, then he is fair game to be bowled over. For the runner, if there is a lane for him to take, the code says to take it. Unless, of course, he is looking to retaliate for something or someone on his team. Then he has a free shot at taking the catcher out and inflicting

Pitcher Jim Kaat on the Catcher's Code

"I didn't intentionally drill a lot of guys over my career, but one of the guys I did drill was Kansas City [Athletics] catcher Phil Roof. We were playing them one night back in the late '60s when I was with the Twins. Harmon Killebrew rounded third base and came in on Phil for a play at the plate. Phil stuck his leg out to block the plate and made contact with him, knocking him over, before tagging him out. Phil didn't mean to be malicious or anything, he was just doing his job. But whenever you take out a future Hall of Famer, guys are going to get upset. I remember our bench erupted because it looked like it was a dirty play.

"Well, I was pitching at the time, and I knew what I had to do. My teammates wanted revenge, and that fell on my lap. So the next time Phil came up, I had to let him have it. It is a tough thing to do. I think I even missed him with the first one, but I drilled him in the ribs with the next pitch to send him a message about getting too physical with our star player. He got pretty upset about it, but that was my job. What is ironic is that several years later he got traded to Minnesota, and we became really good friends."

some bodily harm. When this happens, fireworks usually go off, and the benches empty in a hurry.

The umpires are also involved in this process. They know that the catcher is in a very vulnerable spot and will usually give him the call if he can just hold on to the ball amidst the collision. Much like a second baseman's "phantom tag," which the umpires often award so that fielders don't get run over, catchers, too, will get the benefit of the doubt if there is impact. Even if the catcher blocks the entire plate, which could be considered illegal obstruction, as long as they can just hang on to the ball and make it look close, they'll usually get the out.

There have been some classic plays at the plate over the years, complete with plenty of drama, intrigue, and showmanship. Catchers and runners alike have suffered broken bones, been bloodied, and knocked out cold. That is all part of the deal, though, and it adds an element of danger to the game that is rarely seen. Bad blood can boil over in a heartbeat on a close play at the plate, instigating immediate retaliation. This is why these plays are a real fan-favorite, because you never know what is going to go down.

Perhaps the most notorious play-at-the-plate incident took place in the 1970 All-Star Game, when Cincinnati's Pete Rose ran over Cleveland catcher Ray Fosse at home plate to score the dramatic game-winning run in the twelfth inning. Nobody could believe that Rose would do such a thing in a meaningless All-Star Game, but he had only one speed—full. He never slowed down and he played every game like it was his last. That is what made him so tough. Fosse went down in a heap on the play and never fully recovered from the injuries he sustained during the play. Fosse had blocked the plate, and Rose never thought about slowing down as he barreled over him. It was one of the most brutal plays ever witnessed.

Another memorable incident took place on May 20, 1976, during a game between hated rivals New York and Boston, when the Yankees' Lou Piniella crashed into Sox catcher Carlton Fisk at home plate. It was later dubbed "The Brawl in the Bronx." The situation was ripe for spontaneous combustion—the Sox had just represented the AL in the 1975 World Series, and the Yanks were in first place in the AL East under their combative new manager, Billy Martin.

It all went down in the bottom of the sixth with two outs and New York up 1–0. Dwight Evans fielded an Otto Velez single and threw a one-hopper to Fisk. Piniella rounded third and showed no signs of slowing down, even though he knew that he was going to be out by a country mile. Fisk planted himself in the baseline and braced himself as Piniella tried to run him over.

"He stuck his elbow in my eye and ran me over," said Fisk. "He started kicking. I don't know if he was punching or not. What you've got to remember is each team is up for the other. It has been that way between the Red Sox and the Yankees ever since I started playing."

"I ran into Fisk pretty darn good," Piniella would later recall. "He stuck the ball in my face. We ended up punching a little bit behind home plate. And then it escalated to a different level."

(It is interesting to note that there was no love lost between Fisk and the Yankees. After all, just three years earlier, in 1973, Yankee catcher Thurman Munson had barreled into Fisk at home plate and nearly incited a riot. Fisk went berserk and took on all comers in that fracas, cementing his legacy as one of the toughest backstops of all time.)

With that, the benches emptied and a full-fledged fight broke out. Taking the brunt of the punishment was Boston starting pitcher Bill Lee, who had been a marked man in the Big Apple for comments he had made following a 1973 fight between the two clubs. Lee, who had said that the Yankees fought like "a bunch of hookers swinging their purses," was sought out and attacked by Mickey Rivers and Graig Nettles.

Meanwhile, Carl Yastrzemski, despite being hobbled from being kneed in the thigh, went on to hit a pair of homers en route to an 8–2 Boston victory.

Lee, who wound up suffering a near-career-ending shoulder separation in the incident, and would later have to have two titanium pins surgically put in, remembers it this way:

> I had Otto Velez, who hit the ball, had him wrapped up. Then Rivers, who was sneaking around punching guys, hit me in the back of the head. I let go of Otto, and Nettles ran me over and drove me into the ground, right on my shoulder and elbow. There were actually two separate fights. When I got up, I swung at Nettles, but my arm was dead, and I didn't get much out of it. He came over the top and hit me with a right hook, and I was at the bottom of the pile again.

The next night, Lee showed up at Yankee Stadium with a black eye and his arm in a sling. "I don't think the Yankees started the fight to get to me," he said, "but once it started, I know there were a few Yankees looking for me. My opinions may have caught up with themselves."

Yankees third baseman Graig Nettles, who denied trying to deliberately hurt Lee, later asked rhetorically: "I'd like to know, does he look like he's been hit with a purse?"

The money shot for every play at the plate is that one moment when the crowd waits in nervous anticipation to see whether or not the catcher held on to the ball and applied the tag, or whether the runner successfully

Catcher Tim Laudner on the Catcher's Code

"One thing that has always cracked me up about being a catcher is that we get no damn sympathy back there. If a second baseman or shortstop gets a bump or a bruise on a hard slide into second, the entire training staff will run out there to make sure they are all right. Meanwhile, if the catcher gets absolutely smoked at home plate, I mean completely jacked, you won't hear as much as a peep, other than somebody maybe saying 'walk it off.' Nobody is coming out there to check on you unless you are unconscious. I remember getting my nose busted by Dave Valle one time up in Seattle on a hard collision, and I sure as hell didn't get any sympathy out of any of my guys. But, hey, that is just the nature of the beast if you're a catcher."

Catcher Dan Wilson on the Catcher's Code

"Collisions at home plate are just a part of baseball. You would hope that a runner wouldn't purposely try to hurt you or try to take out your knee, but things can happen. Each incident is unique. If there is bad blood between teams, then maybe a play at the plate will be more of a collision rather than a hard slide. You never know. Again, it is very situational. To be honest, as catchers, we sort of enjoy that kind of thing. Collisions could be just as fun for us, too. To block the plate and tag a guy out in dramatic fashion was pretty exciting, believe me.

"As far as the code goes for stuff like this, if you give a guy a lane to run in and he purposely puts a good blow on you, then you might have an issue to deal with. It depends on the situation. Most guys will try to go around you if you leave them an opening. Some want to make contact, though, and it can be tough, especially if you are watching the ball being thrown in to you from the outfield, and you have to field it and block the plate at the same time. You just never know what could happen. Hopefully, if a guy did plow you over, your teammates would rally behind you and take care of business."

touched home plate with his foot or hand on the slide. If he didn't touch the plate, and the ball scooted away from the catcher, the runner can come back and touch it to make sure he is called safe by the ump. Such was the case back on July 4, 1932, during a game between the Yankees and the Senators at Griffith Stadium in Washington, D.C.

It all started after a collision at the dish when Senators outfielder Carl Reynolds scored on a close play past Yankees catcher Bill Dickey. Reynolds got up and started running toward his dugout but then turned around and headed back to home plate, just to make sure he had stepped on it. Dickey, thinking that he was getting shown up, hauled off and smacked Reynolds, knocking him out and busting his jaw in the process. Both benches emptied and things got so ugly that fans entered into the fracas as well. Dickey would be suspended for a month and fined a cool grand.

One of the most memorable and thrilling play-at-the-plate incidents of all time took place back in Game 4 of the 1939 World Series between the Yankees and the Reds. With runners on the corners in the twelfth inning, Yankees slugger Joe DiMaggio singled to right for what would turn out to be the game-winning hit. Cincinnati right fielder Ival Goodman misplayed the ball and then threw it in to catcher Ernie "the Schnozz" Lombardi, who was unable to hold on to it as he was knocked down and nearly out for the count by the charging Charlie Keller. As the catcher lay in the dirt, DiMaggio was able to circle the bases untouched. The play would later be referred to as "Schnozz's snooze."

Another tactic employed by base runners is to spike the catcher as they slide into the plate. One player who had no problem doing this sort of thing was Giants outfielder Bobby Bonds, who never apologized for his rough style of play.

"I spiked people and I got spiked," said Bonds. "I only went after one person, really: Larry Cox, a catcher for Philadelphia. I slid into home plate one day, 1973, I think it was, or '74. Larry had offered me a part of the plate, and I went after it. And he put down his shin guards in front of me and got me pretty good. My knees were bleeding and everything. He hurt me. Not to the point where I had to leave the game. But I was in some pain. So I went after him to get him back, and I broke his leg. I wanted to hurt him. I mean, not to the point of breaking his leg, because that's a person's career. But I wanted to let him know, 'Don't do this. If you wanna play this way, this is the way I can play. You wanna have rough baseball? Well, let's have rough baseball.'"

11

On Breaking Up a Double Play
by Sliding Hard Into Second Base

Sliding hard into second base to break up a double play is one of the hallmarks of the code; it simply must be done. How aggressively a player chooses to go in, however, is what makes the play exciting as well as controversial. It is understood that when there is a runner on first and the batter hits a ground ball, the runner must do everything in his arsenal to break up the double play at second base. If that means sliding hard into the second baseman or shortstop, whomever is covering the bag, then so be it.

It is the runner's job to disrupt the fielder and try to force him either to throw the ball away or simply not to throw it at all. The runner must sacrifice his body so that the batter can safely reach first base behind him. The best-case scenario will have him break up the double play and somehow force the second baseman to drop the ball, which would ultimately leave both runners safe at first and second. The worst-case scenario is that both runners will be called out as a result of a perfectly executed double play. Not much will get under a manager's skin like a base runner who fails to at least try to knock that second baseman on his ass. It falls under the category of "taking one for the team."

A good second baseman or shortstop will not just stand there like a sitting duck, however. He will move quickly to jump over the approaching hard slide, and if he has to, he will threaten to throw the ball directly at the base runner's head as he barrels toward him. Back in the day plenty of base

Manager Frank Quilici on Sliding Hard Into Second Base

"I had plenty of guys try to roll me over on double plays when I was playing second base. I had guys try to take me out all the time. They would come up my leg if I had to stretch for the ball from the shortstop. They would do whatever they could to take me out. It could be dangerous. One time it happened during a game against the Angels, and I had to leave the game. Well, my roommate, Dave Boswell, got back at the guy for taking me out. Boz was a no-nonsense kind of a pitcher and protected his teammates. So the first time he saw that guy the next time we played them, he drilled him right in the ribs on the first pitch. He even went over to him and said, 'That was for my roommate, you S.O.B.!'

"You know, the guy who taught me the most about how to play second base was my manager, Billy Martin. One time he came up to me and showed me a bunch of newspaper pictures of second basemen and shortstops as they were jumping up in the air to throw the ball over to first base and avoid being hit by the base runner who was trying to break up the double play. He told me that all of those guys were just hotdogging it. I will never forget what he told me. He said: 'Second base is yours. You gotta know your own ability to get to that bag, and then you gotta talk to the other infielders on where you want them to give you that ball. Once you get it in the right spot, then you can throw it over to first base before you jump in the air. Once you release the ball, then you jump in the air. Then, if he is going to try to take you out, you find a spot on his chest to plant your spikes in. You own second base. It's not his—it's yours. So you gotta act like you own it.'

"I never forgot that. And I always tried to make guys pay when they came after me. If I could only get a knee or a foot in there, then that was going to have to suffice. I needed to send them a message that I wasn't going to be intimidated out there. Hell, I didn't want to get injured and lose my job. It was a matter of survival; if those guys were going to try to take me out, then I was going to try to take them out, too. That is what the code is all about in that regard."

runners took it in the kisser under this scenario. The choice is theirs—if the runner stays in the base path and doesn't slide, then he might get drilled with the ball at close range; if he ducks out of the way, then he might be perceived as soft by his teammates. It is a tough call, and one that must be made in the blink of an eye.

In addition to being able to roll over the second baseman, the base runner also has another tool in his arsenal—his spikes. Though illegal and unethical, many players have not hesitated before coming in spikes-high.

It is dirty and cheap, but it is also an intimidation tactic that will certainly make the second baseman think twice about how aggressively he is going to try to turn the double play.

The second baseman, meanwhile, has to be quick and precise. His job is to get to the base so that the third baseman or shortstop can field the ball and throw it to him. Once he gets the ball, he has to catch it for the force-out at or near the bag, pivot, jump to avoid being rolled over by the oncoming base runner, and then throw a bullet to the first baseman in order to complete the second out.

The second baseman is in a pretty vulnerable position at that point, so to prevent injuries, the umpires will allow him to just come close to the bag without actually touching it. They know that if he stands on the bag with his head turned to look for the ball, he could get his legs broken from underneath him. So, the second baseman will stand near the bag, within a foot or two, and turn the play from there. This is known as the "phantom tag." The runner, as a sort of compensation, is then allowed to either slide late, past the bag, or slide at the fielder even though he is nowhere near second base.

If the runner follows or chases him outside of the base path to where he is standing, then he has entered a bit of a gray area. If the runner goes too far over and makes it too obvious that he isn't even attempting to touch the bag, but rather is only interested in running over the second baseman or leg-whipping him to knock him over, then he might get called out for interference. He might also be breaking the code for intentionally trying to injure the opposing fielder.

Sliding hard into second is not only a tactic in breaking up a double-play ball—it is also the biggest form of retaliation for hitters who have been

Infielder/DH Paul Molitor on Sliding Hard Into Second Base

"Taking out the second baseman or shortstop on second base to break up a double play is expected, but if you go too far out of your way to hurt the guy, then that is where you are crossing a line. Those guys expect to be knocked over, but base runners have to do that within the confines of the code. I played a lot of middle infield over my career, and it was definitely a challenge to take on that runner and execute the double play. If you knew he was coming for you, it could be an intimidating thing. Every now and then you would get a guy who would come in with his spikes up, or try to roll you over, but that just came with the territory."

thrown at or drilled by opposing pitchers. Because they can't get even with the pitcher, they will get even with the second baseman instead. That is how the code works. So if a hitter has been thrown at, the second baseman had best be on his toes, because the runner will be coming in high and hard in order to take him out as revenge. It works both ways, though—if a runner takes out a second baseman, then his pitcher might just drill him later in the game as revenge. It is certainly a vicious circle.

"Break up a double play with a good, clean, hard slide," explains ESPN's Tim Kurkjian. "Anything beyond that is unacceptable. No roll blocks. No spikes in the air. No sliding 10 feet to the outside part of the bag. Nothing that could destroy a middle infielder's career. Those guys' knees and legs are exposed, they often can't see the runner coming, they deserve and expect contact, but nothing that could bust a knee in half. Pudge Rodriguez rolled Omar Vizquel a few years ago, knocking him out for a couple months. We've never seen then-Indians manager Mike Hargrove madder than he was that night. There is also no reason to kill

Second Baseman Al Newman on Sliding Hard Into Second Base

"One of the worst collisions I ever had at second base over my career was with Dan Gladden. It happened back in 1986 when I was with Montreal and he was with the Giants. I was playing second base, and Hubie Brooks was at shortstop. With one out and a runner on third, Gladden drew a walk and was standing on first base. The next Giants hitter then hit a ground ball into the hole at short. Hubie fielded it but bobbled the ball and double-pumped it as he threw it over to me at second base. That extra split-second pause was just enough time for me to absolutely get leveled by Gladden, who was a pretty fast runner. He just took me out on a pop-slide, where a runner will slide in early and then quickly pop up and hit the fielder around the hips. I wound up throwing the ball away as he hit me, too, which allowed the guy on third base to score what turned out to be the game-winning run.

"As I was lying in the dirt, I watched him run back to his dugout, where all of his teammates were high-fiving him. I felt awful; I was so pissed at him. Something like that can be a big momentum swinger. What should have been a sure double play now gave them a one-run lead. Ironically, the next season we were both traded to the Twins, and we wound up getting lockers next to each other. I will never forget sitting down next to him and saying, 'Okay, we can either fight right now and get it over with or let it go.' He just looked at me and smiled. Believe it or not, we would go on to become best friends, and still are even to this day."

Third Baseman Ron Coomer on Sliding Hard Into Second Base

"If I got drilled and I knew it was intentional, I was going to try my damnedest to take out their second baseman if I got on base that game. It wasn't personal or anything—it was just playing hard baseball. A good second baseman would know that, too. A lot of people aren't aware of this, but there is sort of an unwritten code amongst infielders that we didn't take each other out, as was the case for catchers colliding with one another at home plate, as well. But when the game got heated and intense and the volume got turned up, then all bets were off. You had to do what you had to do. That was just a part of the game."

middle infielders when it's obvious that there will be no throw to first on the play. Yet that still happens."

One of the most feared base runners of all time was Ty Cobb. Cobb often hated his opponents and would try to hurt them whenever and however he could. He was an antagonist who looked for every angle to exploit in order to get his team a victory. Cobb would announce his intentions, too, oftentimes screaming obscenities at the second baseman while he was en route. He knew that if he could get inside that guy's head, there was a good chance that he would bobble the ball or make a throwing error. Either way, Cobb would win.

As a member of the Detroit Tigers, Cobb enjoyed spiking second basemen and caused many a bench-clearing brawl because of it. Not only would Cobb spike them, but he would come flying in as fast as he could and then leap in order to inflict the most possible damage. He would bloody them in their chests or legs, whichever area was left exposed. The

A Subcode to the Code: Don't Pack Heat in Your Glove

Second basemen can retaliate, too, either by drilling the oncoming runner in the head with the ball or by "packing heat." That's right. Hall of Fame Negro Leaguer Willie "the Devil" Wells used to pack stones into the finger holes of his glove back in the 1920s and '30s so that he could whack opposing base runners when he tagged them. Opposing players would grab a handful of dirt before they took off from first base and then try to throw it in his eyes when they slid in, with the hopes of blinding him just enough so they wouldn't get whacked by his loaded glove.

future Hall of Famer was a mean S.O.B. who loved a good tussle, which is why most players steered clear of him.

Billy Martin, while playing second base for the Yankees back on July 12, 1952, got revenge on St. Louis Browns catcher Clint Courtney, who had a reputation as a guy who would spike players while sliding. On a routine grounder, Courtney was coming hard into second in order to break up a potential double play. Martin held his ground and, instead of tagging him, wound up and drilled him right between the eyes with the ball, breaking his glasses in the process. Courtney got up and went after Martin, but Billy was a brawler and worked him over with several punishing shots to the jaw. And while Courtney was ejected, fined, and suspended, Martin got off scot-free and was allowed to remain in the game. Many speculated that this was the code meting out its own form of justice, as in "what comes around goes around."

One of the most infamous hard-slide retaliation incidents took place on June 15, 1993, during a 12–4 Dodgers victory over the Rockies. Not one but two fights in the span of an inning were spawned as the result of an Andres Galarraga hard slide on Dodgers second baseman Jody Reed. Galarraga, who had hit safely in eight consecutive at-bats, was on fire, and the Dodgers felt as if he needed to be cooled off. So Ramon Martinez threw at him, and that was then followed up with an errant pickoff throw that hit him in the neck while he was on first base.

Upset, Galarraga retaliated by sliding hard into second. The problem was he wound up kicking Reed as he slid in well behind the throw. It was

George Mitterwald on Sliding Hard Into Second Base

"I remember one time when I was with the Cubs back in the late '70s and we were playing the Mets. Mets outfielder Dave Kingman was on first base and came in hard on our shortstop, Mick Kelleher. He was retaliating for being thrown at and just leveled him. He rolled over him and knocked him out. It was crazy. I mean Kingman was about 6'6" and 240 pounds, whereas Kelleher was about 150 pounds soaking wet. So when he hit him he just flew. A brawl broke out and the benches emptied. Then something happened that I will never forget. Mick, this little guy about 5'8", picked up Kingman and slammed him into the ground. It was unbelievable. He was so strong and so pissed off that he just went off and sent a message to them that he wasn't going to take that kind of crap. It really swung the momentum for us, too."

Outfielder Tony Oliva on Sliding Hard Into Second Base

"If you ever had the chance to break up a double play by taking out the second baseman or shortstop, then you had to do it, absolutely. I used to try to slide in about leg high. That way he had to jump at least that high to throw the ball over to first base. I just tried to do whatever I could to break up that double play and keep the inning going for my team. Now you could get hit in the face in the process, but that was just a part of the game. You had to prevent that second out from being made, and if that meant sacrificing your body, then that is what you had to do. If you didn't do it, then you would get a lot of heat from your manager and your teammates when you got back to the bench. You had to go hard. That is good baseball.

"I remember a game back in 1962 against Chicago, and my good friend Orlando Martinez was hit in the face trying to break up a double play. The second baseman went real low, and Orlando couldn't get out of the way. The ball hit him hard and rolled all the way into the dugout. He was okay, but it was really scary. You never knew what was going to happen when you went into second base hard. It was a tough job."

A Subcode to the Code: Use the Hard Tag at Your Own Risk

Another interesting hard-tag subcode deals with how an infielder can use his body to either apply a tag or block the runner's path. Perhaps the most notorious incident that dealt with this issue happened during the 1991 World Series, when Atlanta's Ron Gant hit a single in the third inning of Game 2 and then, after rounding first, started retreating back to the bag. Twins pitcher Kevin Tapani then threw the ball to first baseman Kent Hrbek, where it appeared that Gant had plenty of time to get back safely. That's when Hrbek, a rather large man, leaned into Gant and sort of lifted him off the bag when they became entangled. When Gant's leg came off the bag, umpire Drew Coble called him out, claiming later that it was the runner's momentum that carried him off the base. As for the impact? The out ended the inning, the Twins went on to win the game by one run, and they eventually won the World Series in seven games.

Sometimes a hard tag can set somebody off, too. Such was the case on June 5, 1999, when Dodgers pitcher Chan Ho Park squared off with Angels pitcher Tim Belcher. Park laid down a bunt up the first-base line in the fifth inning. Belcher fielded the ball and tagged Park in the chest with authority. Park took offense, giving Belcher a kick to the midsection. The benches then emptied as Belcher tackled Park and started pounding on him until it was broken up. Park received a seven-game suspension and was fined $3,000 for being the instigator.

Subcode to the Code: You Don't Spike the First Baseman

The act of base runners spiking second basemen and catchers, while considered dirty and disrespectful, has long been a part of the game. Catchers will try to use their shin guards to counter any such attack when a runner slides in at home, and second basemen will position themselves so that they can apply the tag on a would-be base stealer without getting torn to shreds.

The dirtiest and most egregious application of spiking, however, is when a base runner goes out of his way to take out a first baseman. It is just understood that the first baseman owns the left side of the bag, which is where he will anchor his foot as he extends his body in order to catch the ball in an effort to beat the runner. The runner, meanwhile, owns the right half of the bag, which is where he can step freely while running through the base.

Because the first baseman can't see what is going on behind him, he is in an extremely vulnerable position. As such, if a runner went out of his way to spike the first baseman on the back of his foot, he could cause a serious injury. Granted, a runner is going at top speed in this situation and will be trying to contort his body forward in an attempt to beat out the throw by a millisecond. But for him to purposely try to injure an opposing player in that situation is a very serious code violation and will be dealt with accordingly.

Such was the case on May 28, 2007, when White Sox catcher A.J. Pierzynski clipped Twins first baseman Justin Morneau's ankle as he ran through first base while trying to beat out a double play in the sixth inning. Twins manager Ron Gardenhire immediately stormed out of the dugout and began screaming at the umpires, demanding justice for what he felt was a blatant attempt to injure the reigning 2006 American League MVP. Gardenhire's tirade certainly woke the team up though, as they used that incident to kick off a seven-run rally to win the game, 10–4.

Some speculated that Pierzynski, a former Twin, may have had some personal grudges with his former team and was trying to send a message. Nobody will ever know. Afterward, Pierzynski apologized to Morneau and made light of the situation.

"I just don't want it to turn into a big thing," he said. "I don't want it to fester. That's why I went to Gardy right away and tried to clear the air. I would never try to do anything like that. We don't want to make these guys mad. Every time we do, they score 10 runs."

"If a runner intentionally tried to spike me by running on the inside part of first base when I was stretched out to catch an infield ground ball, then that is definitely breaking the code," added Twins first baseman Kent Hrbek. "I mean, you are so vulnerable at that point, and your Achilles tendon could be snapped in a heartbeat. That is serious stuff. That guy would get it. If it was blatant, there would most definitely be retaliation."

Catcher Terry Steinbach on Sliding Hard Into Second Base

"It drove me crazy when I saw a guy who wouldn't go hard into second base to break up a double play and would peel off instead. Teams pick up on that stuff right away, and they remember it. They will be able to play that guy differently from that point on because they know his style and his tendencies. They will ultimately have more confidence to set up and turn the double play the next time because they know he won't be charging hard in to break it up. That sends a clear message. The right way to handle that situation is to try your damnedest to break up that double play and let them worry about you every time you come up to bat. That does not mean rolling over a guy's knee or spiking him. It just means playing the game hard, the right way."

pretty cheap. Martinez then retaliated by drilling Charlie Hayes in the chest, which resulted in a mound charge and bench-clearer. The festivities continued in the next inning when then-Dodgers rookie catcher Mike Piazza hit his second dinger of the game. Rockies pitcher Keith Shepherd retaliated by nailing Cory Snyder with the very next pitch. Thus began round two—the entire Dodgers bench took off toward Shepherd, setting off another round of fireworks.

Not all base-running incidents happen at second base—plenty take place at third as well. There was the brawl between George Brett and Graig Nettles in the 1977 American League Championship Series, when Brett hit a triple and crashed into the Yankees' third baseman. Brett came up and gave Nettles an elbow, at which point Nettles kicked Brett in the face. Then the haymakers started to fly and the benches emptied.

Another doozy at third took place in Cincinnati during the tenth inning of a Reds-Mets game on July 22, 1986. The Reds' Eric Davis slid hard into Mets third baseman Ray Knight, and Knight punched Davis in the face. Knight would later say the reason he punched Davis was because Davis did a hard pop-up slide into him and then pushed off on him. The two went at it, and the cavalries both rushed out in what would turn out to be a 16-minute melee. The Reds dugout was right there, though, and they piled on Knight pretty quickly.

"He looked me right in the eyes, and I felt threatened," recalled Knight. "I had a real short fuse back then, and I unloaded on him. [The Reds' Eddie Milner] charged over and I hit him, too. The next thing I knew, there were guys all over me."

Center Fielder Torii Hunter on Sliding Hard Into Second Base

"If my manager tells me to take out the second baseman on a hard slide and I don't do it, then I should get punished accordingly. I had at least better try to do it and make it look good, or I am going to be in the doghouse. I take that stuff very seriously. If he tells me to take him out, then I am going to nail him and drive him out to center field. It's not personal, it's just business. That is just the way it goes down sometimes. Hey, that's the code."

Another notorious third-base brawl involved one of the game's most aggressive base runners, Cincinnati outfielder Frank Robinson. Robinson was known for his speed and for his ability to take out opposing fielders who challenged him on the base paths. Big Frank didn't back down from anybody and wasn't afraid to get dirty. During a game with the Milwaukee Braves back in 1960, Robinson came in spikes-high on third baseman Eddie Mathews. Words were exchanged, and Robinson swung and missed. Mathews, one of the game's other tough guys, swung back and knocked old Frank right on his can.

For Robinson, however, it was just a small price to pay for being assertive on the base paths. He knew that his aggressiveness would afford him more opportunities over the long run. A few years later Robinson came in hard on Mets second baseman Ron Hunt, who leaped up and then came straight down on Robinson's arm. Although Hunt's spikes tore a huge gash in Robinson's bicep that required a reported 30 stitches, he was back in the lineup in less than two weeks.

Robinson was fearless. When he once tried to take out White Sox shortstop Al Weis, he got knocked unconscious when Weis's knee caught him upside his head. Despite suffering from double vision, Robinson went on to hit over .300 that season. Robinson was a gamer, to say the least.

Sometimes a hard slide into second can incite a riot, as was the case back in the 1973 National League playoffs between the Reds and the Mets. New York was spanking Cincinnati, 9–2, in Game 3 of the NLCS when the Reds came up to bat in the top of the fifth. After pitcher Roger Nelson struck out, Pete Rose singled off pitcher Jerry Koosman. Joe Morgan then grounded into a double play, with Rose getting on his horse and unsuccessfully trying to break it up by steamrolling over Mets shortstop Bud Harrelson, who was much smaller, at second base. The two immediately went after each other, with Rose flipping him around pretty good.

From there, the proverbial shit hit the fan. The benches emptied, and a 10-minute brawl ensued, highlighted by Reds pitcher Pedro Borbon tearing apart a Mets cap with his teeth. When Rose returned to his position out in left field, the fans wanted his head on a plate. They began hurling garbage onto the field in anger. A whiskey bottle came a little bit too close for comfort, though. It was one wild scene. In fact, the Mets would have been forced to forfeit the game had it not been for a plea from the beloved Willie Mays. More than 300 New York cops then surrounded the field, and play resumed.

After the game Rose had no apologies. "I'm no damn little girl out there," he said. "I'm supposed to give the fans their money's worth and try to bust up double plays...and shortstops."

Ironically, Harrelson and Rose would later make up and then get together to sign autographs of their classic fight photos for cold, hard cash.

12

Excessive Celebration Following a Home Run

The code says that if you hit a home run, you had better get on your horse and start running—one of the surest ways of getting plunked is for a batter to hit a dinger and then admire it as it flies through the air and into the cheap seats. That dramatic pause can be interpreted by the opposing pitcher as showing him up, which he might take offense at. Follow that up with a slow trot, and the batter is almost begging for a ball to the ribs the next time he comes up to the plate.

Another violation of the code that can occur immediately following a home run is excessive celebration. This might include a gratuitous fist-pump, a scream or shout, a little dance hop, or the ever-popular bat-flip. The bat-flip might be the most egregious offense to an opposing pitcher, who might choose to have words with the hitter as he heads for first base. Nobody likes to be shown up or humiliated, in whatever his chosen profession is in life, and in baseball, that is a lesson that sometimes must be learned the hard way.

"[In 2001] Phillies shortstop Jimmy Rollins homered off Cardinals reliever Steve Kline," explained ESPN's Tim Kurkjian. "Rollins flipped the bat, but then put his head down and ran around the bases. It was only a slight showing up of Kline, who took it as much more. He cussed Rollins all the way around the bases, later claiming that had it been a veteran player who'd hit that homer and flipped that bat, it wouldn't have been a big deal, but Rollins is a rookie. Thankfully, the Cardinals didn't retaliate against Rollins or the Phillies in that series."

Pitcher Tommy John on Excessive Celebration

"The one thing that has both hurt the game of baseball and helped the game of baseball is ESPN. Nowadays, every player wants to have his highlight shown on *SportsCenter*. You know, there is a line from Shakespeare's *Macbeth* that talks about 'pitying the poor player who struts and frets his hour upon the stage and then is heard no more: it is a tale told by an idiot, full of sound and fury, signifying nothing.' That reminds me of what ESPN does now, by giving everybody their chance to be on stage.

"So when we see the guys doing the bat-flips and the celebrating after they hit home runs, we can thank ESPN for that. The 'Web Gems' have changed the game, too. They really have. I have seen more diving catches in the outfield since they started showing them on *Baseball Tonight* than I have in my entire life. It is unbelievable.

"As far as I was concerned, if a guy celebrated after he hit a home run off of me, I didn't care. He wasn't showing me up. Heck, I was showing myself up by giving up the home run in the first place. If pitchers don't like it when guys celebrate on them by hitting home runs, then they should learn to be better pitchers."

Twins pitcher Frank Viola has similar views on the bat-flip. "I remember pitching in Game 4 of the 1987 World Series and giving up a home run to Tom Lawless," he recalled. "Then, and I will never forget it to this day, he tossed his bat in the air like it was home run number 600 or something. In reality, I think it was career home run number four. Sadly, I never got the opportunity to drill him, but that might be my dying wish, to face Tom Lawless just one more time so I can drill him. I will never forget that. You just don't do stuff like that.

"The bat-flip is the ultimate in one-upmanship in my book. What stupidity. That is one of the cardinal unwritten rules that requires immediate payback. As a pitcher, you already made a mistake by serving up the long ball, and now you have to watch the guy rub it in your face. I mean, I wasn't out there pointing at guys or shooting them down when I struck them out—you just didn't do those things. Hey, I gave up [almost] 300 home runs in my career, so I made my share of mistakes. But I never appreciated it when guys tried to make you pay for it twice. Doing stuff like that was not only showing me up, the pitcher, it was showing up my teammates, too. If you gave me respect, then I gave you respect. When you don't give me respect, then that is when guys get knocked down."

The right way to follow a home run is to put your head down and start running at a pretty good clip. You don't have to sprint, but you should at least break a sweat. Modesty is the best policy here. The players who act like NFL Hall of Fame running back Barry Sanders, who simply handed the referee the ball every time he scored a touchdown, are the ones who are respected most by their peers. If you hit a ball 450 feet, congratulations— act like you have done it before, and don't make a big deal out of it.

Don't slow down to gawk at the ball or give too many high fives rounding third, either. That is reserved for hitting a game-winning walk-off homer, in which case all bets are off. You can celebrate in that scenario because you have earned it. When your teammates mob you at home plate and rub your head with glee, you can smile and give hugs all you want.

Many contend that the godfather of excessive celebration is Hall of Famer Reggie Jackson, a charismatic and outspoken slugger who understood the meaning of sports-entertainment. It all started back in the '70s, when the chants of "REG-GIE, REG-GIE" made the fans go wild. Those same sounds made opposing pitchers cringe. Jackson understood the power of the media and used it to his advantage. He knew that home runs were what the fans and the media wanted, and that is exactly what he gave them. And when he did, he would put his own unique egotistical signature on them, which usually guaranteed him the prime-time slot on that evening's local news.

Jackson was loathed by opposing pitchers. Many couldn't wait to get back at him for all the times he had shown them up. On July 27, 1976, Yankees fireballer Dock Ellis beaned Jackson on the side of the face, shattering his glasses. Jackson, who was playing for Baltimore at the time, went down hard in what was a truly frightening scene. Afterward, Ellis

---

A Celebration No-No

Another no-no when it comes to exiting the batter's box in a timely matter is a hitter immediately removing his batting gloves. This is exactly what Indians center fielder Milton Bradley did in a game against the Dodgers on June 14, 2003. Bradley had just homered off of Andy Ashby and started to peel off his gloves before the ball had even left the park. The Dodgers took offense, and Ashby definitely felt shown up. Tensions mounted after that, and deservedly so.

acknowledged that the reason he did it was for payback from the 1971 All-Star Game: Jackson had hit a home run off of him and stood at home plate admiring his shot. According to Richard Scheinin's outstanding book *Field of Screams,* Ellis felt humiliated and shown up on national TV and was determined to get revenge, no matter how long it took.

When the league cracked down on retaliation several years back, the pitchers had to start getting more creative with their methods of retribution. Because the umpires are now watching for specific acts of retaliation against certain players who may have instigated an incident, the pitchers will oftentimes drill somebody else instead. That way they can just say it was an accident and will have a better chance of not getting ejected.

Such was the case on June 15, 2007, when the Cubs' Alfonso Soriano homered off San Diego pitcher David Wells and showed him up—Soriano stopped and admired the ball and then started his home-run trot by taking a few baby steps backward. Wells, a crafty veteran of more than 20 seasons in the big leagues, was not amused.

The next afternoon, Padres pitcher Chris Young threw at the head of Cubs first baseman Derrek Lee in the fourth inning. Lee was able to duck out of the way so that only his hand got hit. He spun to the ground and then slowly got up. As he walked slowly to first base, he and Young exchanged words. The two then walked toward each other, at which point Lee took a swing at the tall right-hander. Young swung back and the benches emptied. When the dust had settled, both players were ejected for their roles in the altercation. All of the parties involved had a unique perspective on the incident.

"I really don't mind getting hit, but when it's at my head, I feel like it threatened my health," said Lee. "I don't know what his intent was, but it was at my head, and he said some things to me I didn't like. It just escalated."

"I will say this—I didn't throw at him, and that's as far as I'll go," said Young. "I didn't try to hit him. It had nothing to do with anything in the past. I was just trying to throw a pitch inside. It got away and hit him."

"If it happened yesterday, they have to hit me, not Derrek Lee," Soriano said Saturday. "I don't know if he [Young] did it on purpose. If he did, he hit the wrong guy."

Sometimes even the smallest act of disrespect will be enough to set off an opposing pitcher. In April 2005 the Devil Rays and the Red Sox got into a brawl that stemmed from Tampa Bay's Eduardo Perez's bat-flip after a

Pitcher Mike Marshall on Excessive Celebration

"If you hit a home run off of somebody, then you should keep your excitement to yourself until you get into the dugout. It seems to me, however, that a lot of the players have forgotten about that nowadays. I have seen some celebrations recently that I never would have put up with back when I was pitching. No way. It's called 'excessive celebration,' and it is so disrespectful. So is the slow trot around the bases. If a guy did that to me, I would have drilled him the next time he came up. Even if a guy like Reggie Jackson did that to me, who was known for doing that stuff, I would have definitely hit him and hurt him.

"You know, there is a difference between amateur baseball and professional baseball. I had fun in amateur ball, whereas in pro ball I was out there earning a living for my family. I was out there working as hard as I could in order to keep the job I had. So if some jerk wanted to disrespect me, then I took issue with that. Just because he might have guessed right and hit a pitch out of the ballpark, that didn't give him the right to show me up. I would not tolerate that, not in the slightest."

towering home run. The next night, Boston flamethrower Curt Schilling drilled Tampa Bay's Carl Crawford in the ribs with a fastball. Then, as if to make sure they really understood their frustration, Red Sox slugger David Ortiz launched a bomb and proceeded to flip his bat exactly like Perez had done the previous game.

The festivities continued that next afternoon when Sox pitcher Bronson Arroyo nailed Tampa Bay's Aubrey Huff in the sixth. Then, in the seventh, Rays reliever Lance Carter tried to send a message by hurling a fastball behind All-Star Manny Ramirez. Ramirez didn't flinch, though, and homered on the next pitch. Just a few pitches later, Ortiz was buzzed and sent to the dirt by Seth McClurg, who replaced Carter after Ramirez's homer. "Big Papi" got pissed and the dugouts emptied. Following a few ejections, Arroyo nailed Chris Singleton in the bottom of the seventh, which incited yet another bench-clearer and even more ejections, including both managers, Terry Francona and Lou Piniella. Incidentally, Boston won 11–3, but it was an ugly finale to an ugly game, which all started with an innocent bat-flip.

"In a game like that, once it gets out of hand, it gets out of hand," said Arroyo, who received a six-game suspension for his role in the fracas. "People don't care what the consequences are going to be. It's just out of

The Ultimate Celebration

Perhaps the most memorable home-run celebration of all time happened on June 23, 1963, during a game between the Mets and the Phillies, when New York's Jimmy Piersall hit his 100th career home run and proceeded to round the bases while running backwards. Needless to say, Phillies pitcher Dallas Green was not amused.

respect of protecting your players. If the situation calls for it, I have no problem protecting guys on my team."

Every now and then a batter will earn the right to excessively celebrate at home plate and then take his sweet time to chug around the bases. This happened on April 30, 2007, when Orioles pitcher Daniel Cabrera decided to throw high and tight to Tigers slugger Gary Sheffield. Todd Jones, a veteran pitcher of 15 years and Sheffield's teammate, retells the story:

> It's well known that to get Sheff out, you have to pitch him inside. But you need to have control inside. Well, Cabrera didn't. He hit Sheff in the ribs, and our pitcher, Jeremy Bonderman, took offense. When the Orioles' superstar came up to hit, our pitcher tried to send a message. After Bonderman completely missed Miguel Tejada, Tejada pointed his bat at Bonderman. Tejada obviously got the message.
>
> The benches cleared, and there we went. I was in the bullpen, so naturally I was the last to reach the crowd, but from what I could see, Sheffield had cornered Cabrera behind the plate. Sheffield proceeded to tell Cabrera that, although he understood that rib shot, the next one would result in Sheff's rearranging Cabrera's face. Then as soon as one of the coaches grabbed Cabrera to lead him away from Sheff, Cabrera bowed up and started chirping at Sheff. At that point, I wish I could have paid the coach to release Cabrera so Sheff could have taught him a lesson.
>
> Sheffield, however, had other ideas. This was the cool part. Two innings later, Sheff came up to the plate and hit a home run that looked like it was shot out of a bazooka. Not only did Sheff stand and admire his work, he took his time strolling around the bases even as Cabrera watched intently. The ultimate in one-upmanship.
>
> Usually, you don't want to see a hitter show up a pitcher, but if that hitter had earlier taken a ball in the ribs, he's excused. The moral of the story: if you want to send a message to the Tigers, stay away from Sheffield and his midsection. Not only do you risk waking a

sleeping giant, you'll see yourself on *SportsCenter* for the next week as an example of how not to handle a situation.

Longtime pitcher Bert Blyleven has his own unique view of excessive celebration in today's game:

Showing guys up is just such a disrespectful thing to do in this game. You know, I would love to see Bob Gibson pitch in today's game. To think about what he would do to someone like Barry Bonds, who just stands there and watches his home runs leave the park and then does pirouettes around the bases. My God, if he did that on Gibson, the next time Bonds was up he would get the first pitch right in his neck. No doubt about it. You just didn't do those kinds of things back then, but today is another era. I always felt that you should play the game with respect and never try to show up or embarrass the other team. You play the game hard, the way it should be played. When you hit a home run, you should act like a professional and start running the bases. No spinning or bat-flipping or celebrating. That is just garbage.

Guys like Harmon Killebrew, Frank Robinson, and even Mark McGwire never did that kind of stuff. They hit their homers and then acted like they had done it hundreds of times before. They did it with class. To see a guy take forever to get out of the batter's box to start his home-run trot was brutal. Believe me, I gave up a lot of home runs in my career, but I never appreciated a guy trying to show me up. If he did, I was going to let him know how I felt about it one way or another, guaranteed. I understood that if a guy hit a home run that he earned the right to be happy. He can admire it for a split second, but then he had better get on his horse and get around the bases.

One time, I was pitching with the Angels and we were playing in Oakland. Jose Canseco hit a ball over the left-field fence, and I swear, it took him five minutes to get around the bases. He just stood there and watched it and then slowly trotted around the base paths. That really ticked me off. Now, I am from the old school. At this particular juncture of my career, I was 40 years old; my shoulder was killing me, my elbow was killing me, and I did not need to be shown up. Sure, he crushed the ball, and it was a great hit, but what he did was very disrespectful. So when I later came off the field, I told my catcher, Bill Schroeder, that I was going to get the S.O.B.

Well, the next time Canseco got up, Schroeder gave me a sign for a fastball away. I shook my head "no." He came back with a curveball. No way. Finally he gave me the sign for a fastball in. You betcha! I swear to God, I wish I had been 19 again, because I would have thrown that ball right through his chest if I could have. I reared back and drilled him right in the ribs. I remember then walking towards him as he was lying there because the ball bounced back out towards the mound after it hit him. As I bent down to pick up the ball, I said to him, "That couldn't have hurt you, Jose, because you think you are so goddamned big and strong." He just looked at me in disbelief. He couldn't believe that this old, grizzled veteran would have the balls to say this to him. But I was so upset over the way he showed me up, and I had to make a point. I then remember Schroeder coming out to grab me and pulling me away. At that point I said to him, "Hold me tight, Bill, or this f*cking guy is going to knock the shit out of me."

Former player and manager Frank Quilici thinks the problem is a generational one. "Nowadays you have too many hot dogs that only think about themselves," he said. "You know, in my era you learned the game the right way. You came up through the minor leagues and spent several years learning the ropes down there before you got called up. You would go through A-ball, then Double A, then Triple A and play about 500 to 600 ballgames before you would get called up. That is where you learned how to play the game. The older guys would take the younger guys under their belts and explain to them the nuances of the code. They would tell them to not celebrate like a jerk out on the field after hitting a home run. Today, however, things are much different."

Hall of Fame third baseman Paul Molitor spoke candidly on the topic and feels strongly that it is up to the veterans to teach the rookies how to play the game the right way:

> With regards to guys celebrating a bit too much after hitting home runs, that has always been something that was looked down upon by the players. The entertainment value of that seems to be marketed quite a bit now. Reggie Jackson was the first guy to sit back and admire his home runs. It became a part of his routine. He would hit it, watch it, and then walk those first 10 steps or so before he would break into his trot. Certainly guys like Bonds and Sosa have made that a part of their routines, too.
>
> Back in the day, a guy would get drilled for that right away. Now, though, things are different. The fans like it and the media eats it up. I guess it is okay, as long as it doesn't get out of hand. I mean, if a guy abuses the privilege and it becomes more of a mocking of the opposing pitcher, then that guy will have to be held accountable. It depends on whether or not you have an old-school manager on that opposing bench, too. Because if he feels like the guy was being

disrespectful, then that will determine whether or not something will be done about it.

If a fairly respected player who has had a long and productive career hits one out and sits there for a second to watch it, I don't have a problem with that. It is the guys who are all about themselves that piss guys off. If they do the bat-flip and they take forever to get out of the box, those are the guys that are more prone to get drilled for showing somebody up. I mean, we are all in the entertainment business, but there is no place for that stuff in the game, as far as I am concerned.

Now certain guys have a routine that they will insist on doing, like it is their calling card or something. I remember playing with Jeffrey Leonard one season, and he had this thing he did after he hit a home run that he called the "one flap down," which had him dipping his arm as he rounded the bases. It was his signature move, I suppose. Well, some pitchers didn't like him doing it because they thought he was trying to show them up. So he would get drilled a lot. He understood that and just kept on doing it, though. He would get drilled, and then the next time up he would hit a homer and do his move around the base paths. It just didn't faze him because he expected to get hit. He knew what he was doing was disrespectful, but he did it anyway and was willing to pay the price to be able to do it. To each his own, I suppose.

I remember Ken Griffey Jr. telling me one time that when he was a rookie, he hit a home run and stood there and watched it go out. Then, as he was rounding the bases really slowly, he passed me at third base. He said that I said to him pretty loudly, "You had better start running." Well, 15 years later I saw him and he still clearly remembered our brief

Catcher Tim Laudner on Excessive Celebration

"Guys like Reggie Jackson and Mark McGwire came up to the plate looking to hit home runs. If they stared at it a little bit when it went over the fence, they earned that right. They weren't trying to show anybody up, that was just them. You didn't see too many bruises on those guys as a result, either. It was the guys who never hit home runs and celebrated after hitting one—those were the guys you couldn't wait to dirt-back and knock down. Other guys who do or say stuff, they get what is coming, too. I remember when Cleveland outfielder Mel Hall said that the reason he used to put a couple of pairs of batting gloves in his back pockets when he was hitting was so that they could wave bye-bye to the ball when he hit it out of the park. Pitchers have a problem with stuff like that. Comments like that will get a guy a lot of unnecessary bruises."

conversation, telling me that he learned a valuable lesson about how to play the game that day. I was a veteran at that point and was giving him some friendly advice about the code. That was pretty neat because he is a classy player and someone who I respect in the game.

13

On Pitchers Showing Up Hitters

While it is understood that hitters should not show up pitchers by celebrating after hitting home runs or by taking a slow home-run trot, the same is true for pitchers not showing up hitters. Just as a pitcher will watch a hitter when he hits a home run to make sure he doesn't do a celebratory bat-flip, a hitter will watch the pitcher on the way back to the dugout. He will make sure the pitcher doesn't do anything disrespectful, such as pumping his fist, flashing a big smile, or even laughing out loud with his infielders. Players don't want to be embarrassed on the big video screen at the ballpark or, worse yet, on TV for everyone at home to see.

Various pitchers have routines that they will follow on the mound, usually because they are odd creatures of habit and are rife with superstitious rituals. For instance, Dennis Eckersley used to point right at his strikeout victims. He would even occasionally do his signature move, "the windmill," if it was a particularly big K. Dick Radatz used to thrust his arms above his head after striking out the last batter of an inning and then stride off the mound with giant leaping steps. Tug McGraw used to slap his glove against his leg after retiring the side. Juan Berenguer would even go as far as to un-holster his imaginary firearm and then proceed to blast away at his victim after striking him out.

"I used to pull out my six-shooter and shoot guys down after I struck them out. That was just my way of celebrating, I suppose," recalled Berenguer. "I never tried to embarrass another player or show him up.

That was just how I tried to pump up my teammates. Sure, some players got upset over it, but I had been around for a lot of years and guys knew that I did it all the time. It wasn't like I did it to just one person here or there—I did it a lot, and it was something I was known for. It was my signature move, as they would say. It is the same thing for a guy like Sammy Sosa when he flipped his bat and kind of jumped out of the batter's box after he hit a home run. He didn't do it to show up the pitcher. It was just his way of celebrating and pumping up his teammates.

"I remember one time when Bo Jackson shot me back, it was pretty funny. I had struck him out 23 straight times, and he finally hit a home run off of me. He was so happy that he just shot me over and over as he was rounding the bases. I had to really laugh at that one. He deserved to shoot me back after that. I tipped my hat to him and then held my glove over my face to hide my big grin. Then, just for good measure, I struck him out the next time he got up and shot him back. It was a moment I will never forget."

Some relievers even have their own theme music piped through the stadium upon their grand entrance from the bullpen. In hockey, certain arenas will play "Hit Me with Your Best Shot" when a big brawl goes down; in baseball, the home team wants to get the pitcher as well as the fans pumped up. Padres closer Trevor Hoffman enters to the AC/DC song "Hell's Bells," while former Phillies reliever Mitch Williams went with his nickname, "Wild Thing."

Other pitchers will use their physical appearance to gain a psychological edge. The late Rod Beck had one of the nastiest set of sideburns in the business. Ryne Duren looked intimidating as hell in those bottle-thick glasses as he brought 100-mph heat to his victims. Closer Troy Percival squinted at his adversaries, leaving them unable to see his eyes. Dave Stewart used to pull his cap down low, to shield his eyes as he gazed directly at his opponent in a methodical death stare.

When it comes to pitcher intimidation, however, there is one man who clearly stands alone: Al Hrabosky, "the Mad Hungarian." With his patented Fu Manchu mustache and crazy, long hair, Hrabosky's theatrics out on the mound were legendary. Hitters didn't know whether to applaud his performance or be downright terrified, which was exactly what old Al wanted.

For Hrabosky, who pitched for the Cardinals, Royals, and Braves, it was all about the routine. He would start when the hitter was getting set in the batter's box by stomping off the mound toward second base.

Pitcher Joe Nathan on Showing Up a Hitter

"If I am pitching well and I strike out a guy, it's not like I am going to stare him down and fist-pump him. I am going to let my guys throw the ball around the horn and then try to get the next guy out. It is not about showing guys up for me. It is just about being a good professional and respecting my opponents. I know that the guy I am facing worked just as hard as I did to get to this level, so there is no point in me trying to show him up. It is the same for the hitters. If a guy celebrates on me after hitting a home run, it is almost like he is looking down on me and disrespecting what I have done in my career. You remember certain things like that. Then, the next time you face him you will either: A) have the motivation to try even harder to get him out, or B) get back at him and retaliate by coming inside with a purpose."

Then, with his eyes fixed and dilated, he would quickly turn around 180 degrees and pound the ball into his glove as he got set on the mound. The crowd would go nuts. It was what we would refer to as his "controlled hate routine." Hrabosky would later say that he didn't do it to draw attention to himself, but rather so that his teammates could feed off of his adrenaline rush.

One time, Hrabosky's routine actually got him a free strike. It happened when third baseman Bill Madlock, tired of Hrabosky's routine, called time and walked over to the on-deck circle for some pine tar just as Hrabosky had come set on the mound. When Madlock returned to the batter's box, Hrabosky stepped off the rubber and went through his entire routine again, to the delight of the crowd. So Madlock left the box yet again, but this time failed to get approval from the ump. Hrabosky then stepped up and promptly tossed a quick strike into an empty batter's box, at which point the umpire called a strike.

Certain hitters have their routines, too, such as Chicago's Jim Thome, who points his bat out to right field before every pitch. While some might think he is doing his best Babe Ruth impersonation—calling his shot like the Bambino did back in the '32 World Series—it is just his routine. He means no disrespect. Nor does Sammy Sosa, whose hop-skip-and-jump routine, followed by kisses, is just his thing. Veteran pitchers know that is just his style and not an attempt to show them up. Each case and each hitter is unique.

Sometimes a hitter will use a pitcher's signature move to taunt him. Such was the case on May 31, 1989, in a game between the Dodgers and the

Why Walk a Guy When You Can Drill Him Instead?

Throughout baseball's history there have been a handful of pitchers who have chosen to drill hitters rather than walking them. Randy Johnson has long been suspected of doing just that in an effort to keep his pitch counts down and get further into ballgames, where his contract would allow him to reach certain elevator clauses that made him more money. The most notorious pitcher in this regard, however, was Stan "Big Daddy" Williams, a huge 6'5", 230-pound fireballer who was known as one of the most intimidating pitchers of the 1960s. Apparently, Williams had a clause in his contract that stipulated that he got bonuses based on the number of walks he gave up in a season—but there was nothing in there about hit batsmen. As a result, he would simply hit guys instead of walking them. This did a couple of things: first, it made him more money; second, it lowered his pitch counts; and third, it instilled fear in his opponents. If a hitter was afraid that he was going to be drilled by that flamethrower, he just might change his strategy to avoid being in that situation altogether. According to Dan Holmes, author of *An Unofficial History of the Beanball,* Williams's onetime manager, Walt Alston, once instructed him to intentionally walk Hank Aaron. Williams, who didn't want the walk on his record, chose to bean Aaron in the helmet instead.

Expos. Dodgers pitcher Orel Hershiser drilled Hubie Brooks in the first inning, and Brooks had to be restrained by the home plate umpire as the benches emptied. Things settled down from there, but after the Dodgers scored five runs in the seventh, Montreal's Pascual Perez beaned Mike Scioscia on the helmet. Scioscia headed straight to the mound but was cut off by Expos third baseman Tim Wallach. Other Dodgers tried to get at Perez as well, including Kirk Gibson, who had to be wrestled to the ground by no fewer than three Expos. Gibson had helped to escalate the situation earlier in the seventh when he lined a triple to the gap. When he got to third base, he pumped his arm up in the air twice, mimicking Perez's move on the mound after he notched a big strikeout.

Pitcher Bert Blyleven had his own take on the subject:

> If I struck somebody out, I didn't yell or shoot him down or anything like that. Pitchers like Joaquin Andujar, who pulled his imaginary six-shooter out of his holster and shot the guy after he struck him out, they were the worst. When they did stuff like that, hitters on the opposing benches just couldn't wait to get up to smoke a line drive right back at him. They couldn't wait to get him and just undress him.

I never wanted to give my opposition any more reason to get me, so I never did that kind of stuff. It is basic sportsmanship, as far as I was concerned.

"When a pitcher strikes somebody out, they shouldn't make a big deal out of it," added pitcher Mike Marshall. "You should turn around, get the ball back from your catcher or infielder, and then step up to the mound like you have been there before. The epitome of this, in my opinion, was former Detroit Lions running back Barry Sanders, who I believe was the best ever in professional football. When he got into the end zone, he just handed the ball over to the referee like he had been there many, many times before. He didn't spike it or dance around, he just showed class. That is what it is all about in my eyes."

14

On Distracting or Decoying a Player

There is a fine line in baseball between what is fair gamesmanship and what is just plain ol' cheating. Somewhere in between lies the use of deception. Tactics such as sign-stealing, verbal taunting or intimidating, and phantom tags are looked at by most as fair game. But when you talk about issues such as decoys or intentional distractions, which are meant to trick the opposition in a sort of shady manner, then that is where most say the line gets crossed and it becomes a violation of the code. It has been and always will be open for debate.

Take, for instance, the case of Yankees star third baseman Alex Rodriguez, who found himself in a firestorm of controversy following a May 30, 2007, incident in which he "distracted" Toronto Blue Jays third baseman Howie Clark. With the Yanks leading 7–5 in the top of the ninth, Jorge Posada hit a routine two-out pop-up that Clark settled under. Rodriguez, who was running to third from second base, ran by Clark and shouted something. According to Clark he yelled, "Mine!" at which time Clark backed off, assuming he had been waved off by his shortstop, John McDonald. He was wrong, though, and the ball harmlessly dropped in for a single. A-Rod would later claim he said, "Ha!"

The Blue Jays were outraged, and McDonald had to be restrained from going after Rodriguez. The controversy sparked a national debate as to what was cunning gamesmanship and what was dirty play. Was fooling a fielder by breaking his concentration cheating? Nobody knew for sure. A loophole had been exposed in baseball's unwritten code of honor and sportsmanship.

"That's what makes baseball so great," McDonald would later say. "There's the rule book, and there are other things that are passed down from older players when I was first starting my career. So it's something I may take offense to, but other people may not."

According to Rule 7.08(b), a base runner is called out if he "hinders a fielder attempting to make a play on a batted ball." The problem with the interpretation of the rule, however, is that it associates "interference" with contact and not verbal deception. There is a gray area there indeed. When and where can players shout things? Things are screamed out from the dugout all the time during games and that is okay, right? Can players make certain noises but not yell out certain words? If so, how loud can they yell them? When a catcher chases a foul ball over to the opposing dugout, players will yell out, "I got it...I got it," in an attempt to try to fool him or break his concentration. What happens when a player distracts an opposing player and prevents him from doing his job? Is that clever trickery or straight-up bamboozlement?

Seemingly everybody weighed in with an opinion on what was fair and what was foul.

"I would have done it, too," said Chicago White Sox manager Ozzie Guillen. "I don't care what people say. Why not do it? You have to do everything to win games."

"That's Toronto's fault. Catch the ball," said controversial Giants slugger Barry Bonds. "Get over it."

"In a lot of cases, it's an unwritten rule that players respect each other and do what's best for the game," said umpire Rich Garcia.

"Decoying is part of the game," added Mets coach Jerry Manuel. "When you scream or yell, that is not a decoy."

"That probably goes into a different category because players feel that it's up to them to discern, whereas if you're looking up at a pop-up, you can't discern whose voice is whose," said broadcaster Bob Costas. "There are certain things that apparently are okay, and then there are some other things that by some self-defined code are not."

"I'm not sure what the difference between that and the hidden-ball trick is, or a catcher dekeing at home plate that a ball is not coming in, and then at the last second he gets the ball and drops the tag down," said Yankees general manager Brian Cashman. "I'm kind of indifferent to it, because I was looking at it trying to figure out, 'Is this something that's not right?'"

A Subcode to the Code: Don't Swing out of Your Shoes on a 3–0 Count

One subcode deals with batters not jumping all over the first pitch in a blowout game. They had better not dig in too much at home plate, either, or they will be dusting off their backsides. Such was the case on July 22, 2001, when, with his team leading by six runs, Arizona slugger Matt Williams swung hard on a 3–0 pitch in the fifth inning of a game against his former Giants club. Incensed, San Francisco manager Dusty Baker ordered reliever Chad Zerbe to throw at him an inning later, which resulted in a fastball behind the head. After Williams gestured toward the mound and then at Baker, both benches cleared, and Williams went after Baker before being subdued by his teammates.

"I remember one time when Bert Blyleven was pitching for the Twins and we were playing the Yankees in New York," recalled Twins coach Rick Stelmaszek. "Dave Winfield came up to bat—this was when he was in his prime as one of the best hitters in the game—and took a rip on a 3–0 pitch where he nearly came out of his shoes. I mean he really went for it. The next pitch, Bert just flatlined him. I mean, he flipped him like nothing I had ever seen before. It was the best brushback I have ever seen. He just went down hard. He had kind of owned Bert in years past, and it all came to a head that night. Bert made a statement right there, and do you know what? Winfield never hit him very well after that. It had a psychological effect on him and just got him thinking a little bit."

Former Dodgers manager Tommy Lasorda recalled a similar play when he was coaching in the minor leagues with Montreal back in the late 1950s. "I was coaching first base in Miami, and there were two outs in the top of the ninth inning," recalled Lasorda. "We were losing by one run. We had a guy on second base. There was a foul ball. Gene Oliver was going over to catch it. I said, 'I got it! I got it!' He pulled back and the ball dropped. He's screaming at me. And the next pitch a guy hit a home run, and we won the game."

The Rodriguez/Clark situation was probably heightened by the fact that Rodriguez had a reputation as a player known to employ questionable tactics. For instance, in Game 6 of the 2004 American League Championship Series against Boston, he knocked the ball out of pitcher Bronson Arroyo's glove when Arroyo was trying to apply a tag. Rodriguez was called out for interference on the play and was further chastised by the media for his actions.

Another notorious deception took place in Game 7 of the 1991 World Series between the Minnesota Twins and the Atlanta Braves. The game was tied 0–0 in the eighth inning when Atlanta's Lonnie Smith took off from first base on a hit-and-run with Terry Pendleton at the plate. Smith put his head down and started running to second, unaware that Pendleton's hit had gotten between the two outfielders and was heading toward the wall for extra bases. Realizing that Smith hadn't looked up to see where the ball had gone, Twins second baseman Chuck Knoblauch crouched down and pretended to be in position to field a throw from the left fielder.

Seeing this, Smith put on the brakes momentarily, until he realized that he had been duped. He did manage to make it to third, but could have easily scored what would have been the game-winning run to take the World Series. As fate would have it, Smith got stranded on third base, and thanks to Jack Morris's brilliant 10-inning shutout, the Twins went on to win the game, 1–0.

Afterward, Smith was criticized for not paying attention. Most agreed that it was his own fault for losing track of the ball's flight path and then having to watch the reaction of the second baseman to see where it went. Knoblauch, meanwhile, was hailed as a genius for putting down the decoy in that particular situation, which ultimately cemented his team's second world title in five seasons.

Dekeing is an acceptable practice if pulled off in the proper context. Take, for instance, a similar situation that occurred during a 2005 game between the Cubs and the White Sox. With first baseman Derrek Lee on first base, Cubs right fielder Jeromy Burnitz hit a double to right field. Lee took off for second base and had his head down. Seeing this, White Sox shortstop Juan Uribe promptly raised his arms to signal a foul ball. Lee bought the fake and slowed down. Once he realized that he had been deked, he had to hold up at third base. Lee, like Smith, was then stranded on base when the inning ended.

15

You Don't Bunt on a Pitcher Who's Got a No-Hitter Going Late in the Game

One aspect of the code that is rarely invoked deals with bunting on a pitcher who has a no-hitter late in a game. It says that if you are going to break up the no-no, then do it like a man and get a base hit the old-fashioned way. It is a rare occurrence, but there have been a few documented cases of the violation over the years.

The most notorious incident happened in 2001, when Arizona pitcher Curt Schilling had a perfect game going into the eighth inning of a 2–0 game with the San Diego Padres. That's when Padres catcher Ben Davis broke it up with a bunt single. The Diamondbacks fans were livid.

A major debate was sparked as to whether or not Davis was justified in what he did. The Padres didn't care about the rule and were only interested in getting a runner on first base so that they could start a rally in a close ballgame. While the case demonstrated how baseball's unwritten rules are sometimes open to interpretation, most felt that Davis was in the wrong and should have hit away in order to earn his way to first base.

Afterward, Arizona manager Bob Brenly had some harsh words about the play: "Ben Davis is young and has a lot to learn."

The reality is this archaic part of the code exists for the sake of tradition. The fact of the matter is that if a team is in a pennant race, it can and should do whatever it needs to do in order to win every ballgame, especially a close ballgame. So bunting late should be fair game in this situation. Schilling is perfectly capable of fielding his position, whether

> **A Subcode to the Code: Never Remind a Pitcher That He Has a No-Hitter Going**
>
> Players know that after the fourth inning of a game you never, ever remind their pitcher that he has a no-hitter going. That can jinx it all in a nanosecond. They should just stick with their routines and other superstitions and not direct any unwanted mojo toward the pitcher. Some managers will just forbid anybody from talking to him and will have the pitcher sit in the far corner of the dugout by himself. Even players from opposing teams know better than to bring it up or "mistakenly" congratulate him on his performance during the game.

it's the first inning or the eighth. Plus, personal achievement shouldn't come before the team, even if it is the opposing team you are talking about.

A similar situation occurred that next season when the Minnesota Twins were facing the New York Mets in an interleague game. Mets pitcher Steve Trachsel was perfect up to the seventh inning, when Twins outfielder Jacque Jones stepped up and squared to bunt. Leaning toward the first-base line, it was a clear attempt to earn an infield hit on his first pitch. He missed the ball, and the boos started raining down from the enraged Shea Stadium fans.

Perhaps realizing his action was in violation of the code, Jones swung away on the next pitch and grounded out on an infield dribbler. The very next batter, however, Cristian Guzman, then singled to center field and made it all a moot point.

16

On Hitters Wearing Body Armor

A recent phenomenon is players choosing to wear large, protective gear at the plate—commonly referred to as body armor. While many players wear protective batting gloves, some choose to wear protective wrist guards, as well as plastic shin guards. Some players will even wear an extension on their shin guard to protect their foot from a foul tip.

The one piece of protective equipment that stirs up the most controversy, however, is the hockey-like elbow pads that some hitters have begun to wear. Sure, that player may be trying to prevent a serious elbow injury, but most players view it as an unethical violation of the code. These elbow pads allow the hitter to really lean in and crowd the plate with very little fear of getting drilled. Crowding the plate gives you a big advantage over the pitcher, because the hitter will be able to drive the outside corner pitches, effectively owning both sides of the plate.

In fact, many hitters just let an inside pitch hit them in the elbow because the pad absorbs 99 percent of the impact. If there is no fear of pain and suffering, or risk of getting injured and winding up on the disabled list, that is a huge advantage. There are several marquee players who have worn the elbow pads in recent years, including the likes of David Ortiz, A.J. Pierzynski, and Manny Ramirez. But the one player who seems to draw the most ire from pitchers and fans alike is Barry Bonds, who leans in over the plate and swats home runs like nobody's business.

Pitcher Jim Kaat on Hitters Wearing Body Armor

"As a pitcher, you would just paint a big mental bull's-eye on that stuff, especially the oversized elbow pads. That garbage has no place in the game, as far as I am concerned. If you are hurt, that is one thing, but if you wear them everyday…come on. It's ridiculous."

Pitcher Frank Viola on Hitters Wearing Body Armor

"If you look at some of these hitters today, you would think that they own the whole plate. They've got elbow pads, shin guards, and wrist guards. It is crazy. Why not just wear a chest protector and face mask, too? My opinion is that if it is a legitimate injury, fine, wear the pad until it is healed up. They weren't supposed to be worn every day forever. Come on. Be a man. Step up to the plate like a man. These guys like Bonds and Pierzynski think that they own the plate, and they lean way out over it with no fear of retaliation. It just isn't right, in my book. Play the game the right way; that is my opinion. The only person who should be wearing that stuff is the catcher. Period."

Center Fielder Torii Hunter on Hitters Wearing Body Armor

"Players want to be protected from getting injured, and team owners want guys in the lineup—that is the bottom line with this issue. The game has changed so much in recent years, and the money is insane. I tell you what, if I am the owner of a team and I spent millions and millions of dollars for my team, then I for sure want my best players on the field. If that means letting them wear pads to protect themselves from being injured and on the disabled list, then so be it. It is a long season and injuries are a part of the game, but if you can prevent certain things from happening, then I think that is okay. If teams know that they can drill a guy in the elbow and knock him out of a three-game series, then that is a serious tactic. So I say let guys wear what they want to wear out there. That is just my personal opinion."

First Baseman Kent Hrbek on Hitters Wearing Body Armor

"I guess if guys want to wear the big pads, then it would only be fair to in turn let the pitchers have the batting-practice screens out there in front of them, too. The whole thing has gotten pretty ridiculous, if you ask me."

First Baseman Harmon Killebrew on Hitters Wearing Body Armor

"You know, when I first got into the league, we didn't even wear helmets. Heck, we didn't even use batting gloves. So to see how far some of this stuff has gone is pretty ridiculous, in my opinion."

One of the most outspoken players on the topic is former Reds reliever Rob Dibble, who holds nothing back on hitters wearing body armor:

> I think it is absolutely an unfair advantage for guys to wear this stuff, unless they have a serious medical condition that warrants it. And only then should it be used—as a temporary fix, not a permanent thing. A lot of guys wear them nowadays, and I call them "puss pads," because I think they are for pussies. With regards to Barry Bonds's hockey elbow pads, I remember Roger Clemens saying that he was going to test it out to see if it worked. Sure enough, the first time he faced him in interleague play, he nailed him right on the elbow with the first pitch. I thought that was awesome. I mean, come on. I think that thing is made out of Kevlar. So if it can stop a bullet, how much damage is a baseball going to do? Not very much. It is a big psychological advantage for him because he can really crowd the plate without the fear of getting injured.
>
> Now some guys really do need to wear protection from time to time, and I certainly can respect that. Take a guy like Jeff Bagwell, who had broken his hand a couple of times, and just wanted to get back in there and do his job. For me, as a pitcher, if I am good enough at my craft, then I can pick another body part to make sting for a week. I can get him in the ribs or in the thigh, and it's still going to leave a mark. I don't need to go after his hands. That is a sensitive area on a respected guy who is clearly hurt. But Bonds, on the other hand, he has been able to wear these things every time he comes up to bat. I don't agree with that. I know that he has had some surgery on it in the past, but at some point you have to take it off just like everybody else. If not, then what's next? Full body armor?

Pitcher Jim Perry on Hitters Wearing Body Armor

"We didn't have any of that stuff when we played. If we got drilled in the elbow, we would just rub a little dirt on it and run to first base."

Umpire Tim Tschida on Hitters Wearing Body Armor

"The problem with that stuff is that once you let it in, how do you get it out? Players want to know why 'player X' can wear something that is so big, while 'player Y' can't. Wearing that stuff can be an advantage for a hitter, no question. It is easy to stand right up over the plate when you have that big elbow pad on. Getting hit in the elbow hurts, and with no fear of having to worry about that, you can be extremely aggressive as a hitter. In the end, however, we deal with the padding issues on a case-by-case basis and deal with each one accordingly."

For starters, the guy already comes up to the plate as fearless as can be. I mean, he is as big as a defensive end. So he can dig right in and gain a big advantage. It takes away from what a pitcher is trying to do, and I just don't agree with it. As a pitcher, I wanted the batter to have that fear in the back of his mind that I just might nail him in a sensitive area—that is going to keep him honest and back him off the plate a bit. He will know that if I hit him in the elbow or wrist, then he might be out for an extended period of time.

Look at Vladimir Guerrero. He recently got hit in the wrist by Josh Beckett, and he got put on the disabled list. It could have been on purpose or an accident, I don't know, but either way, players are going to fear Beckett just a little bit because they know that he is capable of going after a star player like Guerrero in a sensitive spot. That just helps Beckett, in my eyes. He might not have to drill a single player the rest of the year and beyond because of that. His reputation is set and players will know that every time they face him, they could be next. Fear and intimidation, they are very powerful things in this game.

Former pitcher Mike Marshall had his own unique take on what he would do to hitters who wore excessive padding:

I think that stuff should be outlawed. I don't believe it is appropriate. What they are saying is "If you hit me, I want to make sure it doesn't hurt." I can't believe that baseball allows that stuff to be worn, to tell you the truth. I mean, if Barry Bonds wants to crowd over the plate and hang that big elbow over it, then he should have to pay a price to do so just like everybody else.

As for me, if I was pitching against a batter who was wearing all of that garbage, it would just make me want to hit him even more someplace else. If a guy came up with a big elbow pad, then I had to drill him somewhere that was going to hurt, like in the small of the back. I just had to. He was begging me to with a big pad like that. It was like a big sign that said "HIT ME!" I remember one time a guy came up to bat against me and he had been injured or something, so he was wearing what looked like a football helmet, with a big mask. So I drilled him right in the side of the head just as soon as I could. I just had to. It was simply irresistible to me. It made such a wonderful noise, too—"DONGGGGG!"

17

Friendly Fire

Professional ballplayers understand that even though they essentially play a game for a living, it is still a business. As such, sometimes they will have to do things that they don't necessarily want to do—like having to plunk a friend or a former teammate. It is a dirty job, but it is one that must be done from time to time—the code says so. If a manager feels that a certain player should get drilled, then that pitcher has to toe the company line or risk being disciplined.

Plunkings are just a part of the game, and players understand this. The batters know the situations and usually know when it is coming, and they accept it. The pitchers do, too, but it can still be tough for them to have to plunk an innocent bystander who may even be a close, personal friend outside of the white lines. He can make it easier, though, by drilling his buddy in the fleshy part of the thigh or his backside, where it will sting the least. The bottom line here is that the players must remember that the code supersedes even friendships.

In hockey it has long been understood that players have to fight each other, both in practices as well as in games. For them, it's not personal. Tony Twist, the longtime enforcer of the St. Louis Blues, once knocked out the four front teeth of the best man in his wedding. Former Minnesota North Stars tough guys Basil McRae and Shane Churla were roommates for several years but later got traded away to different clubs. They would have to fight many times after that, with the understanding that the loser bought the beers on the next hunting trip.

Friendly-Fire Story by Pitcher Frank Viola

"I remember one time, when I was with the Twins, sitting in the dugout talking to Bert Blyleven. We were talking about his old catcher when he was in Cleveland, Ron Hassey. They were the best of friends and did everything together. Well, they each eventually moved on to different teams, but whenever Hassey would face Blyleven, he would just own him. I think he hit like .600 lifetime off of him, or some ridiculous number. I mean, who would know better how to hit him better than his personal catcher? So this frustrated the hell out of Bert to no end. Anyway, I am in the dugout with Bert, and Hassey, who is with Oakland now, comes over before the game to say hello and wish him well. They hug and smile and talk for a while, and then just as Hassey is about to walk away, Bert says, 'I'm going to drill you tomorrow.' Hassey is laughing his ass off and just taunting him at this point, almost daring him to do so. Bert just laughed back and that was that.

"Well, sure enough, the next night when Hassey came up to bat, Bert drilled him on the first pitch right in the knee. He went down hard. I don't think he intended to get him in the knee, just his lower leg, but he really nailed him good. I think Hassey had to miss like two weeks after that. It was crazy. Meanwhile, Bert is trying his hardest not to start laughing hysterically out on the mound. Afterwards Bert says to me, 'Hey, I warned him!'"

Pitcher Pedro Martinez spoke candidly on the topic of beaning his good friend Miguel Tejada in the helmet back in 2000. "Me and Tejada are buddies," he said. "We eat in each other's houses. We would eat off the same plate if we had to. If we have to have a beer together, we will. If I have to hit somebody like Tejada, it would be in the safest place. Only if I was ordered to. Only if I were told."

Pitcher Steve Trachsel had his own views on how to handle those situations: "If you have to drill a guy, you might be upset that he's your friend, but you still do it. Mark Grace used to say all the time, 'I know I'm getting hit even though I'm taking the guy out for a couple beers after the game.'"

Orlando Cepeda remembered the first time he had to face his old friend and teammate, Bob Gibson, after he got traded from the St. Louis Cardinals to the Atlanta Braves back in 1969: "The first time I went to the plate, he knocked me back. It was mandatory, know what I mean? In fact, Bob came to my house for dinner after the game, and my son said, 'How come you threw at my dad?' And Bob said, 'It's a game. Baseball.'"

Atlanta Braves catcher Greg Olson remembered a sticky situation that occurred back in the early '90s:

I was with the Braves, and we were playing the Phillies. Otis Nixon was on our team, and something happened between him and Philadelphia's second baseman during a hard slide on a double play. There was some pushing and shoving that went on. We all thought it was a clean play, but the guys on Philadelphia's bench didn't see it that way. Well, the next time Otis was up they smoked him right in the ribs. We were mad, and the benches cleared. Not much happened, so we all came back to the dugout. Our manager, Bobby Cox, then says, "Their next guy is going down." Tom Glavine was pitching for us at the time, and sure enough, that next inning he's got the green light to drill the first guy up. Well, I am catching, and the next guy up to bat is none other than Dale Murphy, one of Atlanta's most beloved all-time heroes, who had just signed with Philly the year before. And he is friends with Tom. So it was very, very uncomfortable for Glavine, for Cox, and for Murphy.

Murphy comes up to bat, looks at me, and says, "Ole, how you doing?" I say "Good, Murph. Thanks." He says, "I know what's happening, so I am backing up." I look over at him, and he was as far back in the batter's box as a player could ever possibly get. I mean he was touching the far outside line, he was that far back. It was hilarious. So Glavine throws the first pitch as far inside as he could, and Murphy actually backed out of the box to avoid being hit. I have never seen anything like it. Glavine didn't want to hurt him, so he only threw it about 75 mph, but had to send a message nonetheless. It was an awkward situation, but some form of retaliation had to be done, regardless of who it was. The code says you drill the next guy up, and in this case, it was a guy nobody wanted to touch. But we had to at least try, and we did. Granted, it was a pretty lackluster attempt at retaliation, but we had to let them know that we were going to protect our players.

18

On Managers Getting Tossed to Swing the Momentum

When a hockey team is down, the team's enforcer will often pick a fight he knows he can win in an effort to swing the momentum. His goal is to get his teammates feeding off his adrenaline, and to get them playing with more emotion. In professional sports, everybody wants to get his juices flowing. It is what makes grown men do things they never thought they were capable of doing.

In baseball, the same theory holds true—however, it's the manager's job to jump out of the dugout on a close play and argue like hell with the umpire. His objective is the same as the enforcer's—he hopes to swing the momentum on his bench and maybe even start a rally. Baseball can be a long, monotonous game, played in the dog days of summer. Sometimes a good wake-up call can be just what the doctor ordered. Hopefully the manager's spirited performance will inspire his boys to get pissed and start playing tougher, meaner, and more passionate baseball.

Perhaps no one in history was better at using this tactic than legendary Baltimore Orioles manager Earl Weaver, who made arguing an art form all his own. Weaver was thrown out of nearly 100 games over his nearly two-decade tenure with the O's, including an ejection from a World Series game. Many in the know felt that Weaver's intimidating style won him a handful of close games a year, which was certainly one of the secrets of his success.

As for Weaver's tactics on arguing with umpires, he disclosed three basic rules in his book *Weaver on Strategy*. First, never curse the umpire or

All-Time Manager Ejection Leaders:

1) Bobby Cox—132 and counting [active]
2) John McGraw—131
3) Leo Durocher—124
4) Earl Weaver—97
5) Frankie Frisch—86

get personal. You could curse the call by saying it was a bleeping bad call, but you should never call the umpire a name. Second, you had to know the rules, because if you knew the rules, you might win one now and then. And third, you had to be yourself when you were dealing with umpires.

Managers know that if their players argue with the umpires, they will get tossed, so managers take it upon themselves to argue on their players' behalf. If they get ejected, the team can go on. But they have to protect their players from doing or saying something stupid, which may get them fined or even suspended. Hopefully the tirade will calm their irate players down and get them to refocus on playing the game.

A good manager will also know the tendencies of certain umpires and will be able to work them in certain situations. For instance, some umps rarely if ever call balks. So a manager might use that to his advantage when he knows that particular ump is on first base. They also might know which umps are more likely to call out base runners on second base, which could come in handy when deciding whether or not to give your base runner on first the steal sign.

The bottom line with managers is that they always need to protect their players, even if it means getting tossed from a game. They need to get in between a player and the umps before a tussle breaks out, and they also need to know when to get thrown out of a ballgame in order to fire up their squads.

"I have seen managers stand up in team meetings, when our team was struggling, and just flat-out say that maybe we needed a good fight to wake us up," said former infielder/DH Paul Molitor. "A good scrap can get people's attention in an effective way and start a rally. Or, the manager himself might go out and get thrown out in order to wake up his players. Sometimes you just need to find some cohesiveness as a team."

19

On Running Up the Score Late in a Blowout

The unwritten rules of baseball are not just about payback and retribution. One of the more fascinating aspects of the code deals with teams running up scores late in games. Again, it boils down to respect—if the losing team is getting hammered, the team in the lead should dial it down. Opposing teams don't want to see guys padding their stats late in a blowout game. That is not to say they should pack it in and tank it. But they should show some restraint.

For instance, if a team is up by a margin of five runs or more late in the game—by the eighth inning or so—then a batter should almost always take a 3–0 pitch. If he swings out of his shoes on that count, he will be showing up the other team and will be opening himself up to be drilled in retaliation. He shouldn't go for broke on the very first pitch, either. Jumping on that one may be a no-no.

Run up the score on a team and payback will be certain, that much is for sure. To many purists, baseball isn't just about winning, it's about winning with dignity and class. Teams have to remember that with 162 games per season, what comes around goes around, and if a team plays like a bunch of jerks, then they will get treated like jerks when the tables are turned. And yes, they will be turned at some point down the road. Even the best teams lose big from time to time. It is a cruel reality in this game.

Case in point: on June 10, 1993, with his Padres ahead 9–2 in the sixth inning, San Diego slugger Gary Sheffield swung hard at a 3–0 pitch. Dodgers relief pitcher Ricky Trlicek took offense and proceeded to hit

Manager Ron Gardenhire on Pouring It On and Rubbing It In

"You never want to bury a team and embarrass them. There has always been a fine line between what certain teams or managers believe is appropriate here. Whether it is a four-, five-, six-, or seven-run lead late in the game, it just depends on what the opposing team feels is their magic number. I mean, if a guy is on a team that is up by six runs in the seventh and drops down a drag bunt and it goes foul, then the next pitch just might flip that guy. That is the code.

"So you have to be careful in those instances not to run up the score or bunt or steal late in a game, otherwise it might come back to bite you later on that season. As for me, I think that if you have a five- or six-run lead late in a game, then stealing and bunting should be thrown out the window. Now that is not to say that we won't try our hardest to get base hits. We just won't try to show up our opponents and disrespect them. There are standards for these things that you have to follow, and each team defines its own set of rules."

Catcher Greg Olson on Pouring It On and Rubbing It In

"This was an automatic retaliation. Each team had their own code rules about this, but for us [Atlanta] it was six runs. So if the other team was up by six runs on us late in the game and somebody stole a base, you could just put a little checkmark by his name, because the next time we played him, he was going down. You may not see that guy for a few weeks or a few months, but we kept track of that stuff in a notebook and would bring it up for that team meeting. You see, every time you would face a team for a new series, you would have a team meeting. The pitchers would talk about where they would want to position their batters, and stuff like that. Then, at the end of the meeting, a player or a coach might say, 'Oh, and by the way, "player X" stole a base on us when they were up by six runs in the eighth inning the last time we played them, so drill him the first time you see him.' It was very businesslike, but it had to be done. Guys couldn't get away with that stuff, or the game would lose its integrity."

Sheffield in the back with a fastball on the next pitch. Sheffield then charged the mound, getting in one pretty good punch to the side of Trlicek's head before steamrollering over him. A wrestling match ensued as the dugouts and bullpens emptied, but not much transpired after that.

Over the past several years, the phrase "comfortable lead" has come under scrutiny. It used to be that if a team had a five- or six-run lead in

Umpire Tim Tschida on Pouring It On and Rubbing It In

"Each situation is unique with regards to teams running up scores late in games. If a team has had a couple of rough outings and their bullpen has been horrible, then they obviously don't feel comfortable with a four- or five-run lead and want to do everything that they can to make it bigger. You just never know. Teams have such loaded offenses nowadays, though, and that is another factor for teams wanting to get big cushions late in games. You have to get up and stay up by a lot of runs to ensure a win over a team like the Yankees or Red Sox. And the new ballparks in today's game are smaller and more conducive to scoring runs in a hurry, too.

"Back in the day the 'five-run rule' was more than enough for teams to essentially shut it down late in a ballgame. Not anymore. Another thing you see now is maybe a team is up by five runs late in the game, and you have a runner on first base with a 3–2 count. They will send him. Years ago they would never do that, but now things are different. Teams are not going to just give their opponents a double play. More and more of those types of things are accepted in today's game."

Manager Tom Kelly on Pouring It On and Rubbing It In

"Back when I was managing, if we were up 9–1 in the seventh, I would bring in new players and that sort of thing. If those guys hit home runs, well that was just the way it went. But the other team knew that we weren't trying to show them up. It also bothers me when I see third-base coaches sending guys around to score for no reason in those situations. Especially if it is a close play at the plate, you just hope your guy doesn't get hurt doing dumb stuff like that. But players want their RBIs, they want to pad their stats, and will complain if they don't get them. Things have really changed. I don't think that is right, but again, I am old school on old codes like that."

the eighth inning, they were content to put things on cruise control and nobody would be shown up.

With today's newer hitter-friendly ballparks, such as Coors Field in Colorado, it seems like no lead is safe. Teams are so explosive now that seemingly any offense can put up seven or eight quick runs in an inning on any given night. In 2000 the Rockies came back from a 9–1 deficit late in the game and won 12–10. Or how about Jacobs Field in Cleveland? In 2001 the Indians came back from a 12-run deficit to beat Seattle, 15–14, in

11 innings. So if you hold back and take your foot off the accelerator, you might just get beat.

"In a blowout game, never swing as hard as you can at a 3–0 pitch," explained Tim Kurkjian. "Again, this is about showing up an opponent, a point we certainly understand. Yet at times, we show too much pity for the losing team. These are professionals, the best in the world, they're making $2 million a year on average; if they can't take getting embarrassed once in a while, that's tough. The idea is always to play every play, every out. There should be no giving up in baseball."

20

On Stealing Bases Late in a Blowout

It is just understood that you don't try to steal a base with a five- or six-run lead in the last two or three innings of a game. That is considered rubbing it in and may warrant retaliation. In addition, when a team is down big late in a game, they will oftentimes stop holding a runner at first base. It is almost an invitation for the winning team to steal on them, something that would merit retaliation at a later date. Teams that take this bait and give the green light to a speedster who wants to pad his stats are just asking for it.

At certain ballparks, such as Coors Field in Colorado, where the air is so thin that a fly ball can turn into a grand slam, even a large lead is rarely safe. As a result, teams never really feel their run total is enough, so they play hard all the way to the end. This may offend some teams. For example, in 2000, Colorado's Tom Goodwin stole a base with his squad ahead 9–1. While Goodwin would later get two pitches thrown over his head in retaliation, the Rockies wound up needing the extra runs, holding on to win by the wild score of 12–10.

Another high-profile incident took place in 2001, when Rickey Henderson, then with San Diego, stole second base uncontested in the seventh inning of a game against the Brewers with the Padres leading 12–5. Many felt that Henderson, who already held the game's all-time steals crown at that point, was just padding his stats. Milwaukee manager Davey Lopes found himself in the middle of a firestorm of controversy when he publicly challenged the incident. Lopes, an old-school guy and a staunch believer that no player was bigger than the code, even threatened that he might have Henderson thrown at the next time he came up to hit.

Again, with explosive lineups and tiny ballparks, the old rules regarding common baseball courtesy may no longer apply. "We're playing in the era now of the lively ball, smaller ballparks, guys are bigger and stronger," said pitcher Dan Plesac. "It's nothing to score four or five runs in an inning now. So when do you stop running? It used to be four or five runs; now it's eight or nine runs."

While Lopes threatened to drill Henderson for stealing in that situation, back in July of 1986 Giants manager Roger Craig found himself in similar circumstances, only he made good on his warning. Craig became incensed when Cardinals skipper Whitey Herzog gave speedster Vince Coleman the green light to steal in a blowout. Craig responded by ordering pitcher Frank Williams to drill Coleman his next time up to bat. The Cardinals took offense and a massive brawl broke out between the two clubs. Coleman charged the mound, and Williams ended up on his back. Herzog and Craig, meanwhile, were both ejected.

Sometimes instead of retaliating, teams may just choose to give their opposition a dose of their own medicine. This happened in 2000, when Giants second baseman Jeff Kent stole second base with San Francisco leading Colorado 5–0 in the seventh inning of a game at Pac Bell Park. Several days later the teams met again, and this time Rockies outfielder Tom Goodwin stole second with his squad up by seven runs late in the game.

While most felt that the situation should have been over at that point, it actually escalated. When the two teams met again a few weeks later at Coors Field, Giants pitcher John Johnstone drilled Goodwin in retaliation. With his team leading by seven runs, Goodwin got back by again stealing second base. Goodwin further infuriated the Giants the next inning when, after catching a hard liner off the bat of J.T. Snow, he began clowning around in the outfield, which the Giants perceived as trying to show them up. The next night, Kent homered and was promptly drilled by Rockies pitcher Scott Karl shortly thereafter. Finally, when Giants pitcher Shawn Estes fired a pitch over Goodwin's head, all hell broke loose. The players began shouting at one another, with managers Buddy Bell and Dusty Baker getting into the mix. Cooler heads would prevail, though, and a truce was called.

On the flip side, the code also says that you shouldn't steal a base if your team is the one being blown out. In May 2007, Rockies catcher Yorvit Torrealba stole a base on Giants lefty Steve Kline with one out in the ninth and the Giants leading 15–1 at Coors Field. Kline was upset and waited patiently for nearly a month before the two teams met again. That is when he plunked Torrealba in the lower back as retaliation.

21

On Bunting Late in a Blowout

Just as stealing a base late in a blowout is viewed as a code violation, so too is bunting in the same situation. It is disrespectful and perceived as trying to show up your opposition, whom at that point just wants the game to end so that they can go home.

Perhaps the most notorious example occurred back in August 1984, in a game between the Braves and the Padres in Atlanta. It all started when Padres second baseman Alan Wiggins got on base with what the Braves felt were several unsportsmanlike bunts late in the game. The next day Atlanta starter Pascual Perez wasted little time in letting Wiggins know how his team felt about being shown up. He drilled Wiggins, the leadoff hitter, right square in the middle of the back to start the game, quickly setting the tone for what was about to come.

Tensions mounted in the second inning when Padres pitcher Ed Whitson tried to drill Perez, rifling his first pitch behind him. After drawing a warning from the home plate umpire, Whitson calmed down and settled for striking him out. Then in the fourth, Whitson faced Perez yet again, this time firing the ball at his midsection. Although Perez was able to back away, the benches emptied for some pushing and shoving at home plate. Things calmed down, but Whitson was determined. His next pitch came way up and in, narrowly missing Perez, but was a bit too obvious for the umpire's liking. Not only was Whitson ejected, but under the rules of the previous warning, San Diego manager Dick Williams was also tossed.

Pitcher Juan Berenguer on the Bunt Code

"I remember pitching one time for San Francisco back in 1986, and we were getting beat by St. Louis 13–1 in the eighth inning. Cardinals left fielder Vince Coleman came up and laid down a bunt for a base hit off of me. I was pissed. That is a clear violation of the code; you just don't do stuff like that in a blowout game. That is very disrespectful. So I walked over to him and told him never to do that to me again. He just looked away and didn't say anything. Well, it took a while, but I finally faced him again later that season on our next road trip and made him pay for it. I drilled him right on his ass on the first pitch. He knew what it was for. My manager, Roger Craig, was okay with it. He knew that I had to send a message to him and make him pay for showing us up."

The Padres knew that their skipper wanted retaliation, so reliever Greg Booker tried to make him proud in the sixth when Perez came up to bat for the third time. Booker whizzed a pair of pitches at the elusive Perez before realizing the same fate as Whitson. This time Booker, as well as San Diego's interim manager, Ozzie Virgil, were both ejected.

Incredibly, Perez came up to bat in the eighth inning for what would prove to be his fourth and final at-bat. This time reliever Craig Lefferts took dead aim and was finally able to drill Perez in the side with a fastball. The benches emptied with both teams going at it pretty good. Nearly half a dozen fights erupted on the field and near the dugouts. It was total mayhem. Atlanta's Gerald Perry sought out Lefferts near the mound and landed a few rights to his face. Perez, meanwhile, sought refuge in the dugout, where he watched from a safe distance.

After a slew of ejections, the game was finally able to resume. But in the top of the ninth, Braves reliever Donnie Moore nailed San Diego's Graig Nettles in the ribs, which promptly emptied the benches yet again. Padres reliever Goose Gossage went after Moore but was intercepted by Atlanta first baseman Bob Watson. The two went at it pretty hard, throwing haymakers back and forth until the cavalry arrived to break it up.

By now several rowdy fans had entered the fracas, making an already ugly situation a potentially dangerous one. One idiot threw a cup of beer on Kurt Bevacqua's head, at which point the Padres' third baseman climbed on top of the dugout in hot pursuit before the police could cut him off at the pass. Atlanta's Chris Chambliss and Jerry Royster got into the mix, too, taking down an unruly fan near the third-base line.

When order was finally restored, scores of policemen had to be stationed around the field. Fearing for the safety of the players, the umps, in an unprecedented move, cleared out both benches for the final three outs of the game.

It is hard to believe, but in a game that featured three hit batters, six brushback pitches, two bench-clearing brawls, 19 ejections, and the arrest of five fans, the impetus of it all was a couple of harmless bunts. In what was later referred to as "perhaps baseball's ugliest game ever," the fireworks continued afterwards in the locker room.

"Dick Williams is an idiot," said then-Braves manager Joe Torre. "It was obvious he was the cause of the whole thing. Precipitating a thing like that was inexcusable. It was stupid of them, period, to take four shots at Perez. It was gutless. It stinks. It was Hitler-like action. I think he [Williams] should be suspended for the rest of the year."

Williams was indeed suspended for 10 days and fined $10,000. But the events served as a catalyst of sorts, and the Padres rallied, going on to reach the World Series that year.

One player who was never afraid to bunt, regardless of the situation, was Pete Rose. Rose drew criticism on several occasions during his career for bunting in circumstances that some deemed questionable. For instance, in 1969 Rose and Roberto Clemente were tied for the batting title going into

---

Subcode to the Code: Bunt Retaliation

There are several ways a hitter can retaliate against a pitcher who has just brushed him back. One is to simply drive the ball directly at him, straight up the middle. An easier way is to employ "bunt retaliation"—the hitter will bunt the ball down the first-base line and then take out the pitcher on his way to first base. The pitcher will instinctively run over to field the ball, and when he does, wham-o!

There were several players through the years who were able to pull this off, including the legendary Ty Cobb, who loved nothing better than to lay down a drag bunt and then tear open the pitcher's leg with his spikes as he ran by. Another player who was able to execute this maneuver with success was the great Jackie Robinson, who was thrown at a lot over his career. In fact, Robinson took out rival pitcher Sal Maglie a couple of times during his career.

the final game of the season. Rose was able to bunt for a base hit in his last at-bat, however, to take the crown.

Then, in 1978, Rose, while chasing Joe DiMaggio's legendary 56-game hitting streak, beat out a bunt against Phillies reliever Ron Reed in his last at-bat of the game to keep his streak alive at 33 games. It came in dramatic fashion, as the Reds managed to bat through their entire lineup in the final frame to give Rose another shot. Some viewed the bunt as a code violation, however, suggesting that hits in that type of situation, with a hallowed record on the line, should be earned the old-fashioned way.

Second Baseman Al Newman on the Bunt Code

"I remember my rookie year playing for Montreal, we opened a series in Houston. Nolan Ryan was pitching that night and I was our leadoff hitter. My teammate, Tim Raines, who hit second, says to me as I am in the on-deck circle, 'Hey, Newman, make sure not to bunt on Ryan.' I am like, 'Why not?' He says, 'Just don't do it, man. He doesn't like it.' Well, I am thinking to myself, I don't like striking out either. So I looked out at that hard Astroturf and said screw it, I'm going for it.

"Just then I look over and Ryan was walking over to look at the third-base line. It was a ritual he did before the start of every game, where he would sort of examine the first- and third-base lines. While he was doing it, he would look right at the on-deck hitter to intimidate him and let him know that he had better not even think about bunting on him.

"So I get up to bat and what do I do? I laid down a perfect bunt on the very first pitch, which was just hugging the third-base line. As I got to first base I was so happy, and then I was crushed when I heard the ump yell, 'FOUL BALL!' I started jogging back to home plate and could sense that Ryan was staring at me, but there was no way I was going to eyeball him. I look back at Tim Raines in the on-deck circle, and he took one look at me and then just dropped his head and turned away. It was like he was looking at a dead man walking.

"Sure enough, the very next pitch I was flat on my back. Luckily he didn't hit me with that fastball of his, but I certainly got the message and never bunted on him again. Nolan was an older player at that point, and that was the respect that players gave him, to not bunt on him and force him to run all over the field. It became an unwritten rule with him that you could only sacrifice-bunt on him, believe it or not. He was such a competitor, though. He challenged you and demanded that if you were going to beat him, it had to be one-on-one. You had to earn your way on base with him by hitting his best stuff. I respected that about him. That is why he is a Hall of Famer."

Writer La Velle E. Neal on the Bunt Code

"I was covering the Twins in Cleveland one night, and the Twins laid down a couple of bunts on Indians pitcher C.C. Sabathia. Well, that guy is like 6'5" and 280 pounds, so if you get him rolling around the infield chasing after bunts, he is going to get worn out and upset. Sure enough, he just started drilling Minnesota players after that to let them know that he wasn't going to tolerate that anymore."

The streak would eventually come to rest at 44 games, when Gene Garber of the Braves struck Rose out in his last at-bat. Ironically, the ultra-competitive Rose was upset after the game, feeling as if the pitcher had broken a code of his own by not giving him a pitch to hit in order to have a chance at keeping his streak going. He blasted Garber and the Braves for treating the situation "like it was the ninth inning of the seventh game of the World Series," and added that "Phil Niekro would have given me a fastball to hit."

22

On Timing a Pitcher from the On-Deck Circle

While a batter trying to gauge the rhythm and speed of a pitcher while he is in the on-deck circle may seem innocent, it is actually considered disrespectful to the pitcher. While each pitcher has his own personal feelings toward this part of the code, retaliation is rare. Hitters will know which pitchers will and won't tolerate it and will act accordingly.

When pitchers do choose to retaliate, they will usually just drill the batter as soon as he steps up to the plate. But some pitchers just can't seem to wait. Take, for instance, Brooklyn Dodgers pitcher Hugh Casey, a brushback artist extraordinaire, who made history when he became the first known pitcher to throw at the on-deck hitter. It happened back in 1946 during a game against the Cardinals.

Casey was throwing some warm-up pitches when he noticed that the Cardinals' Marty Marion had crept out of the on-deck circle to get a good look at Casey's delivery and to better gauge the timing of his pitches. Casey warned Marion to knock it off, but the Cardinals shortstop defiantly blew him off. So Casey responded by firing his next warm-up pitch at Marion's head, sending him sprawling to the dirt. Mission accomplished.

Another high-profile and frightening example occurred on April 23, 1999, during a college baseball game between Wichita State and the University of Evansville (Indiana). Wichita State pitcher Ben Christensen became incensed when he noticed that Evansville third baseman Anthony

Molina was standing between home plate and the on-deck circle, timing his warm-up pitches. So Christensen rifled a fastball toward him, beaning him in the side of the face. The pitch knocked Molina down, fractured his cheekbone, and opened up a cut that required 23 stitches. Furthermore, Molina suffered permanent damage to his vision in his left eye and had to undergo several surgical procedures to help repair it.

While most felt that Christensen was trying to send a retaliatory message to Molina for hitting a pair of home runs off of him in a previous meeting, everybody felt that this was way out of bounds and completely unacceptable. Molina had his head down and never saw the ball coming—he never even had a chance to duck out of the way.

While the Missouri Valley Conference suspended Christensen for the season, ending a three-year college career in which he posted an impressive 21–1 record, the Chicago Cubs later selected the 6'4" right-hander with their first-round draft pick in 1999.

23

On the Umpire Code

Just as there is a code of respect between opposing players, there is also a code between the players and the umpires. There are right ways and wrong ways for hitters and pitchers to interact with the umps. Show one up, and it could be either a long day trying to get a call or a short day, as in "Yer outta here!"

Knowing exactly what can and cannot be said to an ump without getting tossed is an art form all to itself. It is understood that players do not talk about the umpire's mother, or they will be given a one-way pass to the clubhouse. You can curse, but not directly at the ump. You also need to get to the point—there is a limit to the amount of patience an ump has.

If you are standing in the batter's box, you should never turn around to look at the ump while you are voicing any complaints with him either. You can speak to him as long as you are looking toward the field; if you turn back, the fans will know that you are arguing. That may then be viewed as a hostile attempt to turn the crowd against the umpires, which is a big no-no.

Knowing what to say, how to say it, and when to say it are all a part of the code. While the rule book and the umpires say otherwise, it is generally believed that if a batter disrespects an ump or tries to show him up, then he will not be getting any calls anytime soon. Cross the line with an ump, and you will pay for it one way or another.

Perhaps the most infamous act of disrespect toward an umpire occurred on September 27, 1996, when Baltimore Orioles second baseman Roberto Alomar spit on umpire John Hirschbeck during a heated argument over a

Umpire Tim Tschida on the Code Between Umpires and Managers

"With regards to the concept of a manager intentionally getting thrown out of a ballgame in an attempt to swing the momentum for players, there are a lot of different schools of thought on that topic. I recently had a conversation about this with Jim Leyland at a hotel bar after a game in Seattle one night. He said he noticed a lot more young managers in the game today seem to feel obligated to fire up their teams by coming out and arguing with the umpires and ultimately getting ejected. Then he said that if you had to resort to that kind of stuff to get your guys to play for you, then you were in the wrong business.

"He said that in all his years of managing in the big leagues, not once did he ever come out to argue with an umpire just for show. He said he only did so if and when he felt that his team had been wronged or was being treated unfairly. When he did get ejected, he said it was because he was unwilling to accept the umpire's ultimate decision on the issue if he really disagreed with it. So to hear Jim say that, an old-school baseball purist kind of a guy, was pretty insightful.

"More and more today, you see the younger managers fearing that their teams will quit on them if they don't fight for them. There are times when it is just not advantageous to your club to get ejected from the game, and yet they do it anyway. I think that comes from experience and just having enough confidence in yourself to manage your ballclub the way you feel best, rather than what you think you are going to be second-guessed for.

"The managers today are scrutinized much more by the media, by their general managers, by their executives, and by their team owners. I mean, if there is an ownership group and three of the owners think that their guy isn't fiery enough, then he might start to do things that are out of his realm. That is when he may do some questionable things out there that might have previously been out of character for him. I don't blame him, I guess, because he wants to save his job and do what he is told by his superiors. So it can be tough, no question.

"As an umpire, you have to deal with every situation accordingly. If a manager comes out of the dugout to have words with you over a call, you have to be respectful and listen to what he has to say. Usually they say their piece and the game resumes. Sometimes things get hot, though, and the managers want to get tossed to make a point or to get their guys fired up. For the most part, managers are ejected for their words, their behavior, or for prolonging the argument. Not very often is that stuff staged, like it might have been years ago, but you still see it from time to time.

"You can just tell with some managers, too, like Lou Piniella. When you see him start swinging his legs in the dugout, you know it won't be long before he comes out to have words with us. One thing about Lou is that he yells at everybody. He doesn't pick on certain people—he picks on everybody equally, including his own players. As umpires, we don't have a lot of respect for certain managers who scream and yell at us all of the time and yet will always defend their players, even when they are dead wrong. A guy like that won't get a lot of rope with us. We like dealing with guys who are fair."

third-strike call in a game against Toronto. League officials gave Alomar a five-game suspension for his outburst, but his reputation was tarnished forever.

As for the pitcher-umpire dynamic, it too is unique and subjective. If a pitcher whines about calls, they may mysteriously begin to go against him in the future. If he glares at the ump, pouts like a child, throws his rosin bag down in a huff, or shows any negative emotion out on the mound, the ump will take it as an attempt to show him up. The result will be the same—no calls. The ump will only be sympathetic to the pitcher's complaints if he handles himself like a true professional.

Each umpire is different, and each has his own demeanor behind the plate. Veteran pitchers will know which umps they can talk to safely. The pitcher must speak to the umpire in his own distinct language, asking him short questions in a nice way that might or might not warrant a response. He will need to figure out where that particular umpire's strike zone is in the early innings of the ballgame by trial and error. The sooner he figures it out, the sooner he can conform to his parameters. The sooner that happens, the sooner he will get the calls he is looking for.

ESPN's Tim Kurkjian gives his advice on the right way for pitchers to interact with umpires:

> Don't show up an umpire on balls and strikes. Umpires are, on the whole, very good at what they do. If they miss a call, a hitter can tell them, but do it without looking at them, or gesturing. That gets everyone in the ballpark on the umpire. As a pitcher, if an ump misses a pitch down the middle, do what Hall of Famer Fergie Jenkins used to do: don't even flinch, just keep on pitching. As good as umpires are, they're human. If you embarrass them, they'll embarrass you. They'll call you out on a bad pitch if you make them look bad.

The bottom line with umpires is they can rarely ever acknowledge making a mistake. If they do show their human side, then the managers will

Umpire Tim Tschida on the Code Between Umpires and Players

"If a guy starts trying to work over an umpire, either by physical movement or by verbal communication, then you have to ignore that and just keep the game moving along. One thing is for sure: you had better not respond to that by how you start umpiring. You may have to firm up, if anything. You can't be intimidated, and you can't have any sort of favoritism, either. That is against everything we stand for as professionals. Look, you don't factor in a guy's history with regards to whether a pitch is a ball or a strike. It either is or isn't, period. Whether a guy's behavior is unacceptable or not has nothing to do with that fact.

"It is easy to think that if a hitter is being a jerk and is screaming at an umpire about where a pitch was or something, and trying to show us up, that we would hold it against him and not give him any calls. Well, the fact of the matter is that nothing could be further from the truth. We can't do stuff like that, no matter how we might feel personally. We are professionals, and we have all worked very hard to get to the point we are at in our careers as major league umpires. So we are not going to jeopardize our careers or the integrity of the game by doing anything stupid like that.

"If a player has a gripe about a pitch, we will listen respectfully and then move on. If he gets out of hand, we may have to take action, but usually it doesn't ever go beyond a few words or a look or expression. If a player's behavior is unacceptable, then you tell him to stop. If he chooses not to stop, then your only course of action is removal.

"Everybody wants to gain an edge out there and will try to push things as far as he can. Hitters want things to go their way, pitchers want things to go their way, and managers want things to go their way. Well, things are not always going to go everybody's way. That is just baseball. We just do our jobs the best we can and let the players determine the outcomes of their games. We have to be accountable for our actions up there, too.

"Sure, years ago umpires used the strike zone against either the hitter or pitcher as a form of discipline, and it was an accepted part of the game. Even in the early part of my career, back in the early- to mid-1980s, it was done. It was expected, respected, and accepted. Not anymore. You can't do that. You cannot market yourself or your profession as being honest and fair and having integrity and then clearly be subject to that type of criticism. We have had to evolve and change for the good of the game.

"The same is true of pitchers who may complain about location, as well. It used to be that we could settle a situation by just calling a couple of close pitches as balls, figuring that the pitcher would get the message. That is no longer a practice that can be used or accepted. I don't know if it was ever right, or ethical, but it was the way that it was, historically speaking. We have since moved on and grown, which has made the game much, much better."

ride them mercilessly and question every past and future call. They try to avoid controversy like the plague and are trained to show no emotion. They are Switzerland out on the field—completely neutral.

As for make-up calls, they are like Bigfoot: they only exist in our imaginations, or so the umpires would have us believe. There are a few scenarios that make us shake our heads from time to time, though, such as the old "automatic," which happens when a batter takes a pitch with an 0–2 count. As long as it is close, it will always be called a strike. It is one of those unspoken rules that has been around forever.

Umpires also have their own unique code on how to deal with managers. Again, each umpire has his own boiling point and will take only so much abuse before the ejections start to fly. Veteran managers know this and will push the envelope in order to argue their point. Sometimes they come out to argue a call for the sole purpose of getting tossed. It is their own way of swinging the momentum and is intended to serve as a sort of wake-up call for their teams.

Managers will purposely try to show up umpires in situations like that, which might just be a part of their theatrical routine. Certain high-profile skippers, such as Earl Weaver, Lou Piniella, and Bobby Cox, know when the cameras are rolling and enjoy their time in the spotlight. They will choose when and how they are going to get tossed, whether it is in the heat of the moment, following a close play at the plate, or in the middle of a 10–0 blowout and they just want to hit the showers.

"You get turning points during the season: Memorial Day, the Fourth of July, and Labor Day," said crew chief Tim Tschida on why he believes there are spikes in the numbers of managers who get ejected each year. "Teams look at where they are and where they thought they would be at each quarter of the season. If they are not there, frustration and reality probably set in."

The umpires have come under fire in recent years due to a new ruling set forth by Major League Baseball, which mandated that umpires crack down on retaliation incidents that can lead to beanball wars. The commissioner's office put a greater onus on umpires to reduce the number of bench-clearing brawls, and as a result a warning system was put into place back in 2001. Now, when an ump has reason to believe that a batter is being thrown at, he immediately issues warnings to both teams that the next hit batter, intentional or not, will result in the pitcher and manager both getting ejected from the game.

This has changed the landscape of the code, forcing the players to change and alter their tactics to conform to the new rules. It has also put additional strain on the umpires, who must now monitor games throughout the season and gauge whether or not there is any bad blood brewing between certain individuals or teams. An umpire now has the authority, under Rule 8.02 of the rule book, to warn and eject based on his judgment of a player's intent.

Tim Tschida has his own unique insight into this latest effort to cut out the beanball wars:

> There is a program we have now called Heads Up, which dictates that we, the umpires, are required to log on to our computers every day and check in with the league office regarding our particular games that we have coming up that day or for a particular series. In so doing, we may find out that there may be a "heads-up" in place for our game. This information may be in regards to a previous confrontation between the two teams about to play each other or about a previous situation between certain individuals which may not have been resolved. Maybe a fight took place the last time they met, or perhaps somebody got drilled. It might alert you about which pitchers might want to retaliate against which hitters, and so forth. Or it might inform you

Umpire Marty Springstead on the Code Between Umpires and Managers

"The managers are always looking for an advantage and to make sure that their guys get calls and whatnot. As an umpire, you respected that. But you had to call it both ways and just do your best. I didn't get all the calls right, but I tried my best to do the right thing. You know, things are much, much different today than they were 20 years ago, though. Nowadays the managers are very respectful. For the most part, they are college guys and are really a different breed of cat. They are not like the Billy Martins and Earl Weavers, who would throw their hats and really make a spectacle of themselves. I must have thrown Earl out at least 13 or 14 times over my career. We used to really get into it out there. He was my arch-nemesis. As soon as he started pointing his finger in my face, he knew that I was going to run him. That was part of his game—he wanted to get tossed to get his guys fired up. That was his tactic and I understood that."

Manager Tom Kelly on the League's Rules Regarding Retaliation Warnings

"Years ago, back when I played, if somebody threw at one of your guys, you pretty much got a free shot at getting him back whenever the time was right. The umpires knew what was going on and let the game sort of police itself that way. Now the umpires step in and give warnings and throw guys out, which is unfortunate. If he issues a warning after the first guy gets hit in a game, well then the other team is stuck. You either have to wait for another day, or another series, or even another season to get back at that guy.

"Certain umpires get it and know how to handle those situations. I remember an incident one time where one of my guys got hit on purpose, and the umpire knew that. So when I went out there he said to me, 'Tommy, you got a free shot. Take it when you want to.' Now that was the right thing to do. I really respected that guy for doing that. But sadly, most of them don't or won't do that kind of thing today. Some of them can get carried away with the new rules and not enforce them properly. I much preferred the old way of doing things where if you plunked one of our guys, we plunked one of your guys, now let's play baseball. I am old school and prefer the old way. But things change and that is the way it goes."

about what a certain player may have said out on the field or in the newspaper, which might warrant retaliation. Basically, it will fill you in on any bad blood and bring you up to speed.

Baseball players have long memories, and sometimes retaliation can take days, weeks, or even months. So having this system in place really helps us, as umpires, stay on top of every situation and make sure it doesn't get out of hand. To be able to share this information and to know this information ahead of time is invaluable for us. A lot of times we will inform the managers before the first game of the series that there is a "heads-up" in place for that series. What that means is that we may respond quickly, perhaps even too quickly, to something that has the potential to be a confrontation.

The goal of Major League Baseball was to eliminate bench-clearing brawls as much as possible. At worst, we hope to keep them to a minimum and then do everything possible to head them off before they even get a chance to get started. If and when they do occur, the fines and suspensions are immediate, and the appeals process is not dragged out like it was in years past. There will be a decision made very quickly on that person's or persons' fate. Baseball took a hard stand with the Players Association in order to gain that right. It had gotten away from baseball in the previous 20 years because of the

Umpire Tim Tschida on the League's Rules
Regarding Retaliation Warnings

"I like the new rules. I have enough faith in my judgment and in the judgment of my peers to know when a certain guy has to go. For a long time we relied on vigilante justice, if you want to call it that, and those days are long gone. Years ago, when I was a home plate umpire, whenever I was calling a game in which we knew that there was some bad blood, we usually tried to avoid issuing warnings or handing out ejections until there had clearly been an exchange of some sort between the two teams. Rarely back then would we act upon the first guy in a retaliatory situation. Very rarely. It was kind of even accepted, too, that the opposing team wouldn't want you to punish him yet, either. They wanted to get their swing at him first, before we issued our warnings or resorted to ejections.

"Most of the arguments about this today come from when we try to nail the first guy. Usually, the guy who is most upset at this point is the opposing manager, not the manager of the pitcher you just warned or tossed. The opposing club feels cheated because they didn't get their justice. It has taken a while for teams to accept that this is just the way it is today. That is the way this stuff is going to be handled now. The old frontier days of Texas justice are over. The game polices itself differently now, and that is just the reality of how the game has changed and evolved. So if teams really want to retaliate in those situations, they still can. But they are going to lose players to ejections, suspensions, and fines. Regardless of what the players or fans might think about the topic, that is the order that has been handed down to us, the umpires, from our boss at the top. That is our job on the field, and that is what we are paid to do."

strength of the players union to protect its players, but that has all since changed. As a result, it had kind of disarmed the league and the umpires from really doling out discipline that would have served as a deterrent to that type of behavior.

I have to admit that I was skeptical of the program to begin with, but am sold on it now. Our general feeling on retaliation and fighting used to be one of 'it's over when they decide it's over.' Now it is over when *we* say it is over. So the program has actually been very, very successful, and I feel good about that.

Like anything in life, though, the players have evolved and adapted with regards to how they retaliate and protect one another out there. So we as umpires have to look for new ways to stay on top of these situations. We used to be able to predict when the retaliations would occur, but now the teams are not responding immediately on purpose. They are putting those little code violations that they see in the back of their minds and are deciding to retaliate when the time is right. They are convinced that they will still get even, but it will be at a time when it won't cost a player a fine or suspension. In a sense, they try to retaliate now when no one is looking or when no one expects it. They have, in a sense, evolved, and that just makes our jobs that much tougher, to tell you the truth.

You see, another factor we look for is to see if that pitcher is above the 100-pitch count. If he is, that usually means the end of his evening is not too far away. Or, if his five innings are in the books, which will give him the win if his team maintains the lead. You also look to see if there is somebody warming up in the bullpen, too, which means his replacement is getting ready to come into the ballgame. Those are usually the times that he will decide to let one go at somebody and exit with a blaze of glory.

Here is a good example of what I am talking about: I remember one time back in 1998 when I was working a game in Kansas City between the Royals and the Angels. It was around the fifth inning, and Phil Nevin was at bat for Anaheim. Chris Haney was pitching for Kansas City. What is important about the 100-pitch count is that I knew he was about ready to hit the showers.

Anyway, nothing had happened prior to this whatsoever that would have indicated retaliation was coming. But as soon as Nevin stepped up to the plate, Haney reared back and just drilled him with the first pitch, right between the numbers on his back. Haney then took a few steps toward the catcher and put his glove up, signaling

Pitcher Bert Blyleven on the League's Rules Regarding Retaliation Warnings

"In today's game, things are much different with the umpires. There are no longer American League umps and National League umps—they are all Major League umps. As a pitcher, if you are starting 35 to 40 ballgames a year, you would get to know the umpires and their tendencies. Each one had certain nuances that you could pick up on. Some guys would give you the outside part of the plate; others would not. But if you were around long enough, you could do your homework and figure out how to pitch around certain umpires. Well, those days are over. Now you might see the same crew only once or maybe twice a year. So you have to reinvent the wheel every time you pitch. There were certain umpires you could talk to, and others who would toss you out in a heartbeat. Figuring out which ones were the good guys was the hard part. A good umpire, in my opinion, was a guy who was to be seen and not heard."

that he wanted a new ball, like nothing had happened. He was looking at Nevin but not saying anything to taunt him. Meanwhile, I am pretty sure that he just threw at him on purpose, as retaliation for something. But I had nothing to base it on—no evidence whatsoever.

Well, Haney finished the inning and was then replaced by reliever Scott Service. Nevin came up again a few innings later and was again drilled in the back. This time, however, Nevin charged the mound and both benches cleared. So we as umpires have to get the situation under control and figure out who gets to stay and who gets to go. We ejected Nevin from the game for charging the mound and then issued a warning to both teams to 'cease and desist.'

Anaheim then retaliated the next inning by drilling someone. The benches cleared again, only this time it got ugly. Just as the fight was almost broken up, Kansas City's shortstop, this little guy, came up and threw a haymaker from behind on an unsuspecting Angels player, and all hell broke loose. The entire Anaheim team started chasing him toward the dugout, and all of the Royals players followed suit. It was one of the craziest things I have ever seen. It was like that old electric football game we used to play, where all the players just sort of buzzed across the field en masse all the way over to the dugout.

Catcher Terry Steinbach on the Umpire Code

"Back when I played it was still pretty old school in that you had to pay your dues and put your time in before you were going to earn their respect out there. If you are a young catcher and you are turning around and bitching about balls and strikes, you aren't going to get anywhere. Not only are you going to screw your pitcher over, because that ump is now going to be upset that you tried to show him up, but you are also going to screw yourself over when you step up to hit. Those guys have long memories and like to do things their own way. If you screamed and hollered, it got you in hot water.

"So for the first few years, I just sat back and kept my mouth shut. I paid my dues, worked hard, and tried to make the umpire look good, too. I was very aware as to how I received the ball, how I framed the ball, how I blocked the ball, and how I transitioned the ball back to the pitcher. Transitioning the ball back to the pitcher was a big one because if you held it there for too long, they took it as a sign of disrespect and that you were trying to show them up. They appreciate stuff like that, and eventually it paid off. After a while you develop your own reputation with the umpires, and they would talk amongst themselves as to which guys they liked and disliked. And trust me, if they liked you, it made life a lot easier."

Catcher Tim Laudner on the Umpire Code

"I remember one time during a game in Minnesota against Oakland when Kirby Puckett came around on a borderline check swing. The home-plate umpire appealed to the first-base umpire, who was Tim Tschida, a Minnesota native, and Tim banged him—meaning it was a strike. I was sitting on the bench thinking, 'Wow, this is a Hall of Fame player not getting a close call in his home ballpark by a hometown umpire.'

"So the next inning we go out there, and Dave Henderson came up to bat. Well, I immediately appealed the first pitch, which was a ball and wasn't even close to being a check swing. Once I did that, the umpire looked over to Tschida, who then had to make the no-swing call. At that point, 30,000 fans started booing him, which was exactly what I wanted to happen.

"I definitely showed him up on that one, but it was in retaliation for him not giving Puck the respect I thought he deserved. Hey, I think the world of Tim Tschida, but I think that because he was from Minnesota, he had to almost call things even tighter against the Twins so that nobody would think he was a homer."

Now, because we had issued a warning, we automatically ejected Anaheim's pitcher as well as their manager, Terry Collins. So we finally get that mess cleaned up, and wouldn't you know it, Kansas City retaliates again that next inning. So we ejected that pitcher along with Royals manager Tony Muser. This just kept going—it was insane. It continued three times until we nearly ran out of players. We ejected a total of 13 players when it was all said and done. I will never forget that night for as long as I live.

So the next day I finally found out what was behind all of it. It turned out that the year before, when Nevin had played for Detroit, he had bowled over Kansas City's catcher, Mike Macfarlane, in what they considered a dirty play. Well, they never got an opportunity to retaliate, so, figuring the time was right, they finally decided to settle the score. Now get this: Haney figured he had settled the score and it was over, only Service was in the bathroom at the time and never actually saw it happen. So when he came into the game, he thought it was his job to drill Nevin. He had no idea that it had already happened. Nevin, of course, said enough was enough and went after him. Incredibly, this was the genesis of this ridiculous story. Amazing.

Sure, we are accused of overreacting a lot by the players and managers, and for being too quick to warn and or eject certain players, but Major League Baseball stands behind the program and firmly believes it is making a positive influence on the game. It has accomplished what it set out to accomplish, and the statistics will bear that out. The number of bench-clearing brawls has been reduced by over 50 percent, and the amount of fines and suspensions has increased by over 200 percent. So it has worked, and in our eyes that is a good thing for the game both now and well into the future.

One of the most outspoken critics of the league's new rules is former pitcher and current TV analyst Rob Dibble, who explains why he thinks the system needs to be changed:

What has changed over the years, in my opinion, is the influx of money into the game. Baseball is a $6 billion per year industry nowadays. It's huge. The powers that be started to fear that a lot of the everyday players were going to get hurt as a result of all of the retaliation that was going on, so things changed. Umpires got more power, and the rules of the game shifted.

The basic premise behind the new rules is that the umpires can eject the pitcher if they think he was intentionally trying to hurt somebody. What is so difficult with that whole thing, though, is the issue of how do you get inside the pitcher's head and know what he is really trying to do? Or how do you know if he didn't just let a pitch get away from him? So to have an umpire accuse a guy of throwing at someone intentionally, it is almost laughable. Because there are some guys who, when they lose it, they lose it bad. Their control just fails them, and they are all over the place. How do the umps know? They don't.

Case in point: I remember watching a game recently where Boston was playing Seattle, and Brendan Donnelly struck out Jose Guillen. There was some bad blood there with these guys from before, when Guillen had alleged that Donnelly was illegally loading up his glove with pine tar. Well, Donnelly got busted and received a 10-game suspension for it, so there was no love lost there between these two guys. Anyway, after he strikes him out, they start talking smack. Everybody calms down, and the next hitter is Kenji Johjima, whom Donnelly drills. Boom—he is immediately ejected by the home-plate umpire because both benches had just been warned about any future escalation. I am watching this and am like, "Come on, you have got to be kidding me!"

Donnelly didn't mean to hit him. He knew that he was going to receive an automatic ejection and stiff fine if he hit anybody after that, so he was being extra cautious. I believe that because he got rattled, the ball simply got away from him. It was a ridiculous ruling. But that is the rule, so there was nothing he could do. That was a classic case of a guy whose adrenaline was all pumped up, and his command just started to fail him. So for an umpire to stand back there and judge him and accuse him of throwing at a guy is crazy. Again, how can an umpire get in a guy's head like that? I will say, however, that I feel for the umps, too, because that has to be a really tough situation for them to be in as well. It's just a bad rule all the way around.

Catcher Greg Olson on the Umpire Code

"With catchers and umpires, it comes down to years of service and respect. You have to earn their respect the hard way sometimes. I remember my rookie year with Atlanta, and I was catching Tom Glavine against Philadelphia. Paul Runge, the crew chief, was behind the plate. Glavine was the type of pitcher who liked to nibble the corners. Well, he wound up walking a couple of guys in the first inning. So we are in the dugout right after that, and Tom says to me, 'Where the heck are those pitches? I have got to have them.'

"Next inning, the second pitch is right on the black, or the outside corner, and the ump calls it a ball. I then say to the umpire, 'I gotta have that pitch,' reiterating what Glavine had just said to me. Runge then slowly waves his hands and calls a time-out. He then slowly walks out in front of home plate and faces me. He takes out his little brush that he uses to dust off home plate, and fakes like he is sweeping, only he is holding the brush waist-high—just pretending to sweep. He then proceeds to lecture me about what I can and can't say to him. He is just showing me up big-time. He says, 'Listen, young man, you are a rookie. I have been here for 30 years. I know what a strike is, and I will tell you when it is a strike. Don't ever question my calls.' He then slowly walked back behind me and said, 'Play ball!'

"After the inning, I go into the dugout and try to hide from my manager, Bobby Cox, because I knew he was going to be pissed. As I sit down, I see Runge walking up the first-base line, just staring at me. Sure enough, here comes Bobby to ask me what the hell I said out there. I am just thinking, I have got to answer this correctly and quickly, otherwise Runge will have no respect for me. I say to Bobby, 'Mr. Runge told me that he will call the balls and strikes and not to question him.' I then asked Bobby if he could please just let it go. Runge saw all of this and then walked away. Well, the next time I had Runge umpire one of my games, he said to me before the game, 'Kid, I was just checking you out. I was trying to figure out what kind of catcher you were going to be. I wanted to know if you were going to be a complainer or if you were going to be able to work with me. I think you are going to be all right.'"

Pitcher Dave Boswell On What It's Like to be an Umpire for a Day

"I had a lot of run-ins with the umps over my career but finally got to walk in their shoes when I was asked to play the home plate umpire in the movie *Major League II*. I was the guy who couldn't throw the ball back to the pitcher. It was a real blast. There were some scenes where I had to get into it with Charlie Sheen's character, and the director said it was amazing how real I made it look. I told him, 'Hey, I had a lot of experience over the years pissing these guys off.' Luckily, I was a better pitcher than actor, because it took me 33 takes to get my one damn line down!"

Minnesota Twins manager Ron Gardenhire has a strong opinion regarding the new rules as well:

I have had so many issues with the new rules regarding warnings, it isn't even funny. In fact, I think I have gotten thrown out of more games because of it than just about any other manager. What the warning rule did was to tie the hands of the other team. I mean, a pitcher can go out there and blatantly drill your guy, and if the umpire issues a warning, then our pitchers are not allowed to do anything to protect their guys. It just isn't a fair system.

I have always felt that if the umpires know that a certain pitcher drilled a guy, then they should let the other pitcher take care of his business. Let him pitch, and no one will say a word. But when you let that other pitcher whack somebody and then put out a warning, you essentially are no longer letting the players police themselves. That isn't right, in my eyes.

The warning system takes away from what you can and can't do out there. For certain pitchers, it backs them off enough to where they can't or won't pitch inside. They don't want to get ejected or suspended or fined, and I understand that. But, and this is what I have a problem with, if your guys can't pitch inside because they are afraid of hitting a guy, then you are not going to have very much success out there as a result.

The umpires understand that, but they have to follow the new rules that were handed down to them. They have to follow the rules that are set forth in front of them, so I don't blame them. That has been a stickler in my craw for a long time, but you just have to deal with it and move on. So sometimes, when I go out there to talk to them and things get heated, that is usually what it is all about.

I just don't like to have my players get into arguments with the umpires. That is my job. I do all of that stuff, and if that means I get tossed, so be it. Heck, sometimes the umpires need a wake-up call. And they don't want that attention either, believe me. Then when it is all said and done, hopefully the attention and focus is back on the game and not on that one particular incident that was being disputed. The downside to all of this is the fact that the fines aren't cheap. And it is not like the owner picks up the tab on those deals, either. It comes right out of the old pocketbook. My wife just loves me when I do that stuff, believe me.

24

On Pitchers Being Ordered to Retaliate

While a veteran pitcher who has been around the block will know when and where to seek revenge, there are times when the manager will want to make that decision himself. A manager can't just yell out to his pitcher from the dugout to plunk a batter, however, so he must have other creative ways of communicating to his players. Those nonverbal cues are all part of the code. It might be a look or it might be a sign called in to the third-base coach, which is then relayed to the catcher. If justice needs to be served, then the pitcher must react and do as he is instructed—or he, too, will be breaking a code of his own.

Back in the day, old-school managers such as Leo Durocher had no problem barking out orders from the dugout, going so far as to point out which body part he wanted the pitcher to hit on a certain batter. It was as much verbal intimidation as anything else. The batters knew that it was coming and would back off.

Once, back in 1948, Durocher instructed his Giants pitcher, Sheldon Jones, to bean Brooklyn outfielder Carl Furillo. He did, and Furillo had to be hospitalized. Five years later Furillo had a great game against Durocher's Giants club, and Durocher again instructed his pitcher, Ruben Gomez, to get him. He did, nailing the league's batting leader on the wrist. Durocher then began taunting Furillo, at which point Furillo lost it and went after him. According to the book *Field of Screams,* Furillo charged into New York's dugout, put a headlock on Durocher, and squeezed until his "bald head turned purple." Despite suffering a broken hand in the melee, which caused him to miss the rest of the season, Furillo felt it was worth it. "I know Durocher throws at my head, and he knows it," he said. "Why should I be sorry for going after a guy who might get me killed?"

While some pitchers understand and even relish their role in meting out team justice, others simply have no clue. Drilling a guy or even throwing an inside purpose pitch can be excruciatingly painful for some young pitchers. They don't know how to do it, either, because they haven't been taught, or because they just never had to do it in the minor leagues. Then, when they get to the big leagues, it feels completely foreign to them. They are afraid to bean a guy or are afraid of getting ejected or suspended. It is becoming, as many players and managers have said, a lost art.

While managers such as Tony La Russa and Billy Martin have ordered their pitchers to drill players over the years, nothing in recent years can hold a candle to what is now known simply as "The Sean Tracey Incident." It occurred in June 2006, when White Sox manager Ozzie Guillen ordered rookie pitcher Sean Tracey to drill Rangers slugger Hank Blalock. Texas's Vicente Padilla had nailed Sox catcher A.J. Pierzynski twice in recent games, and Tracey needed to retaliate and protect his teammate. Because Padilla is a pitcher in the American League and doesn't have to hit, Blalock, a comparable player in status to Pierzynski, was designated to be drilled instead.

But Tracey couldn't do it. He threw some pitches inside but just couldn't bring himself to hit the guy. It was a surreal scene—enraged and disgusted, Guillen pulled Tracey from the game and could be seen yelling and throwing things in the dugout. After the game Tracey was immediately sent down to the minors. Afterward, Guillen denied that Tracey's failure to hit Blalock resulted in his dismissal from the team.

Sox reliever Cliff Politte consoled Tracey after that game and shared the advice he had given him:

> When the manager calls you in to do something, you do it. This is the guy who runs the team, and if he tells you to jump off a bridge, you have to think about it if you want to stick up here and play. You feel bad for the kid because he doesn't know better and didn't know what he should do after the first pitch.

Guillen, a former player who was known for his toughness, even took a shot at Pierzynski for not charging the mound after Padilla had drilled him the second time. "If Padilla hit me twice, right now I'd be in the hospital

Manager Tom Kelly on Managers Ordering Their Pitchers to Retaliate

"I don't want to speak for all managers, but for myself and from other managers whom I know well and have spoken to, it was pretty much up to us to decide whether or not somebody needed to be hit. If you told your pitcher to drill a guy, then you would expect that to be taken care of. Now that doesn't mean throwing it at his head, either—that is not right. But if I wanted a guy to be hit in the ribs as retaliation for something, then that pitcher had better go out there and do it. I would tell my players right out of the gate that if something needed to be done, then I would tell them when to get it done. That might be the next inning or it might be three months down the road, but it will be taken care of. I didn't want my pitchers to take those situations into their own hands very often, because that is when things could sometimes get out of control. I also tried to make sure I had a veteran pitcher out on the mound who knew how to do it properly. That comes with experience. He will know how to do it right. He won't throw at the guy's head, and he won't start a war, which is what happens when the young guys try to do it with little or no experience."

or I'd be dead," said Guillen. "I will fight because of the way he hit him. I don't care if it was on purpose or not."

Pierzynski played it cool, though, and said he declined to charge the mound because of the consequences.

"Do I want to get suspended for five days?" asked Pierzynski. "Would I like to go out to the mound and get somebody? Yeah, but at the same time, can our team afford me missing four or five games in a row? We are in a pennant race, and we are going to need everyone."

Some speculated that the reason Tracey didn't drill Blalock was because he didn't get along with Pierzynski personally. While that is just speculation, it is widely known that Pierzynski has made his share of enemies in the game over the years. But he was Tracey's teammate on the White Sox at the time, and that means as a Sox pitcher, it was Tracey's job to protect him, regardless of his personal feelings.

The incident elicited opinions from all corners of the baseball world. "Sean Tracey, that was just a young kid, that's all," said manager Tom Kelly. "Kids like that just don't know how to pitch inside. It probably wasn't because he didn't want to do it—he just didn't know how. He probably didn't have the confidence to hit the guy in the ribs in that situation. Hey, that is a tough thing to do. But that is what separates the major leaguers from the minor leaguers."

"Ozzie shouldn't have had to tell him, if you want my opinion. The dumb-ass kid should have been smart enough to just do it on his own," said pitcher Dean Chance. "Hell yes, he should have been sent down to the minors in that situation. If your manager tells you to do something, then you do it. That is baseball. Pitchers need to protect their players and really shouldn't even have to be told when and where to do so. If the other team is throwing at your top guys, then you do the same. If you don't know that, then you don't belong in the big leagues."

"I think that is putting a lot of pressure on a young pitcher, in my opinion, but Ozzie is one of the old-school guys who lets his emotions fly," said pitcher Jim Kaat. "Sometimes people appreciate that, while other times I think it gets him in trouble. If it were me, I might talk to the catcher to see if he could get the pitcher to come around. To blatantly give a young guy an order to hit a guy, though, that can be difficult. Plus, news of that story never should have leaked out. Those types of things are for players' and managers' ears only, in my opinion."

"The pitcher needs to listen to his manager no matter what," said catcher Terry Steinbach. "He needs to be a team player and do what is told of him, otherwise he won't be around for very long. It might not be easy and it might not be fair, but that is your job and you have to do what is asked of you for the good of the team. Young pitchers don't always know and understand the history between certain teams, and that is why you can't

Center Fielder Torii Hunter on Managers Ordering Their Pitchers to Retaliate

"I think it is so important for a pitcher to be able to step up and take care of business when he is called upon to do so. If he needs to sit a guy down and drill him, I know it's not easy, but that is his job, and he has to do it. If he won't retaliate, he will lose the respect and trust of his teammates. And if the manager tells him to do it, or just expects him to do it, and he doesn't, then that is disrespecting the code. A manager might tell a pitcher to hit the first guy with the first pitch, because that is a statement that might need to be made. If the pitcher doesn't do it, or if it takes him a couple pitches to do it, then that is just being disrespectful to the manager. I think that if a pitcher doesn't do what he has to do, then yeah, he should get sent down or even cut."

question the manager's authority. You just do it. Pitchers have to protect their teammates, and that is the bottom line. If that means drilling a guy, then so be it. In Tracey's situation, I am sure Ozzie questioned whether or not he could count on him down the road and decided that he couldn't. So he sent him down. Certain managers are old school like that, and if you aren't going to play that way, then you aren't going to be around for very long."

"When it first happened with the young pitcher, Ozzie was kind of chastised for it," said umpire Tim Tschida. "They said 'You can't do that to your young player. You will destroy his confidence.' But Ozzie doesn't care who you are. If you are not with his program and aren't going to do what he wants done, then you are going to play someplace else. Love him or hate him, that is how Ozzie runs his ballclub."

"That whole situation with Sean Tracey was ridiculous," said pitcher Jack Morris. "I just have to laugh at stuff like that. I always get a kick out of managers who talk like that. I can promise you this, if Ozzie Guillen was a pitcher, he would have never thrown at anybody—and you can quote me on that. In fact, you can call Ozzie right now and tell him I said it, because I know him as a player and know what he was all about. Yeah, he was feisty, but you know what? It's a lot different when you are up on the mound and the whole world is watching you.

"So, if a young pitcher just doesn't have that type of mental makeup, then I don't think a manager should have to ask him to do that type of thing. A pitcher needs to know that situation and the history behind it and then act accordingly. If that means drilling a guy, then so be it. I just don't think it is necessary for a manager to dictate it to him.

"Hey, let's face it, nowadays that could even be considered a criminal offense. I mean, let's say Tracey did hit him, and the guy got hurt. Then what? Could he then retaliate against the manager? I don't know. What I do know is that those types of situations should be discussed behind closed doors. Pitchers need to protect their teammates, absolutely. But to do and say those things out in the open, that is where that situation got way out of hand, in my eyes. Remember, the code is also about 'what happens in the clubhouse stays in the clubhouse.'"

"If the manager asks you to do something, you have to do it," said catcher Greg Olson. "That is the code. It is like being in the army. You don't question authority, you just do it. So in Ozzie's situation, I don't blame him for getting mad. For whatever reason, the pitcher didn't do what he was told to do, and he had to suffer the consequences. He should have been disciplined for that, absolutely. If the manager doesn't have respect for you and the way you play the game, then you shouldn't be on his team. Now did the punishment fit the crime? I don't know. But that is Ozzie's call, and as long as he is the manager, those decisions are up to him."

The bottom line with this episode is that Tracey was wrong. The code says that you have to follow your manager's orders, or else you have to deal with the consequences. Tracey didn't, and had to take responsibility for his actions. Accountability is a big part of the code, and Guillen's actions, as barbaric as they may sound, were for the good of the team. It was obvious that the Rangers had hit Pierzynski on purpose, and Guillen felt justified in his response, as would most big-league managers.

Guillen is a hard-line manager who commands respect from his players. That is why his White Sox were the defending world champions at the time of the incident. As a matter of fact, Guillen showed just how consistent he is with regard to having his players do what they are told. Just a month after the Tracey incident, Guillen went off on his All-Star pitcher Jon Garland for not retaliating in a similar situation. The Sox and Rangers hooked up again, and this time Padilla hit Sox outfielder Alex Cintron in the third inning. Guillen wanted Garland to drill Rangers second baseman Ian Kinsler as retaliation that next inning, but Garland chose not to.

While Garland and the Sox went on to beat the Rangers, 5–0, Ozzie was not pleased. Certainly, with all of the negative press he received regarding the Tracey incident, one can only assume that the matter was handled internally, behind closed doors. Perhaps he cut him some slack because he was a veteran, but needless to say, it probably won't happen again—Garland was traded to the Angels following the 2007 season.

25

On Playing Hurt

Playing hurt is a part of any sport. In the hockey code, it is just expected that players will get stitches between shifts on the bench, not between periods. It isn't quite that brutal in baseball, but these guys are warriors in every sense of the word. Ballplayers have to endure the grind of 162 games per season, and they will inevitably get injured on occasion. They know that they need to keep their butts in the lineup, though, to help their teams and to keep the fans happy who spent a lot of money to come out and watch them.

It is up to the players to keep themselves in good shape, to eat right, get plenty of rest, and stay healthy. If they do suffer an injury in the line of duty, such as diving for a ball or getting drilled in the back, then that is looked at as honorable. If they do something stupid, like fall down some stairs while they are drunk in a Manhattan nightclub at three in the morning after sweeping the Yankees on a road trip, then that is going to require some explaining.

Players who work hard on their rehabilitation and spend a lot of time in the clubhouse getting treatment before and after games and practices are respected. Even if a guy has two broken arms, he can still do sit-ups and ride the stationary bike to stay in shape.

Players who get hurt and stop showing up to practices or blow off rehab sessions are looked upon very negatively. In fact, they may even develop a reputation as a clubhouse cancer, one that needs to be removed before his bad attitude spreads to others.

Baseball Digest's "Unwritten Rules"

Source: *Baseball Digest* (1986)

1. Never put the tying or go-ahead run on base.
2. Play for the tie at home, go for the victory on the road.
3. Don't hit and run with an 0–2 count.
4. Don't play the infield in early in the game.
5. Never make the first or third out at third.
6. Never steal when you're two or more runs down.
7. Don't steal when you're well ahead.
8. Don't steal third with two outs.
9. Don't bunt for a hit when you need a sacrifice.
10. Never throw behind the runner.
11. Left and right fielders concede everything to center fielder.
12. Never give up a home run on an 0–2 count.
13. Never let the score influence the way you manage.
14. Don't go against the percentages.
15. Take a strike when your club is behind in a ballgame.
16. Leadoff hitter must be a base stealer. Designated hitter must be a power hitter.
17. Never give an intentional walk if first base is occupied.
18. With runners in scoring position and first base open, walk the number eight hitter to get to the pitcher.
19. In rundown situations, always run the runner back toward the base from which he came.
20. If you play for one run, that's all you'll get.
21. Don't bunt with a power hitter up.
22. Don't take the bat out of your best hitter's hands by sacrificing in front of him.
23. Only use your bullpen stopper in late-inning situations.
24. Don't use your stopper in a tie game—only when you're ahead.
25. Hit behind the runner at first.
26. If one of your players gets knocked down by a pitch, retaliate.
27. Hit the ball where it's pitched.
28. A manager should remain detached from his players.
29. Never mention a no-hitter while it's in progress.
30. With a right-hander on the mound, don't walk a right-handed hitter to pitch to a left-handed hitter.

Baseball players are tough, make no mistake about it. When you consider the grind of playing in 30 preseason games, 162 regular-season games, and then the possibility of playing in the postseason, it is amazing. It is almost unfathomable to think of Lou Gehrig and Cal Ripken Jr. playing in as many consecutive games as they did.

One of the toughest ballplayers ever to lace 'em up was Pete Reiser, an outfielder/third baseman who played with the Brooklyn Dodgers, Boston Braves, Pittsburgh Pirates, and Cleveland Indians from 1940 to 1952. Some say that Reiser could have been one of the game's all-time greats had it not been for all of the injuries he suffered throughout his career. He played the game tough, though, and that is what made him so revered by his teammates and opponents alike.

Reiser couldn't grasp the concept of moderation and had just one speed: overdrive. He would give it 110 percent at all times, regardless of the consequences, even if that meant running smack into an outfield wall made of concrete while he was chasing down a fly ball. He would do whatever it took to get back onto the field, even if that meant taping up an open wound or just clamping it shut. Once, when he broke his right elbow, he taught himself to throw with his other hand.

Reiser got beaned early and often—it was once estimated he had been knocked out cold nearly a dozen times during his playing days. During his career he would suffer countless injuries, including a broken neck, a broken leg, paralysis, a fractured skull, and a concussion that required brain surgery to repair a blood clot. He was even administered his last rites in the clubhouse by the team chaplain after getting carted off the field.

He made a comeback, though, as he always did. This guy gave new meaning to the word *tough*, and one could only wish that players today performed with a little bit more of the spirit that drove old Pete.

Of course, another reason players are sometimes able to play hurt is because of their use of steroids and other performance-enhancing drugs, which allow them to recover much more quickly. (This issue is addressed in great length later in the book.)

26

The Code Between the Players and the Fans

There is also an unwritten code that exists between the players and the fans. Both sides figured out a long time ago that they need each other, so they had better respect each other.

Fans, for the most part, are decent, law-abiding citizens who come to the ballpark with their families to watch baseball and be entertained. Sure, there are always a few idiots who will come out and try to ruin it for everybody. They are the ones who drink too much, throw things onto the field, and scream obscenities within earshot of young children. They will even occasionally run out onto the field in an attempt to either get on TV or to join in on a bench-clearing brawl. When that happens, they are fair game and usually get pummeled by the first player who is lucky enough to spot them.

Players, for the most part, are decent, law-abiding citizens who come to the ballpark with their teammates and perform their jobs to the best of their abilities. Their objective is to do whatever they can to help their team win. There are always a few bad apples in the bunch who do stupid things both on and off the field. They are the ones who pick fights with teammates in the dugout, throw or yell things at fans in the stands, get drunk and obnoxious on road trips, and break the unwritten rules of the code on a regular basis. They are the team cancer that nobody wants to deal with.

Some of the more notorious incidents in which the player/fan code has been broken involve the infamous Ty Cobb, one of the most hated players of all time. Back in 1912 Cobb got tired of the relentless hecklers in New York and jumped into the stands behind his Tigers bench, where he pummeled a one-armed fan to a pulp. The fans were so rowdy that the Tigers refused to take the field after that and went on strike, vowing to sit out until Cobb, who had been suspended, was reinstated. The Tigers played one game with replacement players until Cobb suggested his teammates return to the field the next day.

Another classic occurred in 1922 at the Polo Grounds, when Yankees slugger Babe Ruth was called out at second base on a close play. Frustrated, Ruth threw dirt in the ump's eyes, at which point he was ejected. As the fans booed, Ruth went after a heckler in the stands. From there, according to ESPN's Jeff Merron, Ruth stood on top of the dugout and shouted, "Come on down and fight! Anyone who wants to fight, come down on the field! Ah, you're all alike, you're all yellow!" Ruth was suspended and fined a whopping $200 for the spectacle.

When fans enter the playing field, things can turn ugly. Such was the case back in 1961 during a game at Yankee Stadium between New York and Cleveland. In the seventh inning, Indians center fielder Jimmy Piersall was attacked by a pair of drunken fans. Piersall quickly landed a stiff right on one of them, knocking him down, and then went after the other one as he ran away. Cleveland's Walt Bond and Johnny Temple caught the guy, though, and let him have it pretty good before the security guards could haul him away.

It can get even uglier when players enter the stands to mix it up with belligerent fans. In one instance, Dodgers outfielder Reggie Smith finally snapped at a heckler during a game against the Giants at Candlestick Park. He flew into the stands behind the Dodgers dugout and went after the guy. He could only land one decent shot before being attacked by an angry mob of San Francisco fans. Several Dodgers jumped in to join the fracas, and the already ugly fight escalated. Smith was ejected, and no fewer than eight fans were arrested to boot.

In 1991, a Cleveland fan yelled out some tasteless comments about Albert Belle's recent alcohol rehabilitation issues. Belle decided that the guy had crossed the line, so he promptly picked up a foul ball and drilled the heckler in the chest from near point-blank range. The fans near the heckler even gave Belle a rousing ovation. The unremorseful Belle received a hefty fine and a one-week suspension for his actions.

For whatever the reason, some fans just want to be a part of the action. In 1995, during a game between the Astros and the Cubs at Wrigley Field, a fan ran out onto the field and messed with the wrong guy. In the eighth inning of the game, Chicago reliever Randy Myers gave up a two-run homer to Houston's James Mouton, giving the Astros a 9–7 lead. So upset was this fan at Myers for serving up the tater that he jumped onto the field and charged toward him. Myers, an experienced martial artist, saw the guy reaching for his pocket and got worried. So he ducked and gave the guy a forearm shiver, which dropped him. He then held him down, holding both of his hands behind him until security could take over. Despite his giving up the lead, the Wrigley fans gave Myers a standing O for his on-field heroics.

Another crazed fan attacked Houston's Bill Spiers in 1999, during a game between the Brewers and the Astros. Spiers did his best to fend the guy off, but the attacker was persistent, leaving the right fielder with several big cuts. Teammate Mike Hampton got there first and was able to land a few kicks to the guy's midsection before the security guards could take over. The fan was arrested on charges of battery and disorderly conduct and then hauled off to the clink.

Sometimes it is the little things that will set a guy off. Back in 2000, during the ninth inning of a tight ballgame between the Dodgers and the Cubs at Wrigley Field, a drunk fan tried to swipe Dodgers catcher Chad Kreuter's cap. Kreuter went berserk and went after the guy, as did a handful of Dodgers players and coaches. They wanted that cap back—it was a respect thing. L.A. wound up winning the game, but no fewer than 16 players were suspended for their roles in the fracas.

Perhaps the granddaddy of all bizarre on-field incidents, however, was the one that occurred on September 19, 2002, during a game between the White Sox and the Royals at Comiskey Park. Royals first-base coach Tom Gamboa was standing in the coach's box during the ninth inning, when all of a sudden a bare-chested fan and his 15-year-old son charged onto the field, slammed Gamboa to the ground, and then started relentlessly punching him. It was straight out of a *Twilight Zone* episode.

Gamboa, who never saw it coming, was grateful that the nearby players from both teams were able to subdue the two attackers pretty quickly. A couple players even got in a few good shots on the duo before the security guards could show up. The pair of attackers even had a folded-up pocket knife with them but were thankfully unable to pull it out and use it.

The two claimed that they had words with the coach earlier in the game, but the bloodied coach vehemently denied it. The father and son were led off the field in handcuffs and later charged with aggravated battery. Gamboa, meanwhile, walked off the field to a standing ovation from the South Side crowd, where, incidentally, his Royals beat the Sox, 2–1.

Another part of the player/fan code is that players need to be courteous to the fans and give back to the less fortunate. One of the most obvious ways that a player can give back is by signing autographs. Fans of all ages love autographs and are thrilled to meet their heroes up close and personal. Sadly, though, some fans will break this code by actually paying kids to repeatedly go back in line to get autograph after autograph, just so they can be sold on eBay or at some other venue. Because of schemes like this, players have become reluctant to do signings.

Another problem that players run into is the issue of time. If a marquee player comes out of the dugout and signs autographs for an hour, huge lines of fans will swarm around him to get in on the action. He might be extremely generous of his time that day and sign 1,000 autographs. But, and this is a big but, that kid who waits patiently and winds up being number 1,001 in line and doesn't get to go home with an autograph—he is crushed. So, too, are his parents, grandparents, brothers, sisters, cousins, and neighbors. They will all bad-mouth that ballplayer who "ignored" that little kid.

What to do? That is a tough one. It's just like in business: a satisfied customer will tell one person, but an angry customer will tell 100. Such are the perils and drama of being a big-time baseball player. If the player is lucky and finds out about it, he will usually have a signed ball or jersey sent over to the kid to make amends.

This situation isn't a violation of the player/fan code, it is just life. Players have to do postgame interviews, get treatment for their injuries, go to team meetings, watch video, and prepare for the next game the following afternoon. Oh, and most of them want to be able to go home and spend some time with their wives and kids, too. Sure, they make a lot of money, but they are human and need to be cut some slack sometimes.

27

On Cheating and Deception

Baseball is a gentleman's game that has always been about winning and losing, but there is another side to the game that exists in its shadows. That side is about players doing whatever they can to gain an edge, both mental and physical, in order to achieve victory. Sometimes they will push the envelope with regard to just how far the rules can be bent without breaking. While some will cheat to gain that advantage, others will use the art of deception. There is a very fine line separating the two. One is illegal according to a rule book, and the other is only illegal if you get caught. The code prohibits cheating, but deception is another story altogether.

Let's take a look at cheating in other sports, beginning with the world's most popular sport: soccer. Soccer players pretend to be injured when they clearly are not, and for whatever the reason, it is an accepted part of the game. Players will dive at the slightest contact and then flop around on the ground, writhing in pain as if their legs have just gone through a wood chipper. The goal? To convince a referee that they are indeed hurt and to draw the elusive yellow card and a free penalty kick.

In the real world we call this faking, but in soccer it is revered as brilliant acting. In fact, there is actually a universal signal for a genuine injury. Apparently, if the player waves one arm over his head, he needs help. Otherwise, it is all for show. Or what about the wall that is set up by a group of players in a line to defend against free kicks? As soon as the referee turns around, the wall mysteriously moves from the mandated 10 yards away to only eight or nine. Some think of this as gamesmanship, while others just see it as straight-up cheating.

In football, a punter will pretend to get knocked on his ass when his leg is in the air in hopes of drawing a personal foul penalty. Veteran punters will even practice how long they can leave their leg hanging out there like live bait. If a defender who is trying to block the punt so much as touches the punter, he will spin and flip over in midair and then pretend that his leg just fell off. And let's not even begin to discuss New England's Bill Belichick and his spy-camera shenanigans.

In hockey, where fighting is legal, players police themselves. There are no facemasks in professional hockey because at that level, the players have to be held accountable for their actions. If a player shows up another player, disrespects him, or takes liberties with his teammate, he will get the crap beaten out of him. That is how the hockey code works. Perhaps the most egregious penalty in hockey, other than whacking a guy over the head with a stick, is diving. The referees hate divers because they feel like they are trying to show them up. Divers in hockey are treated like the lowest of the low, and they usually don't last very long.

In basketball, players will act to get calls from the referees. When a defender is trying to draw a charge, he will fall back at the slightest contact like he was shot in the stomach by a cannon. And the same is true for players on offense trying to set up the three-point play by acting like they were brutally attacked while being fouled. If the referee calls it, then it was a success. If not, better luck next time. There is a human element to refereeing, and players in all sports will always try to push that to the limit—cheating is only cheating if you get caught.

Certain sports have eliminated the need for hands-on referees altogether, such as track and field and swimming, where the fastest man or woman wins. Other sports, such as golf and tennis, have adopted a culture based on honesty, integrity, and honorability. The players follow the rules in those sports, even to their own detriment. The athletes who play these sports value good sportsmanship as much as they value winning.

In tennis, the players can override the umpire and give calls back, even if that means they will lose the match. Such was the case in 2005 when Fernando Verdasco double-faulted on match point against Andy Roddick during the Italian Masters. Roddick, who would have won the match, overruled the call, however, insisting that it was in. The ruling was reversed and Verdasco came back to win the match.

On the links, golfers will actually disqualify themselves if they knowingly break the rules. And in golf, there are a boatload of rules to memorize. Several high-profile golfers have forfeited literally millions of dollars due to their own miscalculations or misinterpretations of the rules. Even if nobody saw them do something, like accidentally ground their club in a hazard, they will still confess and penalize themselves in order to make things right. You have to respect that.

Hale Irwin once blew the British Open because he whiffed while attempting to make a putt. He had to penalize himself even though nobody saw it besides himself. Roberto De Vicenzo won the World Series of golf—the Masters—but then signed an incorrect scorecard, and the win was taken away. Greg Norman disqualified himself from the Australian Open for taking an illegal drop. Greg Chalmers even willingly returned a check just shy of a hundred grand after realizing that he had violated the rule against "giving advice to a playing partner." Lastly, Denis Watson once lost a U.S. Open title because he waited a few seconds too long for a putt to drop. When he learned of the rule, he took the DQ like a man.

While cheating is mitigated in most sports (soccer and basketball have fouls, and football and hockey have penalties), the players get away with whatever they can. Whether it is a power forward on the hardwood pretending to get blown over on a charge, an offensive lineman getting away with a hold, a catcher trying to frame a pitch for the umpire, or a midfielder taking a dive in soccer, the players will take any call a referee will give them, legal or not. That is just the way it is in team sports.

Could any of us imagine what these other sports would be like if they were left to police themselves like they do in golf? In baseball, what if we did away with the umps? How long before utter chaos broke out if each batter, or pitcher, was responsible for calling his own balls and strikes?

Baseball is not without its share of shady plays, though. What about phantom tags at second base? Or what about a pitcher who stands a few inches in front of the rubber to get a little advantage? What about spiking a second baseman? How about beaning a guy in the head, for goodness sakes! Does a trapped catch in the outfield still count as an out if the ump says so? You bet it does.

These issues, for whatever the reason, have been deemed acceptable. Now let's take a look at some of the ways in which players have used cheating and deception to get ahead in other ways over the years.

Corked Bats

One way a hitter can gain an advantage is by corking his bat. It is illegal, but it can be extremely effective. Bat speed is the name of the game when it comes to hitting, and every ounce makes a huge difference. It might be the difference between a ball being hit over the left-field fence or the same ball being caught by the left fielder. It can also make the difference between being a major leaguer and a minor leaguer.

Hitters are bigger, stronger, and faster today than they have ever been, and every nanosecond longer that they can wait before committing to swinging the bat will result in better contact with the ball. The pitchers are faster than ever, too, which is all the more reason to be able to get the barrel of the bat through the strike zone as quickly as possible. A corked bat will allow a hitter to achieve that objective because it will make his bat lighter.

To cork a bat, one must drill down into the barrel and then replace the wood with something lighter, such as rubber balls, epoxy, or cork. The top of the bat must then be plugged back up and sanded smooth so there is no visible trace of the hole left behind. From there, the batter must hope that he doesn't get caught, because he will get fined and suspended.

Several high-profile batters have been caught using doctored bats over the years, including Sammy Sosa, Wilton Guerrero, and Howard Johnson, among others. On September 7, 1974, Yankees third baseman Graig Nettles came up to bat against the Detroit Tigers and hit a broken-bat single that sent six SuperBalls bouncing all over the infield.

Another SuperBaller was Royals All-Star outfielder Amos Otis, who openly admitted to corking after retiring. "I had enough cork and SuperBalls in there to blow away anything," he said. "I had a very close friend who made the bats for me. He'd drill a hole down the barrel and stuff some SuperBalls and cork in it. Then he put some sawdust back into the hole, sandpapered it down, and added a little pine tar over the top of it. The bat looked brand-new."

Tigers outfielder Norm Cash admitted to using a corked bat during the 1961 season, in which he led the AL in batting with a .361 average.

After retiring, he even demonstrated for *Sports Illustrated* how he did it by drilling an eight-inch hole into the bat's barrel and then filling it with cork, sawdust, and glue.

Perhaps the most infamous bat-corking incident took place in 1994, when an umpire suspected that Cleveland slugger Albert Belle was using a doctored bat. So he confiscated Belle's bat and locked it in his dressing room for a thorough inspection after the game. While the game continued, knowing that Belle was guilty, Indians pitcher Jason Grimsley figured he would help out his teammate by replacing the confiscated bat with a clean one. He crawled through a ceiling duct and snuck into the umpire's dressing room.

There, he pulled the old switcheroo, leaving one belonging to teammate Paul Sorrento in its place. After the game, it took the umpires about 30 seconds to figure out that the bats had been switched. It turned out that the replacement bat had Sorrento's name engraved on it, which was their first clue as to whose bat it really was. Belle's bat was later found. When they sawed it in half and saw the cork in it, he was busted and suspended for 10 games.

Boning or Grooving a Bat

Boning is when a player rubs the surface of a bat with a hard object (players actually used to use bones) in order to compress the outer layer of wood, thus making it more rigid and stiff. Grooving, meanwhile, is when a player carves indentations, or grooves, along the grain of the bat with the hope of putting backspin on the ball when making contact. The spin will, in theory, keep the ball in flight longer and thus make it go farther. Both of these practices have been around for eons and aren't necessarily illegal if done in moderation. If the bat is completely flat on one side, or if there are huge grooves on one side of the bat, then the hitter will get busted and be called out.

Pine-Tarring a Bat

Pine tar is a sticky, dark brown substance that players apply to their bat handles and batting gloves in order to get a better grip on the bat. Some players will also smear it all over their batting helmets, so that they can readily get more if they need some while they are up to bat. Pine tar is legal to use on the handle of the bat but illegal to use on the barrel, with the theory being that the bat will grip the ball and give it backspin, similar to grooving.

Perhaps the name that is most associated with pine tar is Royals Hall of Famer George Brett. The notorious "Pine Tar Incident" took place on July 24, 1983, during a game between Kansas City and New York at Yankee Stadium. In the top of the ninth inning, Brett came up and hit a thrilling two-run homer to put his team up 5–4. After Brett rounded the bases, Yankees manager Billy Martin calmly walked out of the dugout and challenged an obscure rule in the books that states that the pine tar on a bat could extend no farther than 18 inches from the bottom of the handle. The bat was measured, and when it was determined that the pine tar indeed extended up to 24 inches, the umpire ruled that Brett was out and the two runs didn't count. Brett then went ballistic and flew out of the dugout to protest the call, at which time he was immediately ejected. The Royals later successfully protested the game, which meant the game had to be resumed later that season, where they hung on to win.

Ball Scuffing

Scuffing balls has been around since the game's dark ages. Pitchers would somehow scuff or cut the ball on a sharp or rough surface with the intent of making the ball move wildly or behave erratically. Scuffing is illegal and is rarely if ever seen in today's game. Back in the day, though, it was all the rage. Legendary manager Leo Durocher used to file the corner of his belt buckle so that he could scuff balls on it for his pitchers. Former Yankees pitcher Whitey Ford later admitted that his catcher, Elston Howard, did the same thing by rubbing the ball against the filed edge of his protective shin guard. The umpires didn't change the balls as much back then as they do today, so scuffing was easier to hide.

Perhaps the most humorous scuffing incident of the modern era came on September 30, 1980, when Mariners pitcher Rick Honeycutt received a 10-day suspension when the umpire discovered a sharp tack taped to his finger. Royals outfielder Willie Wilson spotted the tack while on third base and alerted the authorities. When the umps came out to investigate, they not only found the smoking gun, but they also noticed a cut on Honeycutt's forehead. Turns out he forgot it was there, and when he went to wipe off the sweat from his face he nearly blinded himself.

Sandpaper is also a popular tool for scuffing. And while it is much easier to hide, there have been more than a handful of players who have gotten busted with it. In 1978 Don Sutton was suspended for scuffing and defacing a ball; in 1987 Phillies pitcher Kevin Gross got caught with sandpaper in his glove and was ejected; and in 1999 Tigers pitcher Brian Moehler got a 10-game suspension after the umpire found a small piece of sandpaper glued to the thumb of his glove. Moehler said it was dirt, not sandpaper, but the suspension stayed the same. Afterward, Tigers manager Larry Parrish issued a statement: "There's not a pitching staff in baseball that doesn't have a guy who defaces the ball. If the umpires want to check things like that, I think half to three-quarters of the league would be suspended."

Another classic incident occurred on August 3, 1987, when Twins knuckleballer Joe Niekro got busted on the mound with an emery board. Niekro, who also got caught with a small piece of sandpaper, was trying to look inconspicuous for the umps when it accidentally flew out of his pocket. Busted!

Spitballs

Spitballs have had a long and hallowed place in baseball history. First made legal by the newly created American League back in 1903, pitchers used saliva, mud, and tobacco juice, among other slimy substances, to grease up the balls in order to get them to perform tricks in midair. Pitchers were able to use spitters in two ways. The first was by applying a lubricant to one side of the ball, which would reduce the air friction on that side, thus making the ball break that way when thrown. The other way was for the pitcher to grip the ball with his fingertip right on the lubricated spot. Then when he threw it like a fastball, the ball would slip off his finger and act like a knuckleball, sinking late and with very little spin. Either way, the hitters were left clueless.

Eventually, in 1920 the pitch was made illegal. Due to the tragic beanball death of Cleveland Indians shortstop Ray Chapman, baseball decided to clean up its act, literally. You see, at the time, teams would use the same old ball over and over again, regardless of how dirty it got. One of the factors in Chapman's death was that he couldn't see the dark brown ball coming at his head. So the league mandated that new, clean white balls be used in games. The filthy spitball was no longer welcome.

Another factor that ultimately led to the demise of the spitter was hygiene. Whenever a spitball pitcher took to the mound, by the end of the game the ball would be a slippery mess, full of phlegm and snot. The infielders would cringe when they had to field a ground ball and throw it to first base. Nobody wanted to touch that thing.

There was also the whole unsanitary angle to deal with. If a pitcher was sick, he could infect his entire team. Finally, when a deadly worldwide flu pandemic started heading across the pond following the end of the first World War, the powers that be said enough was enough. With that, restrictions were put into place regarding how many spitball pitchers a team could have. They started with two per squad and then announced that a total of 17 spitballers would be grandfathered into the new era, but for everyone else the pitch would be deemed illegal.

While the spitballers were officially put on ice, every now and then one would pop up. In 1944, St. Louis Browns pitcher Nels Potter became the first player to be suspended for throwing a spitball, ignoring the ump's warning against wetting his fingers before going to the rosin bag. There would be many others who would dabble with the pitch, but none who would be able to master it without getting caught.

That all changed in the early 1960s when a pitcher by the name of Gaylord Perry came onto the scene. Perry did more to resurrect the spitter than perhaps anybody in the modern era. Perry was a junk-baller who would do whatever he could to get guys out. He wasn't a power pitcher by any stretch, but he was extremely smart and could think his way through a ballgame with the best of them.

As soon as the players suspected he was throwing spitters, they would try to bust him. He was elusive, though, and always stayed one step ahead of them. With rules now in place prohibiting pitchers from putting their fingers in their mouths while they were on the mound, Perry found other ways to slime the ball. He would smear Vaseline under the bill of his hat, on his jersey, or even on the tongue of his shoes, and then sneak a dab every now and then.

Even if he didn't throw the spitter, teams still had to account for it. He might throw one early in a game with the hopes of that guy running back to the dugout to tell his teammates. Then they would all be watching for it and worrying about it. It was a psychological battle that he played with them and usually won. He would even pretend to go to his mouth or make other suspicious-looking moves out on the mound, just to keep them guessing.

Perry was always looking for an angle, and one time came up with what was later dubbed the "puff-pitch." Perry would fill up his hand with powdery rosin from the rosin bag and then throw it when he released a pitch, making it look like an explosion went off. The batters, unable to pick up the ball out of his hand, would get completely confused and distracted by the cloud of white rosin dust, which blended with the color of the ball.

Nowadays, the substance of choice for pitchers is pine tar. With the penalties too steep for using Vaseline or spit, pitchers will try to get away with a legal substance that is already smeared all over the place throughout the infield. Pitchers in the National League, who have to hit, have a much easier time getting away with this because they can smear pine tar on their jersey and then play dumb when a smidge winds up on a ball later in the game.

In 1988 Dodgers reliever Jay Howell got busted with pine tar on his glove during the National League Championship Series and was suspended for three games. St. Louis Cardinals reliever Julian Tavarez was ejected for having pine tar on his hat back in 2004, and Angels reliever Brendan Donnelly got tossed for the very same offense the next season. Kenny Rogers got busted in Game 2 of the 2006 World Series for having a dab on his pitching hand. Rogers got off the easiest, though, and was asked to simply wash his hands.

The Hidden-Ball Trick

The old hidden-ball trick is still alive and well, believe it or not. In fact, it usually rears its ugly head once every couple of seasons or so. It is one of those little gray areas to the code. It isn't technically cheating, but it is not a very respectable tactic to employ on your opponents. It is legal, though, and was even once successfully executed in the 1907 World Series by the Detroit Tigers.

The trick requires a base runner who isn't paying attention. It begins when an infielder will have a meeting with the pitcher out on the mound, at which point he will casually take the ball and hide it in his glove. The pitcher will then step off the mound and pretend to be warming up or adjusting his equipment. All the while, he is waiting patiently for the base runner to take a lead off the base. As soon as he does, the infielder will tag him for a free, cheap out.

The base runner immediately feels duped as tens of thousands of fans laugh at his expense. And it just gets worse from there, as every local and national sports show will air it that night, over and over again for all to see. Every season in the big leagues at least a couple of teams will try to use it, but rarely if ever does it work.

28

On the Home-Field Advantage

The concept of home-field advantage has meant many things to many different teams over the years. And while scores of players have perfected the art of deception, so, too, have a whole host of groundskeepers and behind-the-scenes stadium workers, who have cooked up some pretty outlandish schemes in years past in order to help their teams win. Some refer to this as gamesmanship; others just call it cheating. You be the judge.

Let's start in Chicago, where in 1988 and after 44 years of service (1940–83), longtime groundskeeper Gene Bossard was acknowledged in a *Sun-Times* obituary for all of his on-the-field contributions to the White Sox: "The Comiskey Park infield once was known as 'Bossard's Swamp' because he kept it watered down for sinkerball pitchers Dick Donovan, Tommy John, and Joel Horlen. He also soaked the area around first base when opposing base stealers came to town, and he kept the base lines raised so that Nellie Fox's bunts stayed fair."

He wasn't alone. There was a groundskeeper in San Francisco who made the topsoil around first and second base heavy and wet by mixing it with peat moss and sand. That way, when the rival Dodgers came to town and their speedy base stealer Maury Wills tried to run on them, it would be like wading through quicksand.

Watering base paths is nothing new in baseball. Nor is doctoring base lines, altering batter's boxes, contouring the mound, or even moving portable fences in and out from the outfield. That's right, according to

Bossard's grandson, when Bossard was the groundskeeper for Cleveland back in the 1920s, he would move the outfield fences back a good 15 feet when opposing teams came to bat, and then move them back up when the Indians were up. Other teams would do the same over the years, too, including Milwaukee's minor league team back in the '40s, which installed a motorized fence in the right-field corner of Borchardt Field that could be moved in and out between innings.

Teams have long been known to creatively groom their fields. Apparently, Bossard would also slope the dirt on the edge of the baselines at Comiskey Park so when guys like Nellie Fox and Luis Aparicio would lay down a bunt, the ball would stay fair instead of rolling foul. A team might also let the infield grass grow longer if they are facing a team that bunts a lot. Similarly, if the home team has a pitcher going who forces a lot of ground balls, the taller grass will slow the balls down and give the infielders more time to get them out.

There were the little things, too. Take, for example, how some teams would make opposing teams feel pretty unwelcome at their ballparks. From turning off the hot water to providing dim, single light bulbs in the dugouts and bullpens, or even painting their visiting locker rooms soft pink (to calm them down). One that might take the cake, though, is how the Metrodome staff in Minneapolis allegedly turned its powerful air conditioning fans on or off depending on whether the home team Twins were up to bat.

And how about teams doctoring balls by freezing them, baking them, or even storing them for long periods of time in a humidifier so that they will become waterlogged and weigh more? A team that didn't hit many home runs would love balls like that because they would slow down their opposition and give them a fighting chance. Either way, teams have proven over the years that they will try just about anything to give themselves an advantage, fair or otherwise.

29

Signs, Signs, Everywhere a Sign...

One of the most fascinating aspects of the code deals with the issue of signs. Without them, the game would not be able to exist and would fall into utter chaos. There are ethical and unethical ways of decoding signs, and they are probably more a part of the game than many people may realize. There is the issue of how managers and coaches will call in or convey signs to their players, and then there is the issue of sign stealing and sign decoding. Signs have been around since the very beginning of the game, and with them came sign stealers. Teams need to communicate amongst themselves, and conversely, teams want to know what the other team is up to as well. It is constant and never-ending. Many casual fans would be shocked to discover how many hidden lines of communication are going on at any one time during a ballgame.

Let's start on defense. First, the manager and the bench coaches will signal to certain players as to where they want them to position themselves. They put on a shift or move a fielder up or back based on which batter is up and which pitch may be coming. The manager may want to call in pitches to his catcher, who will in turn relay those to the pitcher.

From there, the pitcher and catcher will communicate via signs in order to let each other know what the next pitch is going to be. The catcher will drop down finger signs between his legs while he is squatted down into position. If the pitcher doesn't want the pitch that the catcher has called for, he will shake it off and call for another until he is content.

Pitcher Jack Morris on Catchers
Giving Up the Location of a Pitch

"Good hitters can sense where the pitch is coming when a catcher sets up too early. That was always tough for me because I liked my catcher to set up and show me a big target and then just stay there. I wanted him to stay still. A lot of catchers move around back there late in your delivery, and it can be distracting. I hated that. I wasn't a quarterback, I was a pitcher. I didn't need to throw to a moving target. If it tipped off where I was coming, inside or out, so be it. I didn't really care, to tell you the truth. The guy still had to hit the damn ball, and I was up for the challenge."

They will have a predetermined set of signals for that specific game and may have to deviate from them if they feel that their signs are being stolen by the opposition. If so, then they will have to change up their calls before each inning to make sure that they are staying a step ahead of their opponents. The bottom line here is that the catcher needs to know what pitch is coming so that he can physically prepare himself for it. Otherwise, if he gets a nasty slider when he is expecting a fastball, he could miss it and potentially let a runner come in to score.

Once the decision has been made as to which pitch is going to be thrown and the sign has been confirmed, then other players on the team will adjust accordingly. Infielders may signal to each other regarding positional shifts, or in the case of the shortstop and second baseman in a double-play situation, which man will cover the bag. All of those things will depend on what pitch is coming in that particular situation. Different situations will require different sets of signals.

On offense, a team will have players positioned in the dugout, as well as a man in the batter's box and the on-deck circle. In addition, the manager and bench coaches will be in constant eye contact with the first- and third-base coaches, who are positioned along their respective base lines. The manager will send signals to his coaches, who will then in turn recode that information and signal it to the players. These coaches will then be giving signs to the hitters and base runners regarding bunting, stealing, squeezing, and executing hit-and-runs.

Other signs may come from a runner on second base, who can see the signs between the pitcher and catcher as well as the catcher's positioning. He will then try to relay a coded signal to the hitter as to what sign is coming and as to whether the catcher is set up on his inside or outside. Meanwhile, the hitter is trying to interpret the signs from the pitcher to the catcher in hopes of picking up a tip-off as to which pitch is coming.

Now for the decoding part. While this veritable symphony of signage is going on, players on both teams will be trying to decode all of these signals. Players are looking and listening for any little clue that might tip them off as to what pitch might be coming, what call the manager is signaling in, or whether or not the runner at first base has gotten the green light to steal. And, by the way, the other team may be sending in dummy signs—decoys—in order to see if their signals have been stolen. Fall for that and you are guaranteed that they will all be immediately changed, putting you back to square one.

There are head games going on at all times, with the objective being to either crack the other team's code or to somehow break their concentration in the process. Teams know that they have to protect their signs at all costs. They are the lifeline of a team's ability to communicate in the midst of 40,000 screaming fans in an enormous stadium.

A hitter who knows what the next pitch is going to be has a huge advantage. It is like looking into a crystal ball. He can dig in for a fastball or lay back for an off-speed curveball. If he knows the catcher's location, inside or outside, he can then adjust for where the pitch will be coming from. A catcher who knows that the runner on first base is going to steal can call for a pitchout and get an easy out.

It has been estimated that throughout the course of a game there might be upwards of several hundred signs and signals exchanged between the players and coaching staff. Factor in the umpires and all of their calls, too, and that number could be north of a thousand. While most fans are bored during the lag time between pitches, that is when the designated decoders are busiest, watching intently as to what the opposition is or isn't doing.

To make all of this just a little bit more exciting, the element of danger is also a part of it, too. The unwritten rules regarding sign-stealing are universally understood: you do it at your own risk. If the opposing team knows that you have cracked their code and are relaying in signs, then you are going down. If not you, then your teammate is going down. The code says so.

How Managers and Coaches Call In Signs

At the top of every organization, company, or team, there is a leader, a boss, a head honcho. In baseball, that guy is the manager. The manager's job, among other things, is to orchestrate and implement the strategy that he feels will best help his team win ballgames. It is his job to either call in the signals or to delegate that responsibility to one of his coaches. Like a military commander, the manager must be able to communicate with all of his field generals, who in turn will be able to relay that top-secret information to the soldiers out on the front lines.

Understanding just how the signs are relayed in to the players on the field is an adventure in itself. Managers and coaches will go to extraordinary measures in order to get their signs in to the appropriate people without them being stolen in the process. When on offense, the manager will usually call in signs to his third-base coach, who will then relay those signs to the hitters and base runners. From there, the third-base coach will rattle through a series of signals to notify them of their instructions. They will in turn watch closely and then respond with another signal to confirm the directives.

Some coaches will go through a series of long, intricate gyrations in order to communicate with their players. A coach might touch his nose, rub his belly, adjust his hat, remove his hat, slide his left or right hand down his left or right arm or leg, sneeze, clap, tie his shoe, cross his arms, touch his knee, yawn, tug at his sleeve, stretch, kick some dirt, or even shout something to the hitter. And when he speaks, each word can mean something in code, too.

The hitter may feel like a CIA agent just trying to keep up, but he needs to be on board and pay attention, or he will be letting his team down in a big way. If he misses that sign, he may cost his team an out or a run, which might be the difference between a win and a loss in a tight game. The manager can't get too complicated, either, otherwise the hitters might get confused and start thinking too much. That is when bad things can happen. Some guys can handle complex systems, while others simply cannot. There is an old adage that holds true in this situation: "A manager's signs are limited by his dumbest player."

Sometimes hitters will have to step out of the batter's box and signal to the third-base coach that they don't understand the sign. He may touch the top of his helmet while looking over to him, which will then alert the third-base coach to run through the signs all over again. If a hitter steps out at the last second, he is really going to piss off the pitcher, so he won't want to do that too often. But when he does, rest assured that he is going back to the well to get a new sign. If a hit-and-run is on and he misses it, he is going to be fined and possibly benched. So he will try to make it look inconspicuous by hitting his cleats with his bat, rubbing his hands together, readjusting his batting gloves, or re-gripping his bat. All the while he will be studying his coach to make sure he gets the sign right this time. Once he does, he will confirm it with another touch of the top of his helmet.

Believe it or not, fully 99 percent of the signs are decoys, or "dekes," and are intended merely to confuse and frustrate the other team's players and coaches who are watching intently with the hopes of cracking their opposition's code. The one sign that is "hot," however, is embedded in there somewhere. Where? That's the secret. Mixed in with all of that encrypted symbolism is an indicator, which is then followed by the real sign. They are only active if they are run on a certain sequence, which is critical to the overall success of the play.

There have been some pretty creative ways that managers and coaches have been able to convey their signs over the years. Legendary manager Connie Mack was never too far from his trusty scorecard, which was

Pitcher Mike Marshall on Changing Up His Signs

"My philosophy on this was simple. I always figured that if a guy could pick up your signs, then that was just good baseball. If you were dumb enough to have signs that they could pick up, then you deserved to have them stolen. For me, I never really had that problem because I had my own sign system which was pretty tough to crack. My catcher would give me the sign and then come set. I would then add or subtract to the pitch that I was going to throw. Maybe I would rub the ball above or below my belt as I was getting set. Or maybe I would nod my head one way or the other, or open or close my eyes, or stomp my foot or pat my glove. Whatever the sign was, we would add or subtract to whatever was shown by the catcher. The runner on second base will signal to the hitter what pitch he thinks is coming, but little does he know I was about to change it when I started my delivery. It was a good system that was nearly foolproof. I changed them up so late in the count that there was no way anybody could adjust."

usually in his hand throughout each game. While many opposing players speculated that the card was the key to cracking his sign strategy, the fact is it was nothing more than a clever ruse. In reality, the signs would be sent in via a rookie in the dugout who was riding the pine by the water cooler. Nobody ever caught on.

According to Paul Dickson's outstanding book *The Hidden Language of Baseball,* Arizona State coach Bobby Winkles sent in signals by having certain players stand up in the dugout. If their last name started with the letter "B," it meant that the batter should bunt; if it started with the letter "S," it meant he should steal; and if it started with the letter "H," it meant he should hit and run. All of the other signs he flashed were decoys.

Manager Tony La Russa once signaled in a play by cleaning out the dirt from his spikes with a popsicle stick. Manager Don Zimmer, upon being ejected from a minor league game, actually climbed a light pole and flashed his signs from up there. And similarly, one time a minor league manager, after being ejected from a game, returned to the field dressed as the team mascot so he could continue to send in the signs. Manager

Pitcher Frank Viola on Protecting Your Signs

"If you saw a guy trying to steal your signs, you had to send him a message—absolutely. You can't tolerate it or you won't be pitching for very long at this level. If I was on the mound and had a guy on second base who I suspected of relaying signs back in, I would just step off the rubber and look at him. I might tell him in no uncertain terms that he was going to get it. Maybe I would tell him that the next time he was up that he was going to get one in the ribs. He would knock it off in a hurry. And the next time he was up, he would be back in the batter's box, just in case I followed through on my threat. It was a scare tactic that worked quite well.

"I remember one time when I was with Minnesota and we were playing Texas. Rangers third baseman Steve Buechele was on second base and just flagrantly giving the signs to the hitter. He had a clear view of Twins catcher Brian Harper and was able to relay back to his hitter what was coming. Well, the hitter got a base hit, and Buechele rounded third base to come in and score. Only when he got to home plate, Harper elbowed him right across the face. It was awesome. A brawl ensued from there, but it was worth it. We had to send them a message that if they were going to do those things, especially that flagrantly, then we were not about to be shown up."

Preston Gomez had a foolproof system: he actually had different signs for every single player on the team.

Billy Martin once called in plays by phone from his hospital bed while recovering from a punctured lung. Now *that's* dedication. Martin hated to lose and would do anything and everything in his power to get an edge. Once, tired of getting his signs stolen, he apparently employed a covert wireless microphone get-up to communicate with his coaches, but he canned it after the static drove him crazy.

How Pitchers and Catchers Communicate Covertly

While the signals from the manager and third base coach are critical, they pale in comparison to the importance of the signage system used by the pitcher and catcher. A team might steal or bunt just a few times, if at all, during a game. But the catcher will call upwards of 100 to 200 pitches per contest. Each sign must be painstakingly thought through and analyzed before being given the green light.

Here is how it works: the catcher will usually call a game, meaning he will put down predetermined signs between his legs while he is crouching, and signal to his pitcher as to what pitch he feels should be thrown in that particular situation. The pitcher will usually just accept that sign, but occasionally he will shake it off by nodding no, in which case he will ask for another pitch selection.

Once referred to as "wig-wagging" because of the catcher wagging his fingers, the act of pitchers and catchers using signs to call pitches has been around for about 150 years. And believe it or not, not a whole lot has changed in that time period regarding their deceptive codes. In fact, Paul Revere's famous line "One if by land; two if by sea" is still the norm for the fastball and curve. Nowadays, however, three might be the change-up, four could be the split-fingered fastball, and five might be the knuckleball.

There have been a whole host of different signage systems used over the years, with each having its own varying degree of success. In order to stay a step ahead of any would-be opposing sign stealers, the battery will agree on a numbering system before the start of each game. One finger could still be the fastball, but it might be the "third sign," or the third overall sign that the catcher flashes or "pumps." The catcher might flash five signs in a sequence, but the third one will be the correct one. Or it could be the "second sign," or the "last sign," depending on what they agree on prior to each inning. It also might be as easy as flashing odds or evens—the sky is the limit.

The catcher might have an indicator as well, meaning he will flash through all of his signs, but the hot sign might be indicated by the catcher touching his mask or adjusting his athletic supporter. Everything else might be a decoy. Or he could use that indicator sign, which might be the number three, and then the hot sign will be whatever follows number three. Or, better yet, they might have an addition system whereupon they will go with the first sign, but then add that number to whatever inning it is for a new number, which might mean something completely different.

Some pitchers will choose to call their own signals. One way they might do that would be to look flustered out on the mound by continually shaking off the catcher's signs. But the hidden code is that the number of shake-offs he is giving is actually the sign he wants to use. Four shakes? That means slider. Again, it is a never-ending game of deception, and the possibilities are limitless.

The bottom line, however, is that the pitcher and catcher must have a system which is undetectable as well as appropriately complex. The more difficult it is for the pitcher to remember all of the signs, the more likely he will either get flustered and lose his concentration or simply lose track of what is what. It must also be a pretty quick system, too, because the longer it takes for the battery to agree on a signal, the easier it will be for the opposition to figure it out and steal the sign and then relay that information over to the hitter.

How the Runner on Second Base Steals Signs and Relays Them to the Hitter

Let's suppose there is a runner on second base. It is his job to do anything he can in order to help his teammate in the batter's box. It is universally accepted by all teams that because of the base runner's unique vantage point, he will be able to relay at least some information to his hitter, such as the catcher's location. Location can help determine the pitch type, and in some instances it is nearly as good as knowing what the sign was. So to counter this, the catcher will wait to set up his position behind the plate until the last possible moment, making it harder for the base runner and hitter to communicate.

Pitcher Joe Nathan on Protecting Your Signs

"We cover our mouths out there now, just in case. A lot of the things we say are pretty universal for what we do and can be easily interpreted by people who understand what we are doing out there. I mean, if my catcher walks out and I say 'second sign' or 'last sign,' then that would be pretty easy to pick up. The TV cameras are everywhere now, too. They zoom in on us so tight, it is amazing. So if we are switching signs or something, we have to make sure that the opposition can't interpret them, either from the dugout or by one of their scouts watching the game on TV."

This creates a problem, though. You see, the catcher wants to set up early and give his pitcher an easy target to throw to. He knows that he needs to hold up his glove in the exact position that he wants the ball and then stay as still as possible. If he is bouncing around or jumping into position at the last second, then the pitcher will have a much harder time locating the target. In addition, the catcher doesn't want to impede the umpire's view either. If he gets in his way and hinders his angle to see the ball, he may be less likely to get a strike call.

As for the base runner, there are many tricks as to how to effectively relay signs over to the hitter. For instance, if he wants to let his hitter know the location of the pitch based on where he sees the catcher setting up, he can put his hands on his hips to indicate whether the catcher is on the inside or outside. Or he might let his right arm extend down his side to indicate the right side, and vice versa.

Now if the runner has indeed figured out the sign, he can then relay that, too. He might have a signal to let the hitter know this, such as adjusting his helmet. From there, he might place his hands on his waist to indicate a fastball or put them on his knees for a curve. He may lead off with his right foot first to indicate an off-speed pitch or shuffle them for a fastball. In addition to all of that, he may yell out words of encouragement that will have hidden meaning. For instance, if he yells out the batter's first name, that might mean fastball, whereas his last name might indicate that the curve was coming.

While it is understood that this is going to transpire, there is an unwritten rule that says you don't do it overtly and rub it in. You need to be subtle about it and not show anybody up, or somebody is going to get drilled. Pitchers resent base runners who make them look stupid and will be sure to let them know how they feel about what they are doing. That is the risk that the runner takes when he opts to send signals to his hitter. He may help out his hitter, but at the same time he risks getting that guy nailed, as well as getting nailed himself the next time he comes up to bat.

As for how the retaliation process works in this situation? Simple. Using a prearranged plan, the pitcher and catcher will float out a dummy signal for the runner on second that he will be sure to pick up. They will then call for an off-speed pitch that is low and away. Once they are certain that the runner has relayed this nugget of information to the hitter, they will then come back with a fastball up and in. The surprised hitter, who will have been cheating over to get what he thought was a fat, juicy curveball, will get it right in the ribs.

Case in point: in 1991 Cincinnati's "Nasty Boy" Norm Charlton suspected Dodgers catcher Mike Scioscia of stealing signs while on second and then relaying them to the hitter. So the next time Scioscia came up to bat, Charlton drilled him. Afterward, Charlton was blunt about his intentions, telling reporters why he did what he did and that he would do it again. Turns out that sometimes honesty isn't the best policy—for his comments, Norm was suspended for a week and got a fat fine to boot.

"I'd rather my infielders know them," said Charlton of his signs. "If the guy [running] on second base knows them, that's fine. If he wants to relay them to the guy hitting, there is an easy way to take care of that. One conversation with the catcher: you call for a slider away, I'll throw a fastball up and in. That pretty much cures the sign stealing."

Pitchers make the best of these situations, though, and will try to keep the opposition honest by changing up their signs as often as they can. Some hurlers simply don't want to risk having their signs stolen by a runner on second base peering over his shoulder. Such was the case back in 2005 when Cleveland reliever Bob Wickman intentionally balked the runner on second over to third so that he wouldn't be able to see the catcher's signs.

A good base runner can also help himself. Base runners who want to steal bases have a much better chance of not getting picked off if they can run on a breaking ball, which is slower and harder for the catcher to field cleanly. Every fraction of a second counts when you have to run 90 feet, and knowing which pitch is coming could make the difference between being safe and being thrown out.

One of the smartest base runners of all time was Rickey Henderson, who just happens to be the game's all-time steals leader. Henderson would study pitchers' tendencies throughout each game and figure out when they were going to throw off-speed pitches. He would also study the catcher and try to determine which signs he was laying down. Pitchers feared him while he was on first base, knowing that he was just waiting to take off and pounce, like a cheetah going after a gazelle. Once he had figured it out, that is when he would make them pay.

Some hitters simply don't want to know the signs, claiming it screws up their timing and hand-eye coordination. Others resist for ethical reasons. They want to just step up to the plate and react, without guessing or thinking too much. Reverse psychology can work, too. Back in the early '80s during a game between Montreal and San Diego, catcher Gary Carter started messing with Tony Gwynn about which pitches were coming. Gwynn had been doing extremely well against the Expos, so Carter, in an attempt to get into Gwynn's head, started to tell him which pitches were coming while he was in the batter's box. He would literally say, 'Okay, Tony, here comes a fastball,' and sure enough, there came a fastball. Well, it worked. Gwynn got really screwed up after that and couldn't hit a thing.

"Everything in baseball goes in cycles," recalled White Sox broadcaster Ken "Hawk" Harrelson of sign stealing back in the 1960s and early '70s. "When I played, we stole everything we could. We had guys giving signs from the on-deck circle, telling you where a catcher was setting up. When

Catcher Terry Steinbach on Changing Up His Signs

"The sky was the limit for changing signs—you could get as sophisticated as you wanted, to tell you the truth. But you have to make sure that your pitcher, second baseman, shortstop, and center fielder can follow along. Otherwise you are going to have problems out there. If I am calling for a fastball down and away, and they think a curveball is coming, then things can get real ugly in a hurry. They position themselves out there in the field based on what sign they think is coming, and if they are wrong and a hitter gets an extra-base hit based on that information, then that would be my fault for not making sure we were all on the same page."

we had a runner at second base, he'd give you either a closed hand or an open hand for a breaking ball or fastball. Anything we could do, we did. It was part of the game. Now they treat it like you've committed a mortal sin."

Peeking Back at the Catcher to Steal Signs Will Get You Drilled

When it comes to sign stealing, there is one practice that is simply not tolerated: peeking. The act of peeking entails a hitter standing in the batter's box and covertly peeking back to see where the catcher is setting up, or better yet, trying to pick up some of his signals. If the hitter is caught doing this, he will be lucky to get a warning. Most likely, though, he will get drilled and will be taught a very valuable lesson: there is no peeking in baseball.

Hitters will go through all sorts of gyrations as they are getting set in their stance. During that bizarre ritual, they may dip their head down and sneak a peek. It may be subtle, occurring when they are digging in their spikes to get better footing or maybe when they are adjusting their grip on the bat. They will go to great lengths to disguise their true intentions. One thing is for sure, though—wandering eyes will get you in trouble.

The newer wraparound sunglasses have given some hitters new ammunition in hiding their cheating ways. Experienced hitters will listen intently to hear where the catcher will set up behind them. Maybe it is hot and the catcher is tired, so he is dragging his feet. A veteran hitter will hear this and react accordingly. Or maybe the hitter can peer down and see the catcher's shadow, which can also be effective in seeing both his body location and the location of his mitt.

One thing is for sure, though—with all of the camera angles on the field, if a hitter peeks, there is a good chance that he will get caught.

Pitcher Rick Aguilera on Changing Up His Signs

"The system I used was called 'A, B, and E,' which meant that if I was ahead in the count, or (A), then it was the first sign the catcher put down; if I was behind in the count, or (B), then it was the second sign; or if the count was even (E), then it would be the third sign. This meant that every pitch count could change, which kept it pretty foolproof for me."

Pitcher Jim Perry on Changing Up His Signs

"When I had to send a message, my catcher would flash his thumb. If he pointed his thumb down, that meant to knock the guy down and drill him. If it was pointed up, that meant to throw it up and in and brush him back. And if he pointed it to his right, then that meant to throw over to first base if there was a runner over there."

Teams review the tape, and if they catch a guy peeking, they will retaliate sooner rather than later. As for retaliation in these instances, catchers who catch hitters in the act will pull the old "bait and switch," which usually works like a charm. He will very deliberately set up low and away early to make sure that the hitter can see him. The hitter will immediately suspect an off-speed pitch on the outside corner and will be cheating that way to drive the ball to the opposite field. Then, while the pitcher is in his windup, the catcher will quickly jump back inside, where the hitter will be met with a fastball thrown up and in. The results can be devastating.

In 1979 Kansas City outfielder Al Cowens got caught peeking and had his jaw shattered by White Sox pitcher Ed Farmer on the ensuing pitch. A similar situation occurred in 2001, when Mets outfielder Tsuyoshi Shinjo took a peek and got drilled by Cardinals pitcher Matt Morris. In 2002 Red Sox shortstop Nomar Garciaparra got drilled by Tampa Bay's Ryan Rupe in retaliation for stealing signs from second base that ultimately led to a Shea Hillenbrand grand slam.

"I remember [Orioles outfielder] Paul Blair was looking for a slider off Ken Tatum one time because he thought he had the sign," said Blair's former teammate Don Baylor. "It was a fastball inside, and it fractured Blair's cheekbone. Those are the things that can happen."

"If you thought somebody was stealing your signs, you changed them," said former Giants catcher Bob Brenly. "If they were still stealing them, you warned them. And if that didn't stop, somebody got hit in the helmet. You called for a fastball low and away and told the pitcher to throw it up and in, no matter what."

Former Cardinals and Mets first baseman Keith Hernandez had his own unique take on the topic and wrote about it in his book entitled *Pure Baseball*: "Is peeking cheating? Absolutely not. Poor sportsmanship? No

Coach Rick Stelmaszek on Decoding Signs

"Baseball is a game of percentages and tendencies. We are always trying to study those to learn as much as we can about each and every player. Baseball is also a lot like poker in that everybody has tells that he does, which, if you studied them enough, you would be able to figure out. For instance, some pitchers will make a certain facial expression when they are throwing an off-speed pitch. Or they might raise their hands or legs a little bit higher when they throw certain pitches. Good hitters can read those things and quickly determine what pitch is coming. There is a real game within the game. Managers are playing the game two innings ahead and are always thinking about every scenario that could play out. It is like a big chess game with so many moving pieces. There is so much stuff going on behind the scenes, most fans have no idea."

more than stealing signs or doctoring the ball. I consider all these tricks as part of the art and craft of playing baseball, not as cheating."

Other players, past and present, disagree. "It's like swimming in the water hole down by the creek," said pitcher Norm Charlton. "There's a sign that says 'SWIM AT YOUR OWN RISK.' It would be dangerous to stick up a sign out there on the pitcher's mound that says 'STEAL SIGNS AT YOUR OWN RISK,' but that's pretty much the way it is."

"Sign stealing has been around forever," said center fielder Torii Hunter. "It was way worse back in the day, though, because there weren't all the TV cameras picking up everything. Now the cameras are focused on guys' eyes, and they don't miss a thing. If you get caught up in the batter's box taking a peek back at the catcher, it is all over. You are going to get it. And deservedly so, because it's cheating. Sure, it's an unwritten rule, but it's a definite code violation. If you want to look back at where the catcher is setting up or try to see what his sign is to the pitcher, then you had better watch out.

"There have always been peekers, guys who would stand in the batter's box and then all of a sudden they would mysteriously get something in their eye so they would have to look back towards the catcher to fix it," said pitcher Jim Kaat. "Really, though, they were just trying to see where the catcher was setting up, inside or out. Some catchers could fool them, though, like Johnny Roseboro, who was great at leaning outside just far enough so that the batter couldn't help but see him in his peripheral vision. Once he was convinced that the batter was sure the ball was coming outside, he would jump back inside. It really messed with the hitter's timing and kept him honest."

"When a guy was at bat and while he was digging in took a peek back to look at where the catcher was setting up, then that would really piss me off," said pitcher Frank Viola. "As far as retaliation, I would probably warn him or have my catcher threaten him first. Then, if he did it again, he was getting drilled. No question."

"[Peeking] really bothered me," said pitcher Tommy John. "So if I saw that happening, I would just make sure that the batter saw the sign for a curveball away as the next pitch. Then I would come in on him about neck high with a fastball. They would get the message pretty quickly."

"I have seen guys try all sorts of things to peek back," said pitcher Kevin Tapani. "I remember a guy once tried to act like he was swatting at a mosquito while he was up to bat at the Metrodome. I mean, come on, we are in a domed stadium, do you really think I am going to fall for that? I can't remember, but I think I drilled him for trying to pull that one past me.

"The worst was at Wrigley Field in Chicago. There were long shadows that would appear late in games, so it was really important for the catcher to set up late and to also be light on his feet. Otherwise guys could see pretty well where he was at. Plus, at Wrigley you always had day games, so guys would wear the wraparound Oakley sunglasses, which hid their eyes pretty good. You really had to watch them closely to make sure they weren't peeking back."

Perhaps former catcher Dave Valle said it best: "Peeking is just too blatant. That's when you want to tell a guy, 'Hey, you're doing something that could be dangerous to your own health.'"

On Decoding Signs

There is an old saying in baseball that still rings true today: "If you're not stealing, you're not trying." For as long as there have been signs, there have been sign stealers. With so many signs coming and going throughout the course of a ball game, it is no wonder that there are certain players and coaches who are extremely adept in interpreting and decoding them all.

"I don't understand how somebody gets upset about it," said manager Buck Showalter of sign stealing. "It's not shame on them for stealing; it's shame on you for allowing it to happen."

There are two types of sign stealers in the game: the ethical and the unethical. One is considered a hard-working, well-respected intellectual. The other, who uses electronic devices or optical assistance to steal signs, is considered a big fat cheater. Sound harsh? Welcome to the world of baseball in the 21st century.

Let's start with the ethical. Ethical sign stealers are a part of the established fabric of the game. They are players and coaches who spend their time wisely while in the dugout or bullpen, studying the tendencies of opposing players and managers. To them, sign stealing is an art. They will look for patterns, or tip-offs, which are also referred to as "poker tells."

Good sign stealers are revered in the game as essential components to the overall success of a team. They will crack codes and gather information that can be used to help their team win ballgames. Players are creatures of habit and tend to follow conscious and unconscious routines. Finding them is the key to the puzzle.

If a code breaker is studying a pitcher, he will try to figure out what he does differently on a curveball versus a fastball. If it is a manager he is after, he will try to figure out what the indicator and hot signals are for the steal or bunt signs. If it is a base stealer, he will watch him to see what he does differently on the pitches he chooses to run on.

"Base runners are like thieves. A lot of times, they give themselves away," said former manager Roger Craig. "It could be the way they fix their helmet, or the way they stand at second base, or if they do something different when they squat down."

Reading a hitter's facial expressions can be important, too. For instance, if he is asked to lay down a sacrifice bunt to advance a runner over, he might show a hint of frustration. He would rather hit away with a runner on base and might be concerned that his manager doesn't share that same level of confidence. His eyes will usually indicate his level of frustration. Or he may have other ways of showing emotion. Take, for instance, Texas's Cliff Johnson, who was so upset with third-base coach Art Howe for giving him the take sign on a 3–0 count that he actually flipped him off from home plate. The sign readers on the opposing bench had no problem reading that one.

Ty Cobb was regarded as the greatest base stealer of his era, swiping a whopping 892 bases from 1905 to 1928. And even though he was as speedy

Pitcher Tommy John on Changing Up His Signs

"I tell you what, nobody was better at stealing signs than the old Milwaukee Brewers of the early 1980s, the 'Brew Crew.' Paul Molitor, Robin Yount, Don Money, Sal Bando, Cecil Cooper, and Gorman Thomas, those guys were the best sign stealers I have ever seen in baseball, bar none. They picked up every sign you would put down. It was amazing. If one of those guys was on second, they would get your signs in a heartbeat. Consequently, I had to change up my signs against those guys every time we faced them. I tell you what, I had the same set of signs for 26 years, and they were the only team I ever changed them up for. I normally went with odds and evens, with the first sign for odd innings and the second sign for even innings. I kept it pretty simple. But whenever we faced the Brewers, I would use the first sign after the last pitch. It was a good system unless I had a catcher who wasn't bright enough to remember what the last pitch was."

as they came in those days, Cobb's greatest gift was his ability to read opposing pitchers and catchers. He would study the pitcher's mannerisms and tendencies to figure out when he was going to throw over to first base and when he wasn't. Cobb would also figure out the pitcher's signs for off-speed pitches, which were the ones he was most interested in. Once he had those things down pat, it was just a matter of time before he was standing safely on second base.

There was one guy who had Cobb's number, though, and consistently was able to throw him out. According to the book *The Hidden Language of Baseball*, Buck Crouse, a catcher for the White Sox from 1923 to 1930, noticed that "when Cobb took a big lead, he wouldn't run. When he took a short lead, he was gone. He also realized that just before Cobb would bunt, he would wet his lower lip with his tongue."

Middle infielders need to communicate out on the field, which means that they are also susceptible to having their signs stolen. In his book *Oh, Baby, I Love It!* former big-league catcher Tim McCarver wrote about his former manager with the 1972 Montreal Expos, Gene Mauch, who was able to crack the code between a rival shortstop and second baseman despite the fact that they shielded their conversations with each other with their gloves.

"Mauch couldn't actually see the open or closed mouth—he'd watch the vein in the infielder's neck," wrote McCarver. "If the vein contracted, his mouth was open, and that meant he was saying, 'You!' So Mauch knew the other guy would cover. He was never wrong."

An alert teammate sitting on the bench can also steal signs. Such was the case back in the 1940 World Series when somebody on the Detroit bench figured out that whenever Reds catcher Jimmie Wilson flexed his forearm muscles, he was calling for an off-speed pitch. A similar situation occurred in 1971 during a game between the Cubs and the Reds. Cubs catcher Randy Hundley noticed something odd about Cincinnati catcher Johnny Bench. "He had those long fingers," said Hundley. "I looked up, and all of a sudden I noticed that sometimes I'd see those fingers and sometimes I wouldn't." After a while, Hundley figured that when Bench flashed the sign for a curveball, he'd hang his fingers down real low, whereas on fastballs he couldn't see his fingers. "I told some of our guys, 'I've got his signs. If you hear me before a pitch, it's a breaking ball. If you don't, it's a fastball,'" he continued. "I'd yell out something like, 'Come on, Davey,' or whatever. We came back and won that game."

With regard to studying managers or third-base coaches and trying to figure out their sign system, there is almost always some information immediately available. There will be some consistencies with their rhythms, for starters, as in how slow or fast they are relaying signals. From there, a manager will usually have a "live" sign and a "take-off" sign, which is displayed when he wants the hitter to ignore a sign he may have

Pitcher Kirk McCaskill on Sign Stealing

"I remember a funny story that Jim Slaton told me one time. Slaton was a pitcher with the Angels, and they were playing the Brewers one time back in the late '80s. Milwaukee was really good at stealing signs back then, and they were all over the Angels that night. Well, his catcher Bob Boone finally just came out to the mound and said to him, 'Throw whatever you want, they are picking up all of our signs.' So he did. He spent the rest of the game just rearing back and throwing whatever pitches he wanted, whenever he felt like it, with no signs whatsoever. It worked, and he ultimately wound up winning the game. Afterwards, in the clubhouse, Slaton was absolutely dejected. Somebody came up to him and congratulated him on pitching great game and then asked him what was wrong. Slaton says, 'My career is over. Boone had no idea which pitches were coming all game, yet he didn't have a single passed ball. My confidence is shot!'"

previously given because he has changed his mind based on something that transpired out on the field.

"Here's how you steal a sign every once in a while: if I'm on the bench, I'll see a third-base coach has a rhythm," said former manager Don Zimmer, who was known for his ability to steal signs. "Next pitch, same rhythm. Then the next pitch—wait a minute, uh-oh, something different. It might mean something."

When Roger Craig was managing a ballgame, he would often assign utility players on the bench to watch the opposing manager or coach and chart all of his movements.

"Sometimes I'd have three or four guys look at one person," he said. "You look at when he touches his face, you look at his chest, you look at the belt, and you look at the pants. You keep eliminating stuff."

Studying pitchers is an art form all its own. The smallest subtleties are analyzed and examined by opposing sign stealers. Each pitch will have a signature that makes it unique. Pitchers are creatures of habit and stick to a routine, but their codes can almost always be cracked if studied vigilantly enough. It could be something as insignificant as the way they hold their glove on certain pitches, how they arch their back, the way they grip the ball on a certain seam, how they twist their wrist, where their point of release is, whether or not they leave their fingers out of their gloves, the way they are digging into the rubber to get a better footing, their facial expression, or maybe it is just the way that they shake the rosin bag. Again, the possibilities are endless.

Babe Ruth started out his career as a pitcher and supposedly broadcasted his curveball by the way he would unknowingly curl his tongue in his mouth. Cleveland's Stanley Coveleski would touch the ball to his mouth when he threw a spitball. Similarly, White Sox spitballer Ed Walsh, who covered his face with his glove during his delivery, did the same thing, only in his case the tip-off was when the brim of his cap moved upward when his mouth opened.

Maybe the most unique spitball tell of all time didn't even come from the pitcher or catcher. According to the book *The Hidden Language of Baseball,* back in 1920, during a World Series game between the Brooklyn Dodgers and the Cleveland Indians, it was noticed that Brooklyn's second baseman, Pete Kilduff, was broadcasting pitches. Turned out that each time his pitcher, Burleigh Grimes, threw a spitter, he would reach down and grab a handful of infield dirt. Because the balls were so slippery and disgusting back in those days, Kilduff wanted to make sure he would have a good grip on the ball if it came to him in order to throw it over to first base. Sure enough, the next time the team faced Grimes, they pounded him and won the game by seven runs.

Even today, pitchers will unknowingly give things away, despite their best efforts to study video of themselves. Twins ace Johan Santana had to go to a bigger glove when teams picked up on his excessive hand gripping of the ball inside his glove, which caused it to flare out. Roger Clemens and David Cone used large gloves for the very same reason. Hideki Irabu was leaving tells by the positioning and placement of his feet on the rubber.

Perhaps the most notorious pitch-tipping incident of the modern era came in Game 6 of the 2001 World Series between the Yankees and the Diamondbacks. Yankees ace lefty Andy Pettitte got clobbered early and often in what ended up being a 15–2 bloodbath. Seemingly everybody but Pettitte could see that he was telegraphing his pitches. When he was pitching out of the stretch, he would bring his hands up to his belt in an arc-like motion to throw an off-speed pitch, versus just straight up for a fastball. The Arizona hitters feasted on not only his oversight, but the entire Yankees team, which should have picked up on it earlier.

"One of my favorite tipping pitches stories came from longtime Yankees catcher Yogi Berra, who told me that whenever he faced Connie Johnson, a

Coach Al Newman on Sign Stealing

"When I was the third-base coach for the Twins, I used to have signals with Kirby Puckett. Occasionally, if I could see the catcher setting up inside, I would yell out, 'Hum-Puck!' which was my little code saying with him to let him know. I didn't do it every game, just on some of the tougher pitchers he would face. If teams heard you do that too much, they would get suspicious, so I had to be selective when I did it. Certain teams did it more than others. For years the Yankees used to have their third-base coach cheat up a little bit in the coaching box towards the foul line. He could then peek in to the catcher to see location. So he would signal to the left-handed hitters, who could see him by standing still if it was a fastball and then moving if it was a breaking ball. He would then relay that information over to the first-base coach whenever a right-handed hitter came up."

Manager Tom Kelly on Protecting His Team's Signs

"We had a situation one time when I was managing the Twins where a guy on the opposing team was signaling location to the hitter. I can't remember if he was leading with his right foot or his left foot, or sitting up or bending down, or whatever he was doing—but he was definitely communicating with the hitter. So I went out to the mound and told my second baseman that on the next play I wanted him to cover the bag. Then I told my pitcher to just turn around once he came set and throw it right at the runner and drill him. I didn't care what happened to the ball, I just wanted the runner to get the message. Sure enough, it worked. Yeah, it was probably a little childish on my part, but it put a stop to the situation in a hurry."

black pitcher who played for Chicago and Baltimore back in the '50s, that he could tell if he was throwing his fastball based on whether or not he could see the white part of his hand during his delivery," said Josh Prager, author of the book *The Echoing Green*. "He hit very well against him as a result."

There are countermeasures for pitchers, however, to prevent opposing teams from stealing their signs. One of the most notorious cases of a pitcher going to extraordinary measures to protect his signs came on October 8, 1956, in Game 5 of the World Series between the Yankees and the Brooklyn Dodgers. That was the day that Don Larsen pitched the first-ever perfect game in the Fall Classic's history. What made the accomplishment even more impressive, though, was the fact that he pitched the entire game out of the stretch, not the more effective windup position, which allows for more power to be generated. Worried that he had been tipping pitches out of his windup, he got all 27 outs from the stretch.

Some pitchers, meanwhile, simply didn't care if they were tipping pitches. Such was the case with legendary hurler Sandy Koufax, who many contend might be the game's best ever. It was widely known throughout his career that while in the stretch, he brought his arm straight down when he threw fastballs, versus extending it for off-speed pitches. Koufax just went up and threw strikes and got guys out, oblivious to the fact that they might or might not know what was coming. Now *that* was intimidation.

Occasionally, back in the day, teams would use disinformation campaigns to mess with the heads of opposing hitters as well as the sign stealers. They might even plant nuggets of false information by telling a reporter in confidence about how a certain pitcher on their staff was struggling with certain tipped pitches. They would then make up something, such as whenever the pitcher touched his cap, it meant fastball. Well, the reporter would, of course, run out and start spreading the rumor. Then, after it got back to the opposing players, they would watch for the pitcher to touch his cap while they were hitting and really get messed up. It was brilliant.

One of the premier sign stealers of the modern era was infielder Paul Molitor, who used his time in the dugout wisely in order to study opposing players and managers:

> I always felt that when I was on the field, it was the opposing team's job to keep me from stealing their signs, whether they were from managers to coaches, coaches to players, pitchers to catchers, or what have you. There are so many signs coming in, from sequences used to hold runners, throw-overs, pickoffs, pitch-outs, stealing, bunting, and on and on. I think it is a part of the art of the game to at least have the opportunity to pick up on someone who is not doing his job to protect what he is doing defensively.
>
> It was the same way on the bases, too. If a catcher wasn't hiding his signs from first base, and I could pick something up which would give me an edge, then I would definitely try and do that. It was the same thing whenever I was on second base. If the sequence was such that it was easily detected, then I would transition that information over to the hitter. It was also advantageous with regards to picking a good pitch to run on as well, perhaps a curveball away versus a fastball inside.
>
> When you cross the line is when you take advantage of cameras out in center field or use technology as an unfair advantage. It is tough to see who is doing what, to tell you the truth. There are so many cameras and TV screens in stadiums nowadays, you just don't know. The code is based on playing the game in a 'gentlemanlike' way, and that has definitely changed over the past several years as technology has advanced. I mean, is it inconceivable to think that a player might wear an earpiece like NFL quarterbacks do? It would be a huge advantage if he did because someone on the other end could tell him what pitch was coming and where it was coming, inside or outside. Then what? Do we check every player for earpieces?
>
> In my opinion, that is all a part of the game. If the pitcher takes exception to a runner relaying signs to the batter, then I think the onus is on them to either do a better job of hiding their signs or change them up to protect themselves from being decoded. You know, when

> I teach the young guys about base running at spring training, I tell them to pay attention at all times, even when they are not on base, because there is so much going on. It is the little things in baseball that win you games, but you have to pay attention to the details and do your homework.

While many players have become skilled in interpreting signs from the dugout or bullpen over the years, they usually can't hold a candle to the experts. That's right, some teams even have full-time sign stealers on their payrolls. And they don't come cheap, either. Some have dual roles as assistant coaches within an organization, but make no mistake about it—their expertise lies in the realm of espionage.

The sign stealer will study video until all hours of the night and watch players in person from all sorts of angles and vantage points, hoping to find one of their tells, or tip-offs, that will give something away. His job may be a lonely one, but it also may be one of the most important ones on the team.

Perhaps the most celebrated sign stealer of all time is former Chicago White Sox coach Joe Nossek. Nossek, a statistics major in college, enjoyed analyzing data and finding solutions. This "eye in the sky" kept meticulous notes, studied video, and had incredible patience. While most players and coaches watched the games that they were playing in, Nossek watched *them* watching the games instead. He became so good at what he did that opposing teams would change up their signs whenever they played the Sox, out of both fear and respect. Even if he didn't steal the other team's signs, half the time they thought that he had, which meant that his sheer presence in the dugout served as a psychological advantage.

To Nossek, he wasn't stealing signs, just interpreting them. He felt strongly that there was no sign stealing in baseball, just "giveaways." He knew that old managers were creatures of habit and didn't like to make things too complicated for their players, so sometimes they would get lazy and either not change signs, or just change them slightly based on a small variation. That was like taking candy from a baby for Nossek. It has been said that he knew the other team's signals better than their own players.

He also knew that coaches who learned certain sign systems under certain managers would be more likely to use those same systems when they got promoted and moved on to other teams. Furthermore, if a player ever got traded to his White Sox, they could expect a thorough interrogation from old Joe shortly after their arrival. He understood the value of information and left no stone unturned in order to get it. That is why he was so valuable to his team. Some estimated that over the years, his code-cracking had won his ballclub dozens of games.

Nossek himself was quick to acknowledge his role on the team:

> Anytime a player or coach can pick up signs, then I think it is up to the opposition to recognize that and either change their signs or make them think that they have changed their signs. So much of that stuff is psychological. When I was in my later years in Chicago, I had built up a reputation as one of the top sign stealers in the game. Because of that, teams used to play us very differently. They would either change up their signs just for us, or they would do things to make sure I couldn't get any good looks at them. They would also be hesitant to do certain things as well, because they knew that there was a chance we would figure them out. Either way we won, because they were thinking about it and changing their routines.
>
> That small edge sometimes could be the difference in a tight ballgame. I took great pride in helping my teams from behind the scenes, and I know that every extra out or base hit or stolen base that I might have prevented could have won us a few ballgames. It comes down to the little things in this game. I got to make a contribution to my team even though I wasn't on the field, and that was very satisfying to me.
>
> Everybody has a knack for something, and sign stealing was just my thing. I learned how to do it when I first began playing in the big leagues with Oakland back in the '60s. I spent a lot of time on the bench in those days and figured that I could keep my head in the game by studying the interactions between the opposing manager, the third-base coach, and their dugout. It was a small part of the game that not too many people are aware of, but it really fascinated me. So I watched, and I learned as much as I could. Before long I got pretty good at it.
>
> You know, back then the managers used to go through their signs right out in the open because nobody really paid much attention to them or to whatever signs they were showing. Well, eventually I got a reputation for what I was doing, and before long opposing team managers would try and hide from me in their dugouts. They would do all sorts of things to shield themselves from me so that they could protect their signs. That, of course, made things more difficult for me, but that was just a part of the game.

Umpire Tim Tschida on Sign Stealing

"As an umpire I see sign stealing all of the time. When I am working on second base, I like to stand on the opposite side of the hitter because I like to see the signs. I like to look in to the catcher and try to figure out what the signs are. It makes the game much more enjoyable, and makes it easier for me to see what may or may not be coming, so that I can be fully prepared. I am at the point now in my career where I can usually tell what the signs are after watching just a few batters. That has come from years and years of experience. When you are younger you are only concerned with what is right in front of you, but when you get older and wiser, then you start to see the bigger picture."

The key was being able to pay attention at just the right times and to learn the timing of when the other team displayed their signs. There are so many distractions in the game, and you really had to know when and where to look to gather the right information, otherwise you would miss it. From there, it was all about studying the sequences and tendencies of players and managers. Certain managers liked to do things at certain times, like bunt or hit-and-run. Over the years you pick up who has a tendency to do what and when they liked to do it.

I especially paid attention to the tendencies of base runners. Most good base runners are on their own nowadays and don't require a green light from their manager or third-base coach. That is why we see so many throw-overs nowadays, from the pitcher to the first baseman, so that they can try to get that runner to show them something and give something away. They have routines and tendencies, both when they are going to stay or when they are going to steal. They will give away their tells in subtle ways, and you just have to be patient. You would be surprised just how much young runners will give away on a throw-over at first base. Maybe a little flinch, or perhaps they will relax a bit more when they know they are going to go. They try to hide what they are doing, and sometimes they will give themselves away. So you have to watch them and figure those things out.

As for the pitchers, certain guys will give things away by the way they hold their glove. Some will hold their fingers in a unique way if they are going to throw a certain pitch. They may hold a finger outside the glove on a certain pitch or put it in the glove for another. You have to really pay attention to those little, subtle things. Pitchers are creatures of habit and tend to do things over and over again.

Signs are unique to each player. I have known third-base coaches who have used specific signs for every player. Catchers have unique

Pitcher Mike Marshall on Being a Student of the Game

"I picked up so much over the years from just studying my opponents, their tendencies, their tells, and even their signs. I also kept track of every pitch I ever threw to every batter I ever faced during my 14 years in the major leagues. I can grab my notebooks to this day and tell you any game I played in and which pitches I threw to each hitter. I did my homework before every game I played in and came to work very prepared. I came up with a pitch sequence for every batter I ever faced, too. I never needed to watch any video—I had it all written down. Another thing that really helped was the fact that I always watched the other team's batting practice. I told my managers that I never cared about watching my own hitters take batting practice. I wanted to see how the opposing team was hitting that day and study their tendencies. I would hang around the dugout during that time with my trusty notebook and just watch and listen. That is where you got the really good stuff."

signals for each pitcher that they catch. Managers might use different signs and signals for players, as well. So it can be very confusing if you don't pay attention. Guys forget them and get them twisted around; it was frustrating for us as coaches, for sure. You had to remind them constantly of what the signs were and then hold them accountable. Repetition is the mother of learning. It is so important.

Overall, I really benefited from spending a lot of time in the game as a player and as a coach. Because of that I got to know a lot of people and made a lot of solid relationships over the years. I was able to keep in contact with a lot of those people and collaborate on things, too, which was always very helpful. Gathering information was an art form in itself, I think, and I prided myself on being able to do that. Sometimes my reputation preceded me, though.

I remember a funny story that happened one year when I was with Chicago. We were playing a game against Oakland one night, and Tony La Russa was managing the A's at the time. He was my former roommate in the minor leagues and a very good friend of mine. Anyway, we had just traded a player to Oakland in exchange for one of their guys. Well, I immediately went to our new guy and asked him about what his signs were in Oakland, to sort of interrogate him. I knew that they would change their signs after he had left, but it would give me a good head start into what sorts of things that they did. So I went up to this kid in the clubhouse and asked him for his signs. He looked at me and said, "Mr. La Russa told me that you would ask me that, and he made me promise him that I wouldn't tell you what our signs were." I got the biggest kick out of that. I reassured him that it was okay now that he was with the Sox, and eventually he talked. Tony knew exactly what I was going to do, though, and I got a good laugh out of that one.

Another noted sign stealer was former Mets and Giants manager Wes Westrum. "Wes was sensational at it," said former pitcher Steve Stone of Westrum's uncanny ability to steal signs. "Within three innings, he would have all the pitches down."

While Nossek and Westrum are both retired, one of the best in the business today is Twins bench coach Steve Liddle, who clearly understands the power of information:

> For me personally, what I do is study tendencies. I do my homework and I study the pitchers, the hitters, and even the managers to see what they are all doing. Then, when opportunities come up, we can capitalize on them by having all of that information. When you have that at your fingertips, you are much better than others with regards to making quick decisions.

> Some managers are quite frankly pretty lazy. They might not give very many signs throughout the course of a game, or they just might not change them up very often. Or they may not give any signs at all until a situation arises when they need to act immediately. Then, when they do call in a sign, it is much easier for me to pick it up and steal it. For me, I never pay attention to the third-base coach at all. I watch the dugout. Many times the third-base coach is just a dummy, or decoy. In most situations the hot signs are coming from the dugout to the runner on first as far as when to steal or when a batter should bunt or hit and run. There is a game within the game, as far as signs are concerned, and it all comes down to studying tendencies.

> For instance, if I can see that the pitcher is going to throw an off-speed pitch, then that would be a good time to send your runner to second on a stolen base because he will have an extra-fraction-of-a-second lead on him. Or maybe the pitcher is a lefty who throws over to first base to check the runner only when he is told. If you know his throw-over move or his tendencies as to when he is going to throw, then you can put your base runner in a situation where he will have the best opportunity to have success in stealing the base. Or, better yet, if you steal the throw-over or pitch-out signs, then you will know exactly what he is going to do. That is just a part of the cat-and-mouse game that we play.

> Sometimes third-base coaches will only touch four body parts as their signal routine but then touch nine or 10 when there is an actual

hot sign being called in. So he may "over-give" the signs to make it look like nothing is going on. I will then go back and study those things to figure out what the indicator and signs are. We face teams in our division 19 times a year, so if you know these things it can be very helpful.

I study video a lot, too. That is a very important aspect of what I do. I study game tapes and try to pick up the subtle, little nuances that different players have. Teams will have cameras at their home ballparks focused in on the opposing team's dugouts for that very reason. In fact, during the last four to six weeks of the season, some of the large-market teams will send out a handful of advance scouts to study every possible playoff opponent that they might face in the postseason. They will tape everything and then study it like crazy.

In Minnesota, we only have four cameras in the Metrodome. Other ballparks, however, have dozens of them located everywhere you can imagine. A lot of them are trained on the dugouts to steal managerial signs; others are fixed on the catcher and pitcher, so they can figure out their signs; and others are focused on the first- and third-base coaches, to pick up their tendencies as well. So that way, when their runners get on second base, they will know what sign sequences that particular pitcher is using.

Beyond that, we are a small-market team here in Minnesota, so we don't have any lip-readers on staff, but some teams do use people

Catcher Greg Olson on Changing Up His Signs

"When it came to pitchers having to change up the signs because there was a runner on second base, I would have to say that the starting pitchers were much more intelligent than the relievers. The relievers were mentally geared up for one or two innings max and didn't want to pollute their heads with too much information. They were more hyper. Starters were more relaxed and had routines they followed. They know every fifth day that they were going to the post, so their demeanor and mental capabilities were just better. Relievers are tough. You had to simplify everything for them.

"With the Braves, we tried to go with a universal system that was pretty hard to detect. As the catcher, I would flash a total of four signs, with the first and last sign of the sequence being added together to get a final number. So an inside fastball would add up to five, an outside fastball would add up to six, a curveball would be two, a slider would be three, and a change-up would be four. So if I flashed 'one, three, wiggle, two,' that would be one plus two equals three, or a slider. It was very, very hard to figure out our system. In fact, I don't know of any team that ever picked up on our signs."

to pick up on that stuff. It sounds crazy, but that is why you see the players all hold their gloves up over their mouths now. It is also to prevent the other teams from video-recording them and then figuring out what they were saying after the fact, to try and pick up any tells. You just never know. Everybody is a spy out there nowadays.

On the Use of Electronic Gadgetry or Visual Aids to Steal Signs

Now let's look at the other kind of sign stealers—the unethical ones. Perhaps nothing in the long and storied history of the game of baseball has been as controversial and polarizing as sign stealing through the means of mechanical or electronic devices, or by having somebody not in uniform performing espionage with either a telescope or binoculars from outside of the playing field. Amazingly, while most think of this as dishonorable and cheating, others view it as a form of gamesmanship, which is technically not illegal. While it may not technically be illegal, one thing is for certain—it is a clear violation of the code.

It has long been understood that stealing signs from within the confines of the playing field is okay. Even if a player or coach is located in the dugout or bullpen, that is still okay as long as he is using only his eyes to steal the signs. As soon as a player uses a spyglass, binoculars, telescope, or hunting scope (all of which have been used) to peer into the opposition's signage system, then a line has been crossed. If somebody is getting signs by watching a closed-circuit TV or the actual game telecast and is then somehow relaying that information in to the players, that too is crossing the line.

"Some people think when you steal signs, you're cheating," said former manager Don Zimmer. "If I'm on second base and the other team is dumb enough to let me steal the signs, and I relay that to the hitter, that's just baseball. Now if you're doing something illegal [like having] someone sitting in the stands with binoculars or something, to me, that's not right."

There is a long, interesting history behind these taboos, starting in 1900 during a game between Cincinnati and Philadelphia at Philadelphia's Baker Bowl. According to author Paul Dickson's book *The Hidden Language of Baseball*, Cincinnati was getting beat up pretty badly. That's when Reds shortstop Tommy Corcoran noticed that Philadelphia's third-base coach was oddly stepping on precisely the same spot in an area near the third-base line before each pitch.

Without warning, Corcoran apparently ran over and began using his spikes to kick and dig up the dirt around the area in question. Eventually, with the fans thinking he may have lost his marbles and the umpires looking on, he dug up a small wooden box that contained an electronic buzzer connected to wires that ran underground to the team's center-field clubhouse. In the clubhouse, meanwhile, was a backup catcher whose job it was to steal the signs with binoculars and then buzz them over to the third-base coach. Apparently, one buzz meant fastball, two meant a curve, and three buzzes meant a "slow ball" was coming.

Busted with their hands in the proverbial cookie jar, Philadelphia vehemently denied any prior knowledge of the device. Such was the way most teams responded in those days to accusations of cheating or questionable behavior. In fact, it was just the beginning of many such cheating incidents that would occur over the next half century, the golden age of espionage in professional baseball.

According to Dickson's exhaustively and brilliantly researched book, there were many more episodes to come. Later that season, in a game against Brooklyn, Philadelphia was accused of stealing signs from a building across the street from the stadium and then relaying the signs by waving a folded-up newspaper in the window. Other recorded incidents would include the use of a weather vane as a signaling device, as well as an "L-shaped rod" that was placed in the letter "O" of a billboard ad in the outfield fence. As the years went by, other archaic methods of communication would include the New York Highlanders using a mirror to deflect light from a nearby apartment window. This system was foolproof—unless it was overcast or raining outside. On those days, they would set up shop behind the outfield fence and somehow "manipulate the crossbar in the letter H of the word 'Hats' in an advertising sign."

Dickson also told a story about Ty Cobb that appeared in a 1952 *Life* magazine article entitled "Tricks that Won Me Ball Games." "At our Detroit park there was a fellow in center field with a pair of [spy] glasses strong enough to bring out the fillings in the catcher's teeth," admitted Cobb. "If you watched the 'B' in that advertisement closely [there was an ad on the fence that read 'THE DETROIT NEWS: BEST NEWSPAPER IN THE WEST'], you would watch little slots open and close. If the slot was open

Team Owner Mike Veeck on Sign Stealing

"I would say that my dad [Bill Veeck, owner of the White Sox] was arguably the most beloved owner in the history of the game. Overall, he was a good baseball man and had a deep, abiding love for the game. As far as the sign stealing from the scoreboard, he would tell me that when all of that stuff was going on, the people and fans that he talked to didn't really see it as cheating. They saw it as a kind of sportsmanship or gamesmanship, in the broadest sense of the word. Look, my dad was certainly not above being accused of cheap theatrics, but I think he kind of liked the dimension that it added to the game. He knew that it had been going on forever, and to him it was what it was. To him the decorum, the history, and rituals involved with the game were so fascinating. He felt that the players on the field hadn't changed much over the years, from Ty Cobb on down the line, but that the help around them sort of ebbed and flowed as time went by."

in the top half of the 'B,' our spotter had picked off the signal for a fastball. If the slot in the bottom of the 'B' opened, we knew a curve was coming. I don't know whether the ad sold any newspapers, but it was a great thing for the Detroit batting averages."

Bob Feller would come forward years later to discuss how he, too, was directly involved in a covert sign-stealing saga. According to Dickson, Feller had just returned from World War II in 1945, where he had served as a gunnery officer on the USS *Alabama*. There, he used a telescope to locate nearby enemy aircraft. Feller was able to keep the telescope and brought it home with him when he was discharged. Ironically, it would later find a home perched on top of a tripod mounted in the Cleveland Indians' scoreboard. Apparently, he and fellow Indians pitcher Bob Lemon would take turns using the scope to steal signs from opposing catchers. Once they had the call, they would then relay it to a Cleveland groundskeeper, who would in turn give a variety of signals to the hitters through a space in the scoreboard used to post away-game scores. On some days a head would appear in the space, whereas other days it might be an arm, each carrying its own significance.

"Hey, all's fair in love and war, and when you're trying to win a pennant," said Feller in Dickson's book. "The way I felt about it, it was like in the war. You had to decipher a code, break it down, which we did against the Germans and the Japanese, and we won, right?"

The old center-field scoreboards were a haven for sign stealers. There was very little teams could do to avoid having their signals swiped other than to change up their signs as frequently as possible. According to Dickson, Hall of Famer Rogers Hornsby spoke of a scoreboard incident that might have taken the cake for creativity. Apparently, there was a large advertisement for a water company that featured an Indian head on it. Somehow, after stealing the signs, groundskeepers were able to manipulate the Indian's eyes and make them move up and down and side to side, with each direction indicating a signal to the hitter peering over at home plate.

The granddaddy of all scoreboard sign-stealing incidents, however, took place at the Polo Grounds in New York back in 1951, when the Giants beat the Brooklyn Dodgers to win the National League pennant. Down by nearly 14 games that August, the Giants pulled off one of the greatest comebacks in baseball history by catching their crosstown rival Dodgers in October, thus forcing a three-game playoff between the two clubs. There, behind Bobby Thomson's famous "Shot Heard 'Round the World" walkoff home run against pitcher Ralph Branca, the Giants took the pennant. The moment was forever immortalized when Giants play-by-play announcer Russ Hodges cried, "The Giants win the pennant! The Giants win the pennant!"

The Giants, behind manager Leo Durocher, had posted a gaudy 23–5 record at home up until that point. Eventually, people started talking and news broke that there had been an elaborate sign-stealing system put into place earlier in the season. Apparently, somebody would hide out in the outfield scoreboard with a telescope and then relay the signals to the bullpen through a bell-and-buzzer system that had been installed by an electrician. A player or coach in the bullpen would then tip off the batter as to what pitch was coming.

Thomson's dramatic home run, which would be named as the greatest moment in baseball history by *The Sporting News,* was now tainted. It would all come out years later in Joshua Prager's book *The Echoing Green,* where players finally admitted to taking part in the scheme.

Sign stealing through these means would continue, though, with yet another high-profile center-field scoreboard case being uncovered in 1960 involving the Chicago White Sox. The crux of this operation involved players using binoculars to steal signs and then signaling them to the hitters by flashing a small red light in a corner of the scoreboard. If it was

---

Subcode of the Code: First- and Third-Base Coaches Need to Stay in Their Coaching Boxes

Some first- and third-base coaches have been known to cheat outside of their designated coaching boxes, which are located down the first- and third-base lines. They will walk around nonchalantly, in the hopes of maybe seeing in to the catcher's legs and picking up a sign. When this happens, they will usually get warned by the umpire. If it persists, somebody will go down in retaliation. It is interesting to note that the reason the coaching box even came into existence in the first place was because of Charles Comiskey, who was the St. Louis Browns' third-base coach back in the 1880s. Comiskey, who would later become the owner of the Chicago White Sox, used to parade up and down the line, taunting and cursing at opposing pitchers and batters. He would even supposedly stomp on the umpire's feet with his spikes when he got upset over calls that didn't go his way. As a result, the powers that be came up with a containment plan for old Chuck, which we now know as the coach's box.

---

a curveball, the light would flash on and off, and if it was a fastball, the light stayed on.

What made this particular scheme so unusual, however, wasn't the fact that it was anything new or innovative, but rather because one of the players on the Sox, Al "Red" Worthington, a deeply religious man, took a public stand against what he felt was cheating and quit the team.

"Stealing baseball signs on the field is part of the game," wrote Worthington in his book *I Played and I Won*. "I don't think that using the scoreboard or other such mechanical means is right to do. I knew what our team was doing and I didn't feel right about it. I went to the manager and told him that I could not play with a team that did that...."

"When I found out what was going on, it really upset me," he wrote. "I like to win but I don't want to win if I have to cheat to do it. A call came to the bullpen and I was sent into the game and won in relief. After the game, we flew to Kansas City for a makeup game. The next day in the lobby of the hotel, I got the opportunity to talk with our manager, Al Lopez. I told my manager that it was cheating to have a man in the scoreboard to flash the pitches to our batters. He said, 'Show me in the rulebook where it is cheating.'

"I felt terrible being on a team that had a system that was cheating," he continued. "I had no problem with our players stealing signs on the field.

I did have a big problem with using binoculars from the scoreboard and flashing signs to the batters. As a pitcher, I knew it was hard enough to win a game without someone calling your pitches."

A very principled man, Worthington then went to the general manager, Hank Greenberg, about the matter. Greenberg would later write in his autobiography that he knew it was going on. "We stole the signs from the center-field scoreboard, and I'm sure a lot of other ballclubs do the same," he admitted.

Greenberg sent Worthington to see the team owner, Bill Veeck. The two agreed to disagree, and with that, Worthington left the game he loved and wound up sitting out a season before returning to action with Cincinnati and later Minnesota. It was a pretty gutsy thing for Worthington to do at the time, considering he had five small children to feed at home. He persevered, though, relying heavily on his faith.

"They were cheating, plain and simple," said Worthington years later. "Well, I'm a Christian and I wouldn't stand for it. I couldn't stand for it. I spoke at a lot of churches about lying and cheating, so I couldn't associate myself with that sort of thing. I have no regrets about it now. It was something I felt strongly about then and something I still feel strongly about all these years later. I am proud of what I did. The legacy of that has been a big part of my life even to this day."

Veeck would later comment on the incident in his autobiography *Veeck as in Wreck,* where he defended his team's scoreboard antics. "I doubt if there is one club that hasn't tried it at one time or another in recent years," he wrote. "There is absolutely nothing in the rules against it."

Perhaps the most intriguing episode of sign stealing in Major League Baseball history came in 1975, when the Milwaukee Brewers' team mascot, Bernie Brewer, was accused of espionage by the Rangers. They claimed that Milwaukee had a man stationed in the bleachers with binoculars and would somehow relay the signs over to him on his outfield perch. Bernie, whose signature move was to slide down a gigantic keg and into a beer stein whenever the Brewers scored, would then allegedly signal to the players with his bright white Bavarian gloves. Go figure.

On the Future of Sign Stealing

As the years went by and technology got more and more advanced, so too did the scheming. As manager of the Cubs in the late 1960s, Leo Durocher supposedly had the visiting team's clubhouse bugged. His plan backfired when opposing teams heard about it and announced bogus pitching signs for old Leo to hear.

Eventually, with the advent of television, teams no longer had to deal with dingy old scoreboards in order to steal signs. Signs were now given to them on a platter. There has always been a gentleman's agreement regarding teams not using TVs to steal signs, but who knows what really goes on in the bowels of team stadiums. In 1991 walkie-talkie radios were banned from being used in the press boxes, but with cell phones today, closed-circuit communication is hardly enforceable.

The fact of the matter is that if teams want to cheat, they will find a way. Pitchers and catchers simply have to be diligent regarding their signs and then hope for the best. Teams use cameras to study themselves as well as their opponents and certainly have every opportunity to use them as they wish.

One might assume that when it comes to cracking codes, there's a gentleman's agreement amongst rival teams nowadays that says that they won't start a technological arms race with one another. If they did, then all of them would have to continually come up with new and more complicated systems that would confuse and complicate all of their lives. Most teams have bigger fish to fry than worrying about sign stealers, but they nonetheless have to protect themselves against hidden cameras and other electronic mediums that have yet to be uncovered.

Let's give Joshua Prager, author of the book *The Echoing Green,* the final word on the future of sign stealing: "I researched incidents back all the way to the 1800s and documented many, many examples of elaborate cheating scams where teams used things like telescopes to steal signs. The interesting thing is that every time one of these incidents came up, baseball went bonkers. They would write resolutions, threaten to ban people, and scream and holler about how they weren't going to tolerate it. What is so interesting to me, though, is the fact that even to this day, there has never been a rule to officially ban it. Baseball has basically been schizophrenic about this issue. On the one hand, every time one of these situations comes up, they scream bloody murder about how there is no place for this garbage in the game. On the other hand, they have yet to officially adopt a rule to ban it. That is truly amazing to me."

30

On the Clubhouse Code

"WHAT IS SEEN IN HERE, WHAT IS HEARD IN HERE, WHAT IS SAID IN HERE...STAYS IN HERE." Those 18 words are the basis for what is known simply as the "clubhouse code." This sacred proverb is, or has been, posted on nearly every major league clubhouse wall at one time or another over the years. It applies to all who enter the inner circle, and it boils down to respect and following the principles of the Golden Rule: "Do unto others as you would have them do unto you."

Baseball players truly cherish the sanctity and privacy of their clubhouse. Most will acknowledge that there is a price to pay for enjoying fame and fortune, and that price is their privacy. The clubhouse, for many players, is the only safe haven that they have. If a teammate violates that privilege, then he might be treading in dangerous waters.

As teammates they are all one big family. Together for up to nine months in a row, they actually see more of each other than they do of their own families. They eat together, travel together, live together, socialize together, and work together. With that, like in every family dynamic, there are going to be stresses, squabbles, and disagreements along the way. Not everybody is going to get along, especially when you have such a diverse mix of racial and cultural backgrounds blended together.

Despite the obvious pitfalls that might come from being in such close quarters, it is generally understood that there is no room for public soap operas or airing of any dirty laundry to the press. Nobody wants to read

Pitcher Jim Kaat on the Clubhouse Code

"I remember talking to Chuck Tanner one time, a longtime big-league manager, about how he dealt with all the different things that went on in his clubhouse. He told me that you had to learn how to have one eye and one ear closed at all times. He said you couldn't see or hear everything that went on in there, but just enough to make sure things ran smoothly.

"I also think that part of the code includes talking to reporters. I remember back in 1962 when I was with Minnesota, and we wound up losing a tough 1–0 ballgame in 11 innings to the Angels. Anyway, Leon Wagner came in to pinch hit in the ninth inning and hit a harmless pop-out. He then came in again in the eleventh inning and wound up getting a little broken-bat single that turned out to be the game-winner. Well, the next day I read in the paper where he had said something to the effect that he hadn't seen much of this young newcomer kid out on the mound, referring to me, and that he needed one at-bat to 'figure him out.' I am reading that and thinking, what are you talking about, 'figure me out?' You got a lucky broken-bat single. So the next time they came back to Minnesota, I reared back and fired the first ball right up under Wagner's chin and said to him, 'Figure that one out!' Rarely did I ever let any personal anger get to me, but that time I felt like I needed to retaliate for being shown up."

Pitcher Frank Viola on the Clubhouse Code

As ballplayers, whether we were 20 years old or 40 years old, we were all kids in there. And kids do stupid stuff. None of us have really grown up. We were all getting paid great money to play a kids' game. As far as we were concerned, the clubhouse was fun time and it was our time. It was our sanctuary. What we said in there definitely had to stay in there, though, no questions. If that stuff leaked out, then that would cause all kinds of problems, both internally as well as externally. If a guy broke that code, then he would get blackballed."

Team Owner Mike Veeck on the Clubhouse Code

"I have never been privy to what goes on in the clubhouse, nor was my father or grandfather. That was [the players'] domain, and we respected that immensely. I think one of the biggest mistakes made by rookie owners is to breach that domain. They figure that since they own the team that they can go in, but it is not a place for them whatsoever. That is for the players and for the players alone."

a scathing story about themselves in the paper, nor do they want an off-the-cuff remark about somebody that was made in confidence wind up as "bulletin-board material" for the other team. Those matters are expected to be handled in-house, with no exceptions. Even if a player is really pissed off at another player, they need to settle it like men and behind closed doors. Personal agendas and petty spats can wind up being distractions for teams and can spread like a cancer, infecting the entire clubhouse if not dealt with accordingly.

There have been more than a few clubhouse brawls over the years between teammates and coaches. There is a lot of testosterone flowing between those walls, and sometimes things can get ugly. Such was the case in 1977 when Texas Rangers second baseman Lenny Randle lost his starting position to a rookie and had words with his manager, Frank Lucchesi, threatening to leave the team.

"It's just too damn bad somebody stopped him from leaving," Lucchesi told reporters. "I'm tired of these punks saying play me or trade me. Anyone who makes $80,000 a year and gripes and moans all spring is not going to get a tear out of me."

A few days later, before a spring-training game in Orlando, Randle apparently attacked Lucchesi for his remarks, leaving him with a broken cheekbone, a concussion, and a lacerated lip. For his part, Randle was suspended for 30 days and traded to the Mets.

One of the most publicized clubhouse spats of all time happened on August 20, 1978, between Dodgers teammates Don Sutton and Steve Garvey. When Sutton criticized the first baseman in a *Washington Post* story that was picked up by media outlets across the country, Garvey lost it. He confronted the pitcher in the visitors' clubhouse at Shea Stadium while in New York, and the argument just escalated from there. Once Sutton made a vulgar remark about Garvey's wife, it was on. The two went at it and rolled around on the floor for several minutes before teammates could separate them.

One surefire way for a player to really piss off his teammates and coaches is to write a sordid, tell-all book. This happened back in 1970 when journeyman pitcher Jim Bouton wrote *Ball Four,* a shocking, behind-the-scenes tell-all that named names and featured wild stories of drugs, booze, and illicit sex. It was a breach of the code's policies like none other in history. The code says you don't rat out a teammate. It also says what happens after hours amongst teammates is also an extension of the clubhouse, and therefore stays in the clubhouse.

Another contemptuous book hit the shelves in 2002, when San Francisco Giants infielder Omar Vizquel wrote his autobiography *Omar! My Life On and Off the Field*. In it, he blamed his then-teammate, pitcher Jose Mesa, for the team's collapse in the final inning of Game 7 of the 1997 World Series.

"The eyes of the world were focused on every move we made," wrote Vizquel. "Unfortunately, Jose's own eyes were vacant. Completely empty. Nobody home."

Needless to say, Mesa, who later signed with the Colorado Rockies, was not pleased. In fact, he would go on to drill Vizquel several times in the games following the release of the book. Each time Vizquel would step up to bat, he would get a free pass to first base compliments of a 95-mph fastball in his back. Payback is a bitch.

"I will not forgive him," Mesa told reporters. "Even my little boy told me to get him. If I face him 10 more times, I'll hit him 10 times. Every time. I want to kill him."

In 2005 another bombshell hit when former All-Star Jose Canseco's scandalous biography *Juiced: Wild Times, Rampant 'Roids, Smash Hits, and How Baseball Got Big*, hit the streets. Canseco spoke candidly of his own use of performance-enhancing drugs and went on to paint a disturbing picture of how rampant steroid use was in the '90s. Canseco also named names of other alleged users, particularly those who were his teammates on the A's and Rangers, and shocked baseball fans by implicating potential Hall of Famers Mark McGwire and Rafael Palmeiro.

The clubhouse code has gone through some changes as of late, and that has some baseball purists wondering whether it is being watered down or even deteriorating. They question whether the influence of players' agents has altered certain players' perspectives about loyalty. Whereas in years past teams would show a united front, nowadays the players are speaking more candidly to the media about personal matters.

There have been several high-profile cases of players being publicly thrown under the bus recently, including catcher A.J. Pierzynski being called a cancer by a teammate while with San Francisco, Sammy Sosa being called out for leaving a game early while with the Cubs, and Anaheim outfielder Jose Guillen complaining publicly about his pitchers not doing

Catcher Terry Steinbach on the Clubhouse Code

"This is such a huge part of the code. Whether it is a closed-door meeting or just something said in confidence, it can't leave the room. Nothing will break up the chemistry of a team more than guys talking behind other players' backs and using the media to make a point. You don't rat guys out for showing up to the ballpark hungover or for living a promiscuous lifestyle, or something like that. You might not agree with it personally or ethically, but that gives you no right to talk about it to the media, either. The biggest offender of this was my former teammate, Jose Canseco. What he did was awful. Writing his kiss-and-tell book was such a violation of the code. He had some major financial issues at the time and was clearly trying to make the last buck he is probably ever going to make off of baseball. It is really sad, to tell you the truth. He threw so many people under the bus. I would be hard-pressed to believe that he has any friends whatsoever in the game of baseball. What he said and did disrespected all of us, and guys don't forget that stuff."

Pitcher Tommy John on the Clubhouse Code

"That was our home and it was sacred. What happened in there was no different than what happens between any husband and wife in the sanctity of their own home. What happened in there stayed in there."

Second Baseman Al Newman on the Clubhouse Code

"With the media scrutiny being what it is, sometimes guys just have to get away from the ballpark and settle things like men. I will never forget back in 1987 when I was with the Twins. On the night we clinched the American League West title, Danny Gladden and Steve Lombardozzi got into an argument during that final game in Texas, and it escalated on the team plane coming home. Well, they eventually decided to settle it once and for all, and Lombo drove over to Gladden's house that next day. Sure enough, they went at it pretty good. I lived right by Danny, so I came over just before things escalated, and I watched Danny beat the shit out of him. He even broke his finger while punching him. But from there, it was over. In fact, if you watch the highlight film of the World Series victory just two weeks later, Danny is holding Lombo up in the air as they were celebrating. Those guys settled their differences, made up, and went back to being teammates during the most important stretch of the year. That said a lot in my eyes."

enough to protect him after getting drilled in a game. These are just a few incidents that have occurred as of late, but things that most old timers admit probably wouldn't have happened back in the day.

On Rookie Initiations and Hazing

Whether it is a rite of passage or simply an outdated and archaic tradition, rookie hazing initiations have been around for a long, long time. Players who got hazed are usually the first ones in line to dole out the hazing for the next crop of rookies. That is just the way it goes. While some feel it is demoralizing and humiliating, which it certainly can be, others feel that it acts as a form of team bonding, which brings the players together.

In baseball, the hazing usually gets going around September 1, when the rosters expand to 40 players. During this time, there are usually a handful of greenhorns among them who are getting their first sip of coffee in the bigs. The hazing can range from making the rookies sing their alma mater's fight song to making them carry the veterans' luggage.

Pitcher Mike Marshall on the Clubhouse Code

"You know, a lot of people don't know this, but I actually edited Jim Bouton's notorious book entitled *Ball Four*. I have always felt that we as major league baseball players are not big heroes. In fact, most of us are not even good people in many cases. We are puffed up with self-importance and we take all the advantages of people that we possibly can because of their false perceptions of who we are. So I thought it was good that Jim showed that to the world. And that was exactly what the book did—it showed what kind of people many baseball players really are. As for me, I never gave a damn who was cheating on their wife or who was coming to the ballpark drunk. That was them. I was nonjudgmental and couldn't care less. As long as they played baseball and did their jobs, they were all right with me."

Writer La Velle E. Neal on the Clubhouse Code

"As a beat writer you are privy to a lot of inside information, and you hear things that you simply cannot write about. You get to know guys and you talk to them and they open up. So you have to respect that and not break that trust. If you write about something that was off the record, that is a really unethical thing to do."

There have been some pretty creative ones, though, such as the Kansas City Royals, who in 2001 dressed their call-ups as Hooters waitresses. Not bad. Other indignities might include getting a pie in the face during your first live TV interview, or maybe even getting duct taped to the batting cage by one's jock strap during practice. Sometimes guys will make rookies dress up like hookers and then parade them around, which can fall under the category of cruel and unusual punishment. It is all meant to remind rookies of their place on the food chart, though...just below the rodent.

Rookies eat together, sleep together, work out together, and in many instances, don't intermingle with the veterans. They have a role—they are supposed to be seen and not heard. There is a hierarchy in the locker room, and things are based on seniority. For instance, veterans get the prime seats on the bus, on the plane, and in the locker room. They even get the nicest chairs to go along with them. They are also first in line at dinner time. The rookies get whatever is left over. That is just the way it is. That is all a part of the clubhouse code, which rewards the regulars with perks.

Mo Vaughn recalled his first few years in the league with the Red Sox as tough ones. He said that veteran pitcher Roger Clemens didn't even acknowledge him for the first three years Vaughn played there. Once he became an everyday player and earned a locker along the famed left-side wall in the Red Sox clubhouse, however, everything changed. By then he had gained the respect of the veteran players, and he and Clemens became friends. Things are changing nowadays, though.

"Nowadays it's different because of salaries," said Vaughn. "Unless you're with [the Mets], the Yankees, or another veteran team, there's only four or five clubs like that. The rest of the teams just have four or five veterans and the rest are young guys."

Joe McEwing, a utility player who started his career with the Cardinals, definitely paid his dues. "I had to get Eric Davis coffee every day when he walked into the clubhouse," he said. "I did it for about a month and a half. After that, he knew how much I appreciated the game and respected him. He called me up to his room and had me sized up for four suits."

"The biggest thing when you're a rookie is you respect the people who came before you and don't say a word until you're pretty much spoken to," he added. "That's how I was raised in the game. When I was first called up, I was scared to leave my locker. I didn't want to get in anybody's way, didn't want to tick anybody off."

If the soft-spoken, well-mannered McEwing is the model rookie, he is a dying breed in today's game. Many veterans grouse that baseball has changed considerably since they first came up. Younger players, they say, are more presumptuous than ever before.

31

On Steroids and Drug Use

Drugs and steroids are without question the biggest issue facing the game of baseball as we head into the future. Arguably, nothing has aroused as much debate in recent years as has the specter of players using performance-enhancing drugs to break long-standing records that have stood proudly for decades. The very idea that these hallowed accomplishments could be tarnished by others who have cheated has made for a huge national debate.

Is using steroids cheating? The answer is yes, but it is a complicated and sometimes controversial yes. One thing is for certain, steroids are illegal in society and in sports. Another thing that is for certain is that taking steroids is a violation of the code, a big violation that most players feel very strongly about.

Let's go back and look at the history of drugs and steroids in baseball and try to gain some perspective. The first documented use of steroids occurred way back in 1889 and was chronicled in the book *The Echoing Green*. A pitcher by the name of Pud Galvin took an injection of animal testosterone that was prescribed by a French doctor who thought it would help him to play better.

From there, other than coffee and cigarettes, not a whole lot transpired on the drug front in baseball until the mid-1940s, when our boys started returning from World War II. The ballplayers, particularly the ones who had served as pilots, had been using amphetamines in order to stay awake for long periods of time while on bombing missions. Now, back home, many figured that they would be a great way to stay alert on long doubleheaders or road trips. It didn't take long before "speed" spread throughout the league like wildfire.

Later, in 1968, dubbed the "year of the pitcher," something happened that may have served as a trigger for the problems we are seeing today. *Baseball Digest's* Mark Herrmann summed up what transpired that unbelievable season: "Denny McLain won 31 games," he wrote. "Bob Gibson had a 1.12 ERA and 13 shutouts. Don Drysdale had six shutouts in a row during a record streak of 58⅔ scoreless innings. The St. Louis Cardinals and San Francisco Giants threw no-hitters against each other on back-to-back days. Five American League pitchers finished with ERAs under 2.00. The All-Star Game finished 1-0, as did a Mets–Houston Astros game, once 24 innings had been played."

As for the fallout? While most fans could appreciate good, fundamental pitching, nobody was interested in coming to the ballpark to watch pitching duels night in and night out. They wanted some offensive fireworks, they wanted home runs, and they wanted some action. The owners agreed, and with that commissioner William Eckert was fired and replaced with Bowie Kuhn. One of Kuhn's first acts as the new head honcho was to lower the mound from 15 inches to 10, thus leveling the playing field between the pitchers and the hitters. New balls with seams that weren't as high as they used to be were introduced, making them harder for pitchers to grip and resulting in less break on their curveballs.

It was a good start, but the owners wanted even more offense. So in 1973 the designated hitter rule was put into place, and shortly thereafter a smaller strike zone was adopted. From there, the game expanded, and with all of those expansion teams came a whole host of new and intimate hitter-friendly stadiums, where yesterday's fly ball was now a three-run homer. The writing was on the wall: the teams wanted a more exciting brand of baseball. If they were going to compete with the NFL and NBA, which were becoming more popular, they needed to stay ahead of the curve.

By the late 1980s, while cocaine use was prevalent, it was steroids and performance-enhancing drugs that would become all the rage. With the demand for more home runs, a new breed of player emerged. Weight training, off-the-field workout programs, and personal trainers soon became the norm. With monster home runs being shown around the

Center Fielder Torii Hunter on Steroids

"In my opinion, guys who take steroids have no game anyway. They are losers as far as I am concerned. I think that if you take steroids, then you are disrespecting the game. You are cheating. I just think that if you have to cheat to be successful in baseball, then you shouldn't be in the game at all. It is an unfair advantage, and hopefully the league will get it cleaned up once and for all. They are illegal, they are dangerous, and more importantly they are a violation of the code."

clock on ESPN, players wanted to get bigger, faster, and stronger. And as they did, the big dollars followed. It was a recipe for success, or so they would think.

Before long supplements such as creatine entered into the picture, and with it came players who began to resemble bodybuilders rather than left fielders. The players who chose to use the supplements and steroids found great results. With creatine, a legal, over-the-counter substance, power-hitters could build "twitch muscles," which provided them with more impulse power to swing the bat quicker and harder. Creatine could also help provide quick bursts of energy while also increasing muscle mass, body weight, and overall strength. Hitters could work out much more frequently and recover more quickly from injuries. Young players took them as a shortcut to get ahead, while older players took them as a way to just stay in the game.

As for pitchers, they could recover much more quickly with steroids. They could control the inflammation that occurs following an outing and were able to bounce back much faster. A juiced starter might be able to go eight innings instead of five, while a reliever could throw in back-to-back games versus every other game. They are subtle differences, but advantages nonetheless that many players are willing to take a risk over. With millions of dollars in contract money on the line and a short career window of opportunity, any little edge to keep them at the top of their game—or simply in the game at all—will be explored.

Sure, there have been some high-profile athletes who have suffered from health problems from using steroids over the years. No pain, no gain, right? Wrong. Oakland Raiders defensive end Lyle Alzado asserted that his steroid abuse directly led to the brain cancer that eventually caused his death at the age of 43. There would be others in the future.

Catcher Terry Steinbach on Steroids

"The steroid analogy now is pretty black and white. We all know the good and we all know the bad, but that wasn't the case years ago. I think originally when guys started taking them, there was an infusion of guys wanting to be healthier athletes. Guys were trying to take care of their bodies and not look or live like Babe Ruth, who was out of shape and drank and ate hot dogs all the time.

"The players were being inundated with offers from countless food and drug companies who wanted them to try their supplements and protein drinks. Look at creatine, or andro. When Mark McGwire was taking andro, he went out and bought it at GNC. It was totally legal back then. Now, seven or eight years later, our views have changed on the subject, and we have gotten a lot more information as to what the products really do or don't do.

"So to sit here today and be judgmental is easy. But the reality is back then nobody really knew what steroids and supplements were all about. They were very prevalent in professional sports at the time, and guys wanted to keep their bodies in peak condition all year round. If that could help them, then they were going to look into it.

"Now did some people know exactly what they were taking? Sure. I am not going to be naïve enough to say I know that every athlete took steroids by accident. No way. There were clearly some players who knew what they were doing and what they potentially could do to help them. Whether that meant weight gain or muscle mass, I don't know.

"When I look at Mark McGwire's situation, I feel really bad for him. People are making assumptions about his character, but what was he proven guilty of? Nothing. Sure, people can speculate, but that is just irresponsible, in my opinion. I mean, think of it as grand jury testimony. Okay, if he says he took andro, the media is going to immediately come out and say that he took steroids. No, he didn't admit to taking steroids, he admitted to taking andro-testosterone, which at the time was not illegal. Again, it could be purchased at the corner health-food store at the time and taken legally like any other type of nutritional supplement. Sure, later we all came to the realization that andro became a precursor to steroids.

"We have all learned a lot in the past several years, and unfortunately Mac got wrapped up in all of it and was really scrutinized by the media. Now if he says 'No, I didn't take anything,' then the media will say that he is lying to the grand jury because they knew he took andro. So he was screwed no matter which way you look at it.

"I think what people, and the media, eventually have to get over is that regardless of what players have taken over the last 50 years of baseball, none of that stuff was a substitute for talent. I would assume that steroids don't do a thing for hand-eye-coordination or help someone execute a great swing. Hey, I never took steroids, but even if I did, hypothetically, I promise you I wasn't going to be able to hit 70 home runs. It wasn't going to happen.

"So, all in all, I think the situation with Mac is very unfair. I hope that when he is given his chance to go into the Hall of Fame that he is given his due. Mark and I were teammates together for a lot of years. He was a great ballplayer and a great person. They can't punish him for a crime he hasn't been convicted of. That is the part that upsets me the most."

By the 1990s, steroid use had become rampant in some major league clubhouses. One can only assume that the bigwig execs up in the penthouse just nodded along like bobblehead dolls, never really questioning what was going on. Perhaps, in an odd twist, one of the reasons the problem didn't come to the forefront sooner was because of the clubhouse code, which prohibits players from speaking about anything that happens inside their inner sanctum. If players, trainers, or even coaches saw other players using them, they kept their mouths shut. They may not have agreed with it morally or ethically, but they respected the honor of the code.

Regardless, a culture had emerged in the game that felt bigger was better, by whatever means necessary. While baseball never endorsed or approved of steroid use, they certainly didn't do very much to prevent it. The problem for baseball was that they didn't have a program in place to deal with it. Once it started, it became a Pandora's box. Adding fuel to the fire was the fact that the game was enjoying a boon of recent success.

Following the 1994 strike that led to the cancellation of the World Series, the league was in comeback mode. But there were some clues as to what was happening when certain players started posting some outrageous numbers. So in 1996, when Brady Anderson came out of nowhere and hit 50 home runs after hitting only 16 the year before, people started to wonder. And when he fell back to earth the next season by hitting only 18, they wondered even more.

Leading the charge to win back the fans was the epic Mark McGwire and Sammy Sosa home run chase of 1998, which ultimately led to the shattering of the single-season home run record previously held by Roger Maris. Big Mac and Sammy were like rock stars during that unforgettable season, crushing dingers on a near-nightly basis as the nation watched in awe. While neither has ever admitted to steroid use, it was widely speculated that it may have played a part.

From there, Barry Bonds took over, topping Mark McGwire's eventual single-season home run record of 70 by three long-balls back in 2001. Bonds, who has also been linked to steroid use, would stay in the headlines through 2007, when he eventually broke Henry Aaron's all-time career home-run mark of 755.

Baseball finally stepped up and took action in 2003, albeit on a trial basis, when they started testing for steroid use through an experimental and optional program. Prior to that, they had a pretty weak testing policy focused mostly on recreational drug use. Steroids were something that weren't taken into consideration when they first created the rules regarding illegal drugs, and baseball simply needed to get with the times.

It was a conundrum for Major League Baseball up to that point, to be sure. It was a case of "be careful for what you wish for," in that the league wanted big offense to generate big TV revenues, which it did, but they then looked away at the thought of how that success was achieved. The juiced-ball era was like a runaway freight train, rolling down the tracks with seemingly no way of stopping it.

The league needed to know just how bad the problem was before they got started. But they also needed the players to cooperate, so they issued no penalties to those who tested positive. With that, the league was able to go back to the players union and start the dialogue necessary to lay down guidelines and penalties for those who were caught taking steroids in the future. Most would agree it was a good start.

The biggest hurdle for MLB is that the bad guys are usually always two steps ahead of the good guys with regard to detection. Companies that make illegal drugs, such as the Bay Area Laboratory Co-Operative (BALCO), the now-defunct California nutritional supplements company whose handiwork included the anabolic steroid THG, stand to make a lot of money each time they come out with a new designer drug that cannot be detected by the governing bodies of professional sports leagues. Furthermore, the athletes who make a lot of money for their performances on the field have shown that they will spend whatever it takes to get an edge—regardless of the penalties or side effects.

The latest performance-enhancing drug is called human-growth hormone, or HGH. The problem with HGH is that even though it is illegal, it is very hard to detect without a blood test.

In 2002 *Sports Illustrated* ran a cover story about All-Star third baseman Ken Caminiti, who, following his retirement a year earlier, admitted that he had used steroids during his 1996 MVP season, as well as for several seasons afterward. It was historic in that it was the first public admission of steroid use by a big leaguer, and it sent shock waves throughout the sports world. Sadly, Caminiti died of an apparent heart attack in 2004 at the age of 41.

As for the ongoing investigation regarding the issue of steroids in baseball, there is still a lot to be determined in figuring out just who did what, why, when, and where. Back in 2003 a federal grand jury heard testimony from several players, as well as from executives of BALCO who were implicated in the scandal. A lot of big-name power hitters were named in the case, which would leave a cloud of suspicion hanging over them. The evidence presented was strong. Some players were caught red-handed, others denied any wrongdoing, and some admitted using.

Giants slugger Barry Bonds testified to the grand jury that in 2003 he used undetectable steroids known as "the cream" and "the clear," designer drugs created by BALCO, which he received from his personal trainer and friend Greg Anderson, who was indicted in a steroid-distribution ring. According to Bonds, the trainer told him the substances were the nutritional supplement flaxseed oil and a pain-relieving balm for the player's arthritis and fatigue. According to the *San Francisco Chronicle,* Bonds said he didn't know they were steroids.

The prosecutors also questioned Bonds about "doping calendars," which contained his name and notes about performance-enhancing substances,

Pitcher Kirk McCaskill on Steroids

"I think that there was a consensus amongst the owners, stated or unstated, to get the fans re-interested in the game several years ago. They knew that offense sold tickets, and that is exactly what they gave them. I firmly believe it was the home-run race which got the fans back into the stadiums. I think that the owners figured that an offensive game was a more profitable game, too, because they usually take longer, which means the fans are there longer and will ultimately spend more money. So it went on, and now they are trying to figure out how they are going to put a stop to it. I don't know the answers, but I hope that they can figure it out for the sake of the game."

Pitcher Mike Marshall on Steroids

"Steroids are such an egregious violation of the code. Players using steroids, in my opinion, is worse than betting on baseball. I think players who use them should be suspended for life. And I don't mean on the third time, either. I mean on the first time. This whole thing is absolutely absurd how they coddle these people. What a joke.

"It was clear to me as a pitcher early on that bat speeds were way greater than they should be. There was no question in my mind that a lot of these guys were using steroids. So I made comment of it at the time, but nobody paid attention. As far as I was concerned, baseball condoned it. I mean, if they didn't know what the hell was going on when McGwire and Sosa were having their home-run derby a few years back, they had to be blind. Yet they were celebrating every minute of it. I said take a damn blood test. Both of these guys are so juiced that they can't see straight. Baseball let it go, though.

"So I put the blame on the owners. I warned people about it back in the '70s when I took a course on advanced internal endocrinology while working towards my doctorate degree in Exercise Physiology and found out about the increasing availability of growth hormone and steroids. I told Marvin Miller, the head of the Major League Baseball Players Association, about it and said that we needed to get a policy together to ban it before it got out of hand. He didn't do a thing about it and neither did Don Fehr, his successor. I am ashamed of both of them. I really am.

"The thing with pitchers who use steroids is that eventually they will injure themselves. Sure, they do it for recovery, but they also do it for velocity, too. Here is the thing: steroids increase muscle mass, but they don't increase bone density. They don't increase ligament or tendon density or strength, either. So you can generate more velocity, but you have less ability to withstand it. So they wind up hurting themselves, especially their elbows. A pitcher will throw 97 or 98 mph for a few weeks, and then he is on the disabled list for a few months or longer.

"The only ones who can really get away with it are the hitters. Eventually their knees go bad, though, and that is probably one of the reasons why Mark McGwire is out of the game right now and why Barry Bonds has problems, too. Steroids will eventually tear up your knees because they soften the connective tissues between the bones. It weakens your body in that regard. So hitters lose it in their knees, and for pitchers it happens in their elbows. Eventually, their bodies are just a mess. And that is exactly what this whole fiasco has become—a big filthy mess."

and other documents that were seized from Anderson's home. Bonds denied knowing of the calendars and also said he had never discussed steroids with the trainer, had never asked what the products he was given contained, and was certain Anderson wouldn't give him illegal substances without his knowledge.

Several of Bonds's former teammates admitted using performance-enhancing drugs provided by Anderson: Armando Rios, Benito Santiago, and Bobby Estalella, as well as former Oakland A's Jason and Jeremy Giambi. All the players testified because they were offered immunity as long as they told the truth to the grand jury.

"As I have repeatedly stated, I am fully committed to the goal of immediately ridding our great game of illegal performance-enhancing substances," said commissioner Bud Selig. "The use of these substances continues to raise issues regarding the game's integrity and raises serious concerns about the health and well-being of our players."

All of the testimony, combined with Jose Canseco's scandalous book, eventually led to an even bigger hearing before Congress. On March 18, 2005, an all-day, nationally televised hearing was held before the House Government Reform Committee. The goal of the committee was to examine baseball's much-criticized drug-testing program and its subsequent impact on steroid use among kids. The committee would deduce that baseball's policy was full of holes and threatened to legislate tougher testing policies and sanctions if they didn't get serious about the problem and bring it in line with that of the Olympic testing program. (MLB's policy at the time mandated a 10-day suspension for first-time offenders, as opposed to two years for Olympians.)

The investigation featured riveting testimony from a handful of the game's biggest stars, including Canseco, Mark McGwire, Sammy Sosa, Rafael Palmeiro, Frank Thomas, and Curt Schilling. Schilling and Thomas were invited because of their outspoken views against steroids, while the others had all been connected to or accused of using. Barry Bonds, meanwhile, wasn't invited because, according to the committee's leaders, "his presence would have overshadowed the substance of the hearing."

McGwire, who had retired in 2001, was asked repeatedly whether he had used steroids, to which he would deflect each question, finally acknowledging that "there has been a problem with steroid use in baseball in the past," but that he was "not here to discuss the past."

"Asking me or any other player to answer questions about who took steroids in front of television cameras," he added, "will not solve the problem. My lawyers have advised me that I cannot answer these questions without jeopardizing my friends, my family, and myself. I intend to follow their advice."

Palmeiro had the most dramatic testimony. "Let me start by telling you this," he said, dramatically pointing his finger at the committee chairman. "I have never used steroids, period."

Sosa, meanwhile, speaking in Spanish, read a statement in which he said that he "has never used illegal performance-enhancing drugs," has never "injected myself or had anyone inject me with anything," and has not "broken the laws of the United States or the laws of the Dominican Republic."

Perhaps the most vocal politician who spoke was Kentucky Senator Jim Bunning, a Hall of Fame pitcher himself, who told the panel: "When I played with Henry Aaron, Willie Mays, and Ted Williams, they didn't put on 40 pounds, and they didn't hit more home runs in their late thirties as they did in their late twenties. What's happening in baseball is not natural, and it's not right."

Bunning went on to say that the records of steroid users should be marked by an asterisk and that their records should be cleaned from the books. "If they started in 1992 or '93 illegally using steroids," said Bunning, "wipe all their records out. Take them away. They don't deserve them."

The image of McGwire, a beloved national hero, nearly reduced to tears and then refusing to testify about the subject under oath hit the media like a Mack truck. Suddenly, everybody was talking about steroids in baseball. If some good had to come from some bad, then history will likely view this moment as the catalyst for cleaning up the game.

Ironically, Palmeiro tested positive for steroids shortly after his finger-pointing display, but he was able to stick around with the Baltimore Orioles. But as soon as he tried to blame teammate Miguel Tejada for his problems, the O's gave him the boot. He had crossed the line and broken the code.

Another publicized clubhouse code incident involving steroids occurred in 2006, when Diamondbacks reliever Jason Grimsley was caught possessing human growth hormone. Grimsley, like Canseco, named names and was immediately chastised by his baseball brethren. "To go and start throwing

First Baseman Harmon Killebrew on Steroids

"That is just plain old cheating in my book. Steroids have put a big cloud over the game, no question. I know that most of the players, especially the older ones of my generation, are pretty upset about it. You know, I saw recently where the players union was upset over some issues regarding drug testing. If it was me, I wouldn't be upset because I never used drugs. If you don't have anything to hide, then what is the problem? It is a mess. I guess I would have to agree with Senator Jim Bunning's recommendation of what to do with players who were caught using steroids: ban them from the game and strip them of all their records."

other guys under the bus is definitely wrong as well," said White Sox reliever Jeff Nelson, a former teammate of Grimsley's with the Yankees. "Take the blame. You should take the hit and not have to be putting it on anybody else."

When it comes to drugs and the clubhouse, you simply cannot expose your teammates. Maybe nobody has been more guilty of this than Barry Bonds. The aloof Bonds, who prefers to sit alone in the corner of the clubhouse in his personal recliner rather than hang out with the boys, even blamed a positive test for amphetamines on a teammate a few years back, which did not sit well at all with the fellas in the locker room.

This of course came after telling a federal grand jury in the 2003 BALCO case that he'd never knowingly taken steroids. Bonds implied that if he had somehow used them, perhaps accidentally, then it was the fault of his trainer and boyhood friend, Greg Anderson. Anderson, by the way, went to prison for refusing to testify whether or not his friend and client had indeed told a fib.

It is interesting to note that for the most part, other than Palmeiro, the players who have been getting busted for steroids since the league started implementing its tougher testing policy aren't the big-name stars. Rather, the vast majority of suspended players have been anonymous minor leaguers. This could be because the bigger-name players have more funds necessary to purchase masking agents, as well as trainers who can regulate their cycles to ensure clean tests.

Regardless, fully half of the guilty parties hail from Latin American countries. As a result, this has been a point of contention amongst the players in the Hispanic community.

Red Sox slugger David Ortiz, a Dominican, expressed his concern about the language barrier, which he felt was leading to confusion and a disproportionate number of positive tests among Latino players. "You might think everyone's got the message," Ortiz said, "but they don't."

Venezuelans, who make up nearly 12 percent of all major league rosters, accounted for a whopping 35 percent of performance-enhancing-drug–related suspensions in 2006. For young Latino players who come from lives of poverty and crime, it is their lifelong dream to change their lives as well as their families' lives by making it to the big leagues. A drug suspension, however, can end all hope and become tantamount to a death sentence.

While most of the guilty players claim to have legitimate medical misunderstandings as alibis, some baseball officials see it differently. One high-ranking MLB executive had this to say about the subject in a 2007 *ESPN The Magazine* story: "If you do this as long as I have, there's

Pitcher Jim Kaat on Steroids

"Things have changed so much over the years. I remember when team doctors and trainers used to hand out diet pills, or amphetamines, which were used as pick-me-ups because of the travel conditions. As for steroids, I remember talking to players in the late '80s about this stuff. I was broadcasting at the time and would spend time with players before the games and whatnot. I would ask certain players about so and so, and how many home runs he was suddenly hitting, and they would say, 'Yeah, he's on the juice,' very matter-of-factly. The players were not about to rat each other out, that was for sure. That is a part of the code, too. I think that baseball in general knew about it and could see how it was starting to get out of hand. They let it go on too long, I think, and it became a real mess. The big thing now is how steroids are skewing all of the records. That is too bad.

"And believe me, a lot of pitchers have been getting free passes on this stuff, too. There are a whole lot of pitchers who are guilty of juicing as well. I am not going to name names, but there are a lot of them out there. If you followed the game closely, you would see the pitchers who threw exceptionally hard and then broke down, and then came back in a cycle like that. You can talk to scouts nowadays who have scouting reports on certain pitchers who have lost a lot of velocity in their fastballs over the past few years since testing has become an issue. So it is a big problem and thankfully it looks like baseball has finally decided to do something about it. Let's hope they can clean it up once and for all, because it has no place in the game, as far as I am concerned."

one thing you learn: people who are positive under these policies, it's never their fault. It's always, 'Somebody didn't tell me,' or 'The dog ate my homework.'"

They speculate that because of looser pharmaceutical regulations in places such as Venezuela, some players don't pay as much attention to the labels of banned substances that are sold either as legal dietary supplements or as illegal ones sold in outdoor markets. Eventually, it just becomes too much to keep track of, and that is when things can go from bad to worse.

Major League Baseball has said that it is conducting educational sessions in those areas and is also printing copies of the current drug policies in both English and Spanish to avoid further confusion. One of the game's most outspoken figures, White Sox manager Ozzie Guillen, who hails from Venezuela, said that the problem stems from the country's unregulated network of wannabe baseball trainers, scouts, and agents—all looking for a quick buck at the expense of a naïve youngster.

"I think the main problem is the people who surround these kids, who lie to these kids, who give them supplements they're not supposed to, who say they're going to be better, richer," said Guillen. "I think those are the people we have to control."

So just how big is the actual problem of steroids in baseball? Nobody knows for sure, nor will they. With all of the masking agents out there and the lack of testing capabilities, players can still get away with cheating pretty easily. Is it a big problem? Sure. But who can you believe when it comes to the question of just how big? Jose Canseco alleged in his book that 85 percent of players today were juiced, while Ken Caminiti guessed that at least half of the league was doping. There are roughly 750 players on the active rosters of all 30 teams in Major League Baseball. To assume that half, 375, or a whopping 638 players in Canseco's case, are on 'roids is utterly ridiculous. But there is a certain percentage out there that is guilty, that much is for sure.

In 2007 commissioner Bud Selig announced that there would be an investigation of steroid use headed by former Senator George Mitchell. "Any admission regarding the use of illegal performance-enhancing substances, no matter how casual, must be taken seriously," Selig said at the beginning of May 2007. "It is in the best interests of baseball for everyone, including players, to cooperate with Senator Mitchell in his investigation. Discipline for wrongdoing is important, but it is also important to create an environment so players can feel free to honestly and completely cooperate with this important investigation."

One of the players whom Selig threatened to discipline if he didn't speak to the panel was Jason Giambi, who on May 18, 2007, finally came clean...sort of.

"I was wrong for doing that stuff," said Giambi of his steroid use. "What we should have done a long time ago was stand up—players, ownership, everybody—and said: 'We made a mistake.' Steroids and all of that was a part of history."

More importantly, Giambi stayed true to the code and vowed not to implicate other players. "I will address my own personal history regarding steroids and will not discuss in any fashion any other individual," he said.

Today, if a player tests positive for steroids or any other performance-enhancing drugs, he will be given a 50-game suspension under the league's new policy. The league has taken the initiative to get its house in order and appears willing to stay the course. This is good for baseball.

As for the legacy of steroids in baseball? I think author Derek Zumsteg puts it into the proper perspective in his outstanding book *The Cheater's Guide to Baseball*:

> The argument about the integrity of records is overwrought. A record is only a story of what happened. A hitter on steroids hit those home runs, just as a spitballer struck out those hitters and a bat-corker got those extra hits. The statistics aren't tainted; they just require us to remember their context, as has always been true. Every era's statistics are skewed. Barry Bonds took drugs for a few years. Babe Ruth is a spot below him on the all-time home-run leader board, and Ruth never had to face a pitcher who wasn't white as a lily. Who had the bigger advantage? All the triple leaders played in gigantic parks, where line drives could drop and roll forever and the fielders had poor equipment. Pitchers before 1920 could use trick pitches to their hearts' content. And so on, through the last game that was played.

One thing is for sure—players of all eras have extremely strong feelings about the subject. One of the most interesting perspectives came from former Reds pitcher Rob Dibble, who remains close to the game as a national TV analyst:

> I think steroids are as much ego as anything. It is all about keeping up with the Joneses, and everybody wants to get huge and hit 50 home runs. There is big money to be made, and everybody is looking for

an edge. Some guys, sadly enough, will go past the edge and cheat. Because, make no mistake about it, taking steroids is cheating.

I think in my era guys didn't think that they needed a chemical edge. For me, my edge was running 10 extra sprints or long-tossing before the game. When it comes to chemicals, however, whether it was amphetamines or steroids, that just shows a weaker-minded player, in my mind. The word *supplement* is the perfect word, because it describes how he needs to take something like HGH [human growth hormone] in order to supplement his inadequacies. I understand why, because guys want to get bigger, faster, and stronger, and they want to recover quicker. I get it. Play better and you get more money; I understand that. I just think it is cheating.

For me, the beauty of baseball and other sports is trying your hardest and doing whatever it takes to help your teammates win. To have to cheat to do that, though, really dilutes what sports are all about, in my book. So when guys break records after having cheated, it means nothing, in my opinion. They haven't done anything. It's hollow. It's a chemically enhanced performance that shouldn't count. It's like when Ben Johnson won the gold medal in the Olympics and then got busted for steroids. It meant nothing. How proud can you be of that accomplishment if you had to cheat to get it? It's a tarnished achievement.

I guarantee you this: if I would have taken steroids, I would have played for more than seven and a half years in the big leagues. That is for sure. I hung it up not because my arm was shot at the end, it was because of other body parts that started to fail. I eventually lost my location on my fastball and finally said screw it, I don't need this. I had other things I wanted to do with my life, and fortunately I am doing them. Some of these guys, who are playing into their forties and making a boatload of money and breaking records, it's hollow.

I am not accusing all of those guys of cheating, by any means, but some of them are, and I think in the end it will all come out. I also think that one day when those guys are long gone from the game and they are sitting at home looking at their trophies and awards that they will realize that they didn't earn them. To me, that is the ultimate. I wouldn't be able to look at myself or my wife or my kids and feel good about accomplishing anything in life if I had to cheat in order to do it. I am very proud to say that I won a world championship and that I was clean. I wasn't enhanced in any way, and that makes it even more special.

I remember serving as a player rep for the union back in 1994, when we were on strike, and dealing with the issue of steroids back then. There were a lot of goofballs in those meetings with holier-than-thou attitudes who were like, "They want to interfere with our civil rights. They can't test us." Come on, what a joke. If you have nothing to hide, then what is the problem? For me, I was actually more worried about the players' health than anything else. I wasn't worried so much about who got caught. I mean, if you get caught then you are an idiot anyway, as far as I was concerned.

It is an unfair advantage, not to mention the fact that it is extremely dangerous. Big egos oftentimes get in the way of common sense, and that is too bad. So to me, if guys are willing to sacrifice their reputations, then they should be willing to suffer the consequences. If you hit 50 home runs or win 25 games and you are juiced, then you are a disgrace, as far as I am concerned. You deserve what comes to you when you get caught. Period.

Steroids won't make a player instantly able to hit home runs. Rather, they will allow the player to stay healthy so that he can train to get bigger, faster, and stronger, which will ultimately allow him to gain much more muscle. As a result, he will be able to have quicker hand-eye coordination and more power to hit the ball. Most players who take them don't want to look like Jose Canseco or Mark McGwire. They just want to gain an extra five mph on their fastball or be able to hit a fly ball an extra 30 feet. Those aren't huge differences by any stretch, but they might just be the difference between being in the majors versus being in the minors for somebody. Or, for an established star, they might mean the difference between signing a $25 million contract versus a $75 million contract.

Either way, it is a violation of the code of honor. Baseball has seen its share of scandals over its illustrious history, from the 1919 Black Sox scandal to Pete Rose's gambling problem. It has always come through it, though, stronger and wiser. Let's hope that baseball can get it right with steroids, not only for the sake of the players' health, but so that no more hallowed records will have to fall unnecessarily.

Outfielder Dave Winfield on Steroids

"Steroids are definitely a violation of the code. Players are looking for any way to enhance their performance, though, which ultimately enhances their paychecks. There are people out there who are willing to break the law if they think that they can get away with it, and some of them are compensated handsomely for cheating, which is really sad in my opinion."

Sources

Chapter 1
Field of Screams, by Richard Scheinin, W.W. Norton & Co., 1994.

Chapter 2
"Unwritten rules? Baseball's code of conduct is blurring," by Brian E. Fallon, *The Washington Times,* Page C1, June 25, 2002.

"Cracking baseball's secret code of ethics," by Stan McNeal, *The Sporting News,* July 7, 2005.

"An Unofficial History of the Beanball," by Dan Holmes, www.thebaseballpage.com, 2003.

"When should baseball players swing away?" by Evan Grant, *The Dallas Morning News,* September 14, 2006.

"Angels striking back on beanball incidents," by Cheryl Rosenberg Neubert, *The Orange County Register,* March 11, 2002.

Chapter 3
"Back in the box," by Avani Patel & Teddy Greenstein, *Chicago Tribune,* August 12, 2000.

"Beanball leaves a cut, and a score to settle," by La Velle E. Neal III, *Star Tribune,* April 26, 2007.

"Minor League Legends: Steve Dalkowski," by Jared Hoffman, *The Sporting News,* August 24, 1999.

Chapter 4

"Court: Calif. athlete can't sue over 'beanball' pitch," *Community College Week*, April 24, 2006.

"Calif. Supreme Court: Ballplayer Can't Sue for Bean Ball," by Mike McKee, *The Recorder*, April 10, 2006.

"All-Stars defend Clemens despite beanball incident," by Gary Washburn, *Contra Costa Times*, July 10, 2000.

"Unwritten rules? Baseball's code of conduct is blurring," by Brian E. Fallon, *The Washington Times*, Page C1, June 25, 2002.

"An Unofficial History of the Beanball," by Dan Holmes, www.thebaseballpage.com, 2003.

"Maybe Piazza should have seen the beanball coming," by Randy Galloway, *Fort Worth Star-Telegram*, September 13, 2000.

"Walter Johnson Quotes," http://www.baseball-almanac.com/quotes/quojhns.shtml

"Back in the box," by Avani Patel & Teddy Greenstein, *Chicago Tribune*, August 12, 2000.

Chapter 5

"Can Baseball Change Macho Culture of High and Tight Fastball?" TV Transcript: ESPN's *Outside the Lines with Bob Ley*, April 30, 2000.

Chapter 6

"Can Baseball Change Macho Culture of High and Tight Fastball?" TV Transcript: ESPN's *Outside the Lines with Bob Ley*, April 30, 2000.

"Unwritten rules keep the peace in baseball," by Ray Buck, Tribune News Services, November 25, 2004.

"Baseball is back," by Charles Krauthammer, Townhall.com, October 17, 2003.

"Put up your dukes," by Jeff Merron, ESPN.com Page Two, April 23, 2003.

"When should baseball players swing away?" by Evan Grant, *The Dallas Morning News*, September 14, 2006.

The Echoing Green, by Joshua Prager, Pantheon, 2006.

Chapter 9

"Put up your dukes," by Jeff Merron, ESPN.com Page Two, April 23, 2003.

"Offerman Charged With Assault After Bat-Wielding Incident in Minors," by Frank Litsky, NYTimes.com, accessed August 16, 2007.

Chapter 10

"25 years ago, Red Sox and Yanks had a battle to remember," by Joe Gergen, NYYFans.com, May 21, 2001.

Field of Screams, by Richard Scheinin, W.W. Norton & Co., 1994.

Chapter 11

"The codes of baseball," by Tim Kurkjian, *ESPN The Magazine,* May 31, 2001.

"The Ray Knight–Eric Davis Brawl," by John Erardi, *The Cincinnati Enquirer,* June 9, 2002.

"Put up your dukes," by Jeff Merron, ESPN.com Page Two, April 23, 2003.

Chapter 12

"Twins fired up after manager's outburst, bounce ChiSox 10–4," CBS SportsLine.com, May 28, 2007.

"The codes of baseball," by Tim Kurkjian, *ESPN The Magazine,* May 31, 2001.

"Let's fight, too: Zambrano loses no-hit bid, ejection-marred game," the Associated Press, June 16, 2007.

"Francona, Piniella suspended three games each," the Associated Press, April 29, 2005.

"Plunking a superstar can wake a sleeping giant," by Todd Jones, TSN.com, May 8, 2007.

Chapter 13

"Remembering 'The Mad Hungarian,'" by Gordon Edes, *Baseball Digest,* August 2003.

Chapter 14
"Rodriguez Keeps Straddling Baseball's Foul Line," by John Branch, June 1, 2007, *The New York Times*, P.1a.
"Did A-Rod break the code?" by Ronald Blum, the Associated Press, May 31, 2007.
"Torre: A-Rod was out of line," the Associated Press, June 1, 2007.

Chapter 15
"Unwritten rules? Baseball's code of conduct is blurring," by Brian E. Fallon, *The Washington Times*, Page C1, June 25, 2002.

Chapter 17
"Pedro has foggy memory on beanball controversy," by Gary Washburn, *Contra Costa Times*, July 28, 2000.
"Unwritten rules? Baseball's code of conduct is blurring," by Brian E. Fallon, *The Washington Times*, Page C1, June 25, 2002.
Field of Screams, by Richard Scheinin, W.W. Norton & Co., 1994.

Chapter 18
"Leader in the clubhouse," by John Donovan, CNNSI.com, May 31, 2007.

Chapter 19
"The codes of baseball," by Tim Kurkjian, *ESPN The Magazine*, May 31, 2001.

Chapter 20
"Unwritten rules? Baseball's code of conduct is blurring," by Brian E. Fallon, *The Washington Times*, Page C1, June 25, 2002.

Chapter 21
"Put up your dukes," by Jeff Merron, ESPN.com Page Two, April 23, 2003.
"Former reliever Gene Garber recalls 19-year career and his role in baseball history," by Joe O'Loughlin, *Baseball Digest*, February 2004.

Chapter 23
"The codes of baseball," by Tim Kurkjian, *ESPN The Magazine*, May 31, 2001.
"Holidays hit managers," by Charley Walters, *Pioneer Press*, June 4, 2007.

Chapter 24
Field of Screams, by Richard Scheinin, W.W. Norton & Co., 1994.
"White Sox top the Rangers; Guillen speaks on beanball issue," by Mark Gonzales, *Chicago Tribune*, June 15, 2006.

Chapter 25
"Unwritten Rules," *Baseball Digest*, 1986.

Chapter 26
"Fighting through the years," by Jeff Merron, ESPN.com, November 20, 2004.

Chapter 27
"Biggest cheaters in baseball," by ESPN.com's Page 2 staff, ESPN.com, 2004.

Chapter 29
The Hidden Language of Baseball, by Paul Dickson, Walker & Co., 2003.
"Sign language: the art of baseball communication," by Larry Stone, *Baseball Digest*, August 2003.
"Stealing signs in baseball is as old as the game itself," by Michael Martinez, Tribune News Services, June 8, 1997.
The Echoing Green, by Joshua Prager, Pantheon, 2006.
Pure Baseball, by Keith Hernandez, Harper Perennial, 1995.
Oh Baby, I Love It!, by Tim McCarver, Dell, 1998.
I Played and I Won, by Allan Worthington, Xulon Press, 2004.
Veeck as in Wreck, by Bill Veeck, University of Chicago Press, 2001.
"Heroes and Steroids," by Dave Studeman, TheHardballTimes.com, December 3, 2004.

"Stealing signs: fair or foul?" by Greg Couch, *Baseball Digest*, August 2002.

"Masters of sign-stealing get in opponents' heads but aren't proud of it," by Larry Stone, *Seattle Times*, May 11, 2003.

"The art of baseball: Sign language is game's lifeblood," by Larry Stone, *Seattle Times*, May 11, 2003.

Chapter 30

"Put up your dukes," by Jeff Merron, ESPN.com Page Two, April 23, 2003.

"Beanball," by John Dawson, www.worldmag.com/articles/11807, May 6, 2006.

"Detroit 6, Seattle 3," by Tim Booth, the Associated Press, July 14, 2007.

Ball Four, by Jim Bouton, Bulldog Publishing, 2001.

Omar!, by Omar Vizquel, Gray & Company, 2003.

Juiced, by Jose Canseco, HarperEntertainment, 2006.

Chapter 31

"Unwritten rules? Baseball's code of conduct is blurring," by Brian E. Fallon, *The Washington Times*, Page C1, June 25, 2002.

"A hitter's game: rule changes promoting offense have favored batters over pitchers," by Mark Herrmann, *Baseball Digest*, July 2003.

"Bonds testified that substances didn't work," ESPN.com, December 3, 2004.

"Baseball Has a Day of Reckoning in Congress," by Dave Sheinin, *The Washington Post*, Page A1, March 18, 2005.

"USA Today reports that Selig may suspend Giambi," ESPN.com news services, June 13, 2007.

"Code of silence," by Dan Connolly, *Baltimore Sun*, July 20, 2006.

"Other Voices: Bonds broke code by smearing Sweeney," by Nancy Armour, the Associated Press, January 13, 2007.

"Caught Looking," by Ian Gordon, *ESPN The Magazine*, June 4, 2007.

"MLB officials mum on discussions in Giambi-Mitchell meeting," the Associated Press, July 13, 2007.

The Echoing Green, by Joshua Prager, Pantheon, 2006.

The Cheater's Guide to Baseball, by Derek Zumsteg, Houghton Mifflin, 2007.